Winning
Commitment

Winning Commitment

How to Build and Keep a Competitive Workforce

Gary Dessler

McGraw-Hill, Inc.

New York   San Francisco   Washington, D.C.   Auckland   Bogotá
Caracas   Lisbon   London   Madrid   Mexico City
Milan   Montreal   New Delhi   San Juan
Singapore   Sydney   Tokyo   Toronto

Library of Congress Cataloging-in-Publication Data

Dessler, Gary.
    Winning commitment : how to build and keep a competitive workforce
  / Gary Dessler.
        p.   cm.
    Includes bibliographical references and index.
    ISBN 0-07-016630-7 (alk. paper) :
    1. Corporate culture—United States—Case studies.   2. Employee
motivation—United States—Case studies.   3. Commitment
(Psychology)—Case studies.   I. Title.
HD58.7.D485   1993
658.3′14—dc20   92-40329
                                                                              CIP

1 2 3 4 5 6 7 8 9 0   DOC/DOC   9 9 8 7 6 5 4 3

ISBN 0-07-016630-7

*The sponsoring editor for this book was Karen Hansen, the editing supervisor
was Jane Palmieri, and the production supervisor was Suzanne W. Babeuf. It was
set in Palatino by McGraw-Hill's Professional Book Group composition unit.*

Printed and bound by R. R. Donnelley & Sons Company.

This book is printed on recycled, acid-free paper containing a
minimum of 50% recycled de-inked fiber.

*To my son, Derek, and
to the memory of my father, Alexander*

Contents

Preface   xiii

Part 1. The Challenge Today

1. Employee Commitment as a Competitive Advantage   3

The End of Predictability   3
The Commitment Factor   4
The Commitment Dilemma   7
The Keys to Commitment   8
The Commitment Wheel   10
References   15

2. Toward a New Theory   15

Commitment in Utopia   15
   Sacrifice   16
   Investment   16
   Communion   16
   Transcendence   17
Commitment at Work   17
Creating Commitment   19
References   20
Additional Readings   21

Part 2. The Keys to Commitment

3. People-First Values   25

Know What You Want   26
Put It in Writing   28
Hire and Indoctrinate   29
"Walk the Talk"   30
A Summary: People-First Values as Key to Commitment   33
References   34

4. Double-Talk   37

Guaranteed Fair Treatment Programs   38
  Federal Express's Guaranteed Fair Treatment Procedure   38
  Toyota's Concern Resolution System   41
  IBM's Open-Door Program   42
Speak Up Programs   43
  IBM's Speak Up!   43
  Informal Open-Door Concepts   44
  Federal Express's Open-Door Policy   45
  Toyota's Hotline   46
Periodic Survey Programs   46
  Federal Express's Survey Feedback Action Program   47
Top-Down Programs   48
Double-Talk and Commitment   49
A Summary: Double-Talk as a Key to Commitment   50
References   50

5. Communion   53

Homogeneity: We've Got So Much in Common   55
Communal Sharing: I Own a Piece of the Rock   57
  The Penney Policy   58
  Ben & Jerry's Communal Sharing   58
  The Mary Kay System   59
Communal Work: Get on the Team   60
  Small Work Teams   60
  Job Rotation   63
  Top-Down Involvement   63
Regularized Group Contact: Let's Get Together   64
Ritual: It's a Tradition   64
A Summary: Communion as a Key to Commitment   66
References   67

6. Transcendental Mediation 69

Creating the Ideology 70
Creating the Charisma 78
Achieving Ideological Conversion 81
  Value-Based Hiring 81
  Value-Based Orientation 82
  Value-Based Training 84
Symbols and Stories, Rites and Ceremonials 85
A Summary: Transcendental Mediation as a Key to
  Commitment 86
References 87

7. Value-Based Hiring 89

Quality, Kaizen, and Commitment: The Toyota Story 90
  Past and Present 90
  The Hiring Process 91
  Traits and Skills Sought 94
Unions and Team Selection: The Saturn Story 95
  Past and Present 95
  The Hiring Process 96
The Certified Interview: The J. C. Penney Process 97
  The Hiring Process 98
The Best and the Brightest: The Goldman, Sachs Story 100
Self-Selection: The Process at Delta, Ben & Jerry's,
  and Mary Kay 101
  Delta Air Lines 101
  Ben & Jerry's Homemade 102
  Mary Kay Cosmetics 102
Common Themes 102
A Summary: Value-Based Hiring as a Key to Commitment 103
References 104

8. Securitizing 105

Security and Commitment 106
Lifetime Employment Without Guarantees 107
  Toyota's Policy 107
  Saturn's Contract 108
  Delta's Experience 109
  Federal Express's Commitment 110
  Publix Practices 110
  IBM's History 111

Strategies for Maintaining Full Employment   113
A Summary: Securitizing as a Key to Commitment   114
References   114

9. Hard-Side Rewards   **117**

Can You Buy Commitment?   117
Employee Compensation in High-Commitment Firms   119
    J. C. Penney's Policy and Programs   119
    Federal Express's Policy and Programs   121
    Ben & Jerry's Policy and Programs   125
    Toyota's Policy and Programs   125
    Saturn's Policy and Programs   128
    Mary Kay's Policy and Programs   129
Common Themes   130
A Summary: Hard-Side Rewards as a Key to
    Commitment   131
References   131

10. Actualizing   **133**

Actualizing in Theory and in Practice   133
A Commitment to Actualizing   134
Front-Loading Entry-Level Positions   136
Enriching and Empowering   138
Promoting from Within   142
    Value-Based Hiring   143
    Developmental Activities   143
    Career-Oriented Appraisals   145
    Career Records and Job Posting   148
A Summary: Actualizing as a Key to Commitment   149
References   150

11. In Summary: Using the Keys to Commitment   **153**

People-First Values   153
    Know What You Want   153
    Put It in Writing   154
    Hire and Indoctrinate   154
    "Walk the Talk"   154
Double-Talk   155
    Guaranteed Fair Treatment Programs   155
    Speak Up! Programs   155
    Periodic Survey Programs   156
    Top-Down Programs   156

Communion   156
  Homogeneity: We've Got So Much in Common   156
  Communal Sharing: I Own a Piece of the Rock   156
  Communal Work: Get On the Team   157
  Regular Group Contact: Let's Get Together   157
  Ritual: It's a Tradition   158
Transcendental Mediation   158
  Create the Ideology   158
  Create Charisma   159
  Achieve Ideological Conversion   159
  Use Symbols and Stories, Rites and Ceremonials   159
Value-Based Hiring   160
Securitizing   160
Hard-Side Rewards   161
Actualizing   161
  Commit to Actualizing   162
  Front-Load   162
  Enrich and Empower   162
  Promote from Within   162
References   163

The Workers Speak: Selected Comments by
Employees of High-Commitment Companies   165

Ben & Jerry's   165
Delta Air Lines   171
Federal Express   174
Goldman, Sachs   181
IBM   184
Mary Kay   185
J. C. Penney   190
Publix   198
Saturn Corporation   199
Toyota Motor Manufacturing, U.S.A.   208

Index   219

Preface

In today's fast-changing business environment, the future belongs to those managers who can best manage change, but to manage change you must have committed employees. Whether you run a law firm, a retail store, a manufacturing firm, or some other business, committed employees—employees who do their jobs like they own the company—are your firm's, as well as your competitors', competitive edge. The firms described in this book—Delta, Toyota, Ben & Jerry's, and the others—have survived and often thrived, in part, because their managers knew that in a rapidly changing world competitive advantage lies not in machines or patents but in people, people who will improvise and innovate and treat their companies and their customers like their own.

I have studied these companies and their documents and have spoken with their employees, and I believe that what these companies have accomplished, your company can too. As explained later in this book, committed employees aren't just a product of some mysterious "culture" that is impossible to see or bottle or measure. Instead, I've found—as we'll see—that managers in these firms took concrete steps and formulated concrete personnel policies that combined to create the intense employee commitment that these firms are famous for.

Will employee commitment guarantee your firm's success? I think not. IBM is a good example. Historically, commitment and IBM have gone hand in hand, and yet IBM's sales, profits, and market share have been sliding fast throughout the past few years. Their employees, I think, were as committed in the 1980s and 1990s as they had been in earlier years (although that commitment could start eroding if the practices it was built on, such as job security and hefty pensions, continue to erode). But high commitment won't compensate for a strategy that focused for too long on mainframe computers, nor will it overcome the inherent inefficiencies of overstaffing or of a slow-moving product-approval process.

Committed employees will help you to compete more effectively in good times and react to adverse conditions when things turn bad. They will help you gain a responsiveness and (hopefully) also quality and service and productivity levels your competitors will envy. More than anything, though, committed employees will do their best for you even when you're not looking, and more and more jobs today are carried out far from the watchful eyes of your supervisory staff.

This book can start you on the road to creating commitment; translating commitment into corporate success depends on you.

Gary Dessler

PART 1
The Challenge Today

1

Employee Commitment as a Competitive Advantage

The End of Predictability

For managers, the age of predictability is over; the age of uncertainty has begun. Intensified global competition, deregulation, and technical advances have triggered an avalanche of change, one that many firms have not survived. Consider some facts: Bank failures rose from single digits in the 1970s to 10 in 1980, 120 in 1985, and almost 200 annually in the early 1990s.[1] Some estimate that almost 20 million people were displaced in the 1980s by restructuring in manufacturing, and the percent of those employed in service jobs jumped from 70 percent in 1980 to almost 78 percent in 1991.[2] American firms, once dominant players in the market for phonographs and TVs, have seen their market share drop to 1 percent for phonographs and 10 percent for TVs; in 1990 the United States, once the undisputed leader in telecommunications apparatus, exported just over $9 billion worth of such apparatus and imported over $22 billion worth.[3] In the past 10 years three U.S. airlines—Eastern, People's Express, and Braniff—have ceased operations, while others, including Pan Am and U.S. Air, have either been taken over or have had to sell substantial shares. Still other airlines, including TWA, Northwest, and Continental, are barely holding on; even the giant of the industry—American—lost $280 million in the two years ending 1991, in spite of revenues of $13 billion in the second of those two years, and Delta—long known for its stability and job security—had to turn to layoffs toward the end of 1992.[4]

Major currency prices, once stable, now swing as much as 30 percent per year, and our banking system faces a crushing trillion dollars in developing-country debt.[5]

In the United States, cutthroat competition has been fed by deregulation, the increasingly global nature of competition, and a tapering off in population trends. (The U.S. labor force should grow at 1.3 percent per year through 2005, compared with 1.9 percent annual growth for 1975–1990.) Japanese auto firms have bypassed Chrysler as this nation's third-largest auto maker, and Intel Corp. President Andrew S. Grove predicts an industrywide shakeout among PC makers, noting that "There are 500 suppliers—and 450 shouldn't exist."[6] In 1991 IBM suffered its first drop in companywide sales since the 1940s.[7] By 1993 its stock price had fallen to an 11-year low, and the firm was contemplating the first forced layoffs in its history. A wave of junk-bond-financed mergers continues to reverberate in restructurings in industries ranging from apparel to retailing to financial services. Everywhere, new competitors spring up overnight, consumers demand ever-better quality, factories demand ever-smarter workers, and computers increasingly link buyers and sellers in symbiotic chains.

The U.S. public debt ballooned from just under $1 trillion in 1980 to $3.2 trillion in 1990,[8] and in country after country household debt as a percentage of annual disposable income jumped: from 80 percent in 1980 to over 100 percent in 1990 in the United States, from under 80 to almost 120 percent in Japan, and from barely 60 to 118 percent in Great Britain.[9] America's favorable balance of trade evaporated in the 1970s and 1980s: U.S. exports exceeded imports by over $9 billion in 1975, but imports exceeded exports by $24 billion in 1980, $132 billion in 1985, and $101 billion in 1990.[10] Executives everywhere understandably ask themselves what's coming next.

The Commitment Factor

In this environment, the future belongs to those managers who can best manage change; but to manage change you must have committed employees. The firms described in this book—Delta, Toyota, Ben & Jerry's, and others—have survived and most have thrived—in part because their managers know that in a rapidly changing world competitive advantage lies not in machines or patents but in people, people who will improvise and innovate and invest themselves personally in their companies. Under conditions of rapid change *committed employees* give the competitive edge to these firms.

What these companies have accomplished, yours can too. Committed employees aren't just a product of some mysterious "culture" that's impossible to see or measure. Instead, I've found that managers in these firms engaged in practices—they took concrete steps and formulated concrete personnel policies—that combined to create the intense employee commitment that these firms are famous for. I've given names to these practices, and you'll be hearing about them throughout this book: people-first values, double-talk, communion, transcendental mediation, value-based hiring, securitizing, hard-side rewards, and actualizing. Together these practices are the keys to creating employee commitment.

The need for creating commitment derives from the new nature of workers' jobs. The imperatives of quality, service, and rapid change that have marked the 1980s and 1990s have required dramatic changes in the way firms are managed. Rosabeth Moss Kanter, for instance, writes that rapid change, increased competition, and the need to get closer to the customer have created changes in how organizations are managed.[11] She says that position, title, and authority are no longer adequate tools for managing in a world where workers are required to think for themselves; workers, she says, must be given more control of their jobs, continuous learning, empowerment, and a share of the value they produce. Peter Drucker similarly describes our era's shift from "blue-collar production to white-collar knowledge-intensive work." He argues that knowledge workers like those in medicine, engineering, and programming need to be left to direct and discipline their own performance through "organized feedback from colleagues and customers."[12] The firms of today and tomorrow will have to rely not on yesterday's "command and control" management practices, Drucker says, but on self-discipline; simple, clear, common objectives; and self-governing work teams.

In a study of several manufacturers, the authors of *Made in America* similarly argue that "In successful firms, the role of the production worker is shifting from one of passive performance of narrow jobs to active collaboration in production." These firms promote participation, teamwork, flatter hierarchies, and much broader responsibilities for their workers. As a result, "Best practice firms have recognized that quality and flexibility improvements require levels of commitment, responsibility, and knowledge that cannot be obtained by compulsion or cosmetic improvements in human resource policies."[13] Service management expert Karl Albrecht argues that the "GM model"—with its focus on control and compliance and its reliance on the chain of command—can't be used to run a service business, because "managers do not control the quality of the product when the product is a service."[14]

Examples of managerial changes like these appear in the media almost everyday. When Chairman Robert Allen took over AT&T, one of the first things he did was to flatten the structure and give lower-level managers more autonomy.[15] "In today's organization," says Kenan Sahin, president of Kenan Systems Corp., a Cambridge, Massachusetts, software consulting firm, "managers will have to change gears readily, following the lead of the person who knows most about the subject." He goes on to say, "Before, when markets were slower, leaders had time to absorb information from experts. Now markets and technologies are becoming so complex, the experts will have to do the leading."[16] At a General Mills cereal plant in Lodi, California, work teams "schedule, operate, and maintain machinery so effectively that the factory runs with no managers present during the night shift."[17]

When it opened its Blacksburg, Virginia, plant in 1989, Corning "decided to use multi-skilled, team-based production in tandem with automation as a means of 'challenging people instead of forcing them to do dumb, stupid jobs,'" says plant manager Robert D. Hoover. "The firm sorted through 8,000 job applicants and hired 150 with the best problem-solving ability and the willingness to work in a team setting. The majority had finished at least one year of college."[18] The relative expense of this kind of practice has really paid off. A Blacksburg team, composed of workers with interchangeable skills, can retool a line to produce a different type of filter in only 10 minutes, six times faster than workers in traditional filter plants. "This is crucial for a plant that must constantly change product lines, and it's one reason why Blacksburg turned out a $2 million profit in its first eight months of production, instead of losing $2.3 million as projected for the start-up."[19] Corning is now converting its 27 other factories to team-based production.

But such management systems require, as never before, committed employees—those who identify with and adopt the goals of the firm and thus treat the firm as if it were their own business. One behavioral scientist has said that the most significant attribute of commitment is its capacity for "fusing individual and organizational goals."

> The committed manager will act in the interests of the organization just as he would in his own interests, for he has come to perceive

them as identical....The fear of personal failure and the lure of financial rewards [alone] can't unleash the same degree of creativity or
the kind of empassioned concern that results from dedication to [the
firm's] shared purpose.[20]

Increasingly, *committed employees* are the keys to a firm's competitive
edge.

The Commitment Dilemma

Yet just as the need for it is on the rise, employee commitment is becoming more elusive. Several things account for this, but perhaps the most
serious threat is what one expert calls "the rash of corporate downsizings and restructurings that have seen tens of thousands of employees
terminated in the last few years."[21] In fact, all the evidence points to the
fact that downsizing today has become a continuing corporate activity,
not just one linked to the recent recession. For example, fewer than half
the employers who downsized in 1988–1989 cited "business downturn,"
actual or forecast, as the reason. About 57 percent of the human
resources managers in one survey listed improved staff utilization,
mergers and acquisitions, and other reasons (such as budget cuts) for
their staff reductions. Only 43 percent of the 1084 employers responding were forced to make cuts because of economic slowdowns. Of the
424 companies that downsized, 30 percent said they planned to do so
again in the next 12 months.[22]

In his book *Pack Your Own Parachute*, Paul Hirsch says these downsizings and restructurings have wounded "perhaps fatally, the very
concept of employees' commitment and/or loyalty to their companies."
Furthermore, "the resulting message to chief executives is that if the
firm is free to sack its managers and downsize at will, it can no longer
expect the same levels of commitment, involvement and caring from its
own employees." His recommendation to employees reflects that of
most recruiters, career counselors, and outplacement experts today: As
an employee "you must make the best deal you can for yourself short-
term and don't worry about the long-term, because the chances are
you're not going to be there." Hirsch argues that all sensible employees
and managers should become free agents, focusing on their own career
needs first and foremost.[23]

And he's not alone. William Morin (of outplacement firm Drake Beam
Morin) says that employees and managers must develop what he calls
"non-dependent trust." As he puts it,

As an individual and as a professional—you must care for yourself and assume responsibility for your future. No longer do you look to the company, or your boss, or your colleagues or friends for a ready-made sense of security. Instead, you realize that you are the only one who can create and maintain a personal scenario for happiness and success.[24]

It is not surprising that a survey by one consulting firm concluded that loyalty is the number 1 employee virtue chief executives seek: "In today's chaotic business climate, more than 60% of the CEOs surveyed considered employee loyalty a top priority problem."[25]

We'll see that creating commitment—synchronizing employee and company goals to create self-motivated employees—is nothing new. Its desirability, particularly for jobs requiring self-discipline and responsiveness and service, has long been known. What *has* changed today is that these sorts of jobs now prevail. In terms of the jobs to be done, we have entered the age of unpredictability and innovation and initiative. As a result, we have entered an age in which employee commitment is not just laudable, it's indispensable.

The Keys to Commitment

What are the keys to employee commitment? How do managers create employee commitment? That is the basic question addressed in this book.

Answering it involved me in a four-step process. My first step was to review almost 30 years' worth of literature regarding employee commitment: how it is defined, how it is measured, how it is created, and what impact it has on organizations. This information provided a basic direction for my study, in terms of the sorts of practices I should look for as I went from firm to firm. In Chapter 2 we'll look at some of these earlier studies of commitment.

My second step was to identify high-commitment companies. My aim here was to find 10 firms that most businesspeople would instinctively agree have highly committed employees. Many sources were useful to me in devising this list of firms. For example, I asked many business-people what companies came to mind when they thought of committed employees; it was soon apparent that the names of certain firms appeared again and again. People remember that Delta Air Lines employees voluntarily bought their firm its first Boeing 737 to say "thank you" for all the firm had done for them; people are also aware of the quality-conscious employees at GM's new Saturn subsidiary who are seeking to achieve the highest car-quality standards in the United States. There is the overwhelming enthusiasm for Mary Kay Cosmetics among the firm's tens of thousands of sales consultants, and there is the commitment of Ben & Jerry's employees to the firm's environmental and social goals. These firms and others—Toyota Motor Manufacturing, U.S.A.; Federal Express; Goldman, Sachs & Company; and J. C. Penney—were mentioned often by the many people—managers, executives, friends, business professors, human resource managers, and others—whom I questioned in the process of devising my list. I also went to books such as *The 100 Best Companies to Work for in America, Thriving on Chaos,* and *In Search of Excellence* to find yet more names—and was not surprised to find there confirmation of many of the firms cited in my original poll.[26] An analysis of news and academic articles and books and annual reports regarding these and other firms also helped me fine-tune my list.

As I narrowed the list, I looked for outward signs of high commitment in the literature I read. I noted employees who continually "talked up" their companies as good places to work; employees who expressed a willingness to accept internal transfers—even to lesser jobs—to stay with a firm; employees who expressed genuine concern about the fate of their firms. On the basis of such research, I cut my list to 15 high-commitment firms, 10 of which agreed to participate in my study: Ben & Jerry's Ice Cream; Delta Air Lines; Federal Express; Goldman, Sachs & Company; IBM; Mary Kay Cosmetics; J. C. Penney; Publix Supermarkets; Saturn Corporation; and Toyota Motor Manufacturing, U.S.A.

In step 3 I studied these firms to discover the management practices that created employee commitment. Was it the people they hired? Job security? Job advancement? High pay? To establish the cause for commitment, I conducted interviews with employees of the 10 firms, usually on-site; reviewed their company documents and particularly their human resource management policies and procedures; double-checked that my first impressions of employee commitment were sound; and analyzed everything I could find in writing. As I zeroed in on the management practices that seemed to drive employee commitment, I also had as a guide the work of those earlier studies. It soon became apparent that a number of practices were common from firm to firm.

Finally, I found eight high-commitment practices that appeared and reappeared in the conduct of business in each of the 10 firms I was studying. They were actually *sets* of practices, each set composed of specific, concrete management actions, and I gave each of these sets of practices a name: people-first values, double-talk, communion, transcendental mediation, value-based hiring, securitizing, hard-side rewards, and actualizing. One thing that became increasingly obvious as my study progressed was that creating commitment requires a comprehensive management program, one consisting of a package of concrete management practices and personnel policies. In the absence of such a program, results from relatively one-dimensional efforts like quality improvement programs or incentive plans are bound to disappoint.

Figure 1-1 summarizes my findings in this search for the keys to employee commitment. Not all the firms that made my list make use of all the keys to commitment, but all the firms use most of them. *All* the firms use people-first values, communion, transcendental mediation, value-based hiring, securitizing, hard-side rewards, and actualizing, for instance. What I've called "double-talk" practices—formalized two-way communication systems that guarantee fair treatment and upward access for all employees—were used by nine of the ten firms.

The Commitment Wheel

Since creating commitment requires a comprehensive program, the question arises, where do you start? My recommendation is summarized in the "commitment wheel" seen in Figure 1-2. Launch a program by instituting what I've called people-first values (a subject we'll cover in Chapter 3). Actions are the products of values; it's futile to try to create commitment unless people-first values—top-management trust and respect for people—exists.

The second ring in the commitment wheel holds the keys explained in Chapters 4 through 6: double-talk, communion, and transcendental mediation. These practices are the foundations for the two-way communication practices, the sense of shared fate, and the sense of mission that commitment programs are based on.

Next come the value-based hiring, securitizing, and hard-side reward practices, which are explained in Chapters 7, 8, and 9. As we'll see, instituting these practices may require modifying your personnel policies and will only succeed if you have already committed yourself to the basic keys of people-first values, two-way communication, a sense of shared fate, and a sense of mission.

Finally, Chapter 10 discusses the final ring in our wheel, actualizing employees. Here, building on the foundation of the first seven keys, firms institute practices that help employees become "all they can be," the final key to ensuring commitment.

Company

KEY	Ben & Jerry's	Delta Air Lines	Federal Express	Goldman, Sachs	IBM	Mary Kay Cosmetics	J. C. Penney	Publix Super-markets	Saturn Automobile Corp.	Toyota Motor Mfg., U.S.A.
People-first values	•	•	•	•	•	•	•	•	•	•
Double-talk										
Guaranteed fair treatment programs	•	•	•	•	•		•	•	•	•
Speak Up! programs	•	•	•	•	•		•	•	•	•
Periodic survey programs	•	•	•		•	•	•	•		
Top-down programs	•	•	•	•	•		•	•	•	
Communion										
Homogeneity	•	•	•	•	•	•	•	•	•	•
Communal sharing	○	•	•	•	•	•	•	•	•	•
Communal work	•	•	•	•	•	•	•	•	•	•
Regular group contact	•	•	•		•	•	•	•	•	•
Ritual	•	•	•		•	•	•	•	•	•
Transcendental mediation										
Company ideology	•	•	•	•	•	•	•	•	•	•
Company charisma	•	•	•	•	•	•	•	•	•	•
Ideological conversion	•	•	•	•	•	•	•	•	•	•
Symbols, stories, and rites	•	•	•		•	•	•	•	•	•
Value-based hiring										
Clarification of values	•	•	•	•	•	•	•	•	•	•
Rejection of most applicants	•	•	•	•	•	•	•	•	•	•
Exhaustive screening	•			•	•	•	•	•	•	•

Figure 1-1. How top companies get and keep employee commitment.

KEY	Ben & Jerry's	Delta Air Lines	Federal Express	Goldman, Sachs	IBM	Mary Kay Cosmetics	J.C. Penney	Publix Super-markets	Saturn Automobile Corp.	Toyota Motor Mfg, U.S.A.
Value-based hiring (*continued*)										
Matching of values	•	•	•	•	•	•	•	•	•	•
Realistic job previews		•	•	•	•	•	•	•	•	•
Self-selection & sacrifice	•	•	•	•	•	•	•	•	•	•
Securitizing	•	•	•	•	•	•	•	•	•	•
Hard-side rewards										
Above-average pay	•	•	•	•	•	•	•	•	•	•
Risk participation	•		•	•	•	•	•	•	•	•
Limited pay grades	•	•	•		•	•	•	•	•	•
Salaries, not wages	•	•	•	•	•	•	•	•	•	•
Above-average benefits	•	•	•	•	•	•	•	•	•	•
Actualizing										
Commitment to actualize	•	•	•	•	•	•	•	•	•	•
Front-loading	•	•	•	•	•	•	•	•	•	•
Enrich and empower policy	•				•	•	•	•	•	•
Promote-from-within programs	•	•	•		•	•	•	•	•	•

Figure 1-1. (*Continued*).

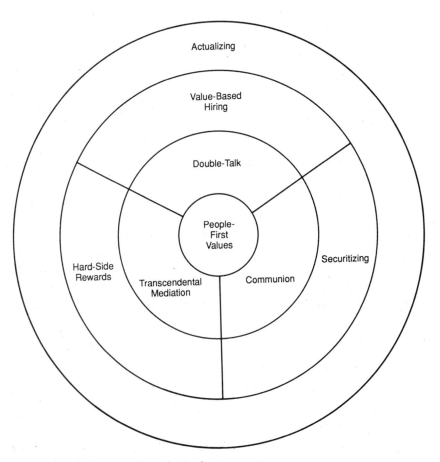

Figure 1-2. The commitment wheel.

References

1. *The World Almanac and Book of Facts: 1992*, World Almanac, New York, 1991, p. 157.
2. Diane Herz, "Worker Displacement in a Period of Rapid Job Expansion: 1983–87," *Monthly Labor Review*, vol. 113, no. 5, May 1990, pp. 21–41; U.S. Department of Labor, *Occupational Outlook Quarterly*, "Outlook: 1990–2005," Spring 1992.
3. *World Almanac*, p. 673
4. Wendy Zellner, Andrea Rothman, and Eric Schine, "The Airline Mess," *Business Week*, July 6, 1992, p. 51.

5. *World Almanac*, p. 823; *The Economist Yearbook: 1992*, The Economist Books, London, 1992, pp. 330–331.

6. Katherine Arnst, "This Is Not a Fun Business to Be In Now," *Business Week*, July 6, 1992, p. 68.

7. *The Economist Yearbook*, p. 167.

8. *World Almanac*, p. 140.

9. *The Economist Yearbook*, p. 222.

10. *World Almanac*, p. 673.

11. Rosabeth Moss Kanter, "The New Managerial Work," *Harvard Business Review*, no. 6, 1989.

12. Peter Drucker, "The Coming of the New Organization," *Harvard Business Review*, no. 1, 1988, p. 45.

13. Michael L. Dertouzos et al., *Made in America: Regaining the Productive Edge*, The MIT Press, Cambridge, Mass., 1989, p. 139.

14. Karl Albrecht, *At America's Service: How Corporations Can Revolutionize How They Treat Their Customers*, Dow Jones–Irwin, Homewood, Ill., 1988, p. 165.

15. John Keller, "Bob Allen Is Turning AT&T into a Live Wire," *Business Week*, November 6, 1989, p. 140.

16. Brian Dumaine, "The Bureacracy Busters," *Fortune*, June 17, 1991, p. 50.

17. Brian Dumaine, "Who Needs a Boss?" *Fortune*, May 7, 1990, p. 52.

18. As quoted in John Hoerr, "Sharpening Minds for a Competitive Edge," *Business Week*, December 17, 1990, p. 72.

19. Ibid.

20. Bruce Buchanan, "To Walk an Extra Mile: The What's, When's, and Why's of Organizational Commitment," *Organizational Dynamics*, Spring 1975, pp. 67–80; in Jerome Schnee, Harold Lazarus, and E. Kirby Warren, *The Progesss of Management*, Prentice-Hall, Englewood Cliffs, N.J., 1977.

21. Paul Hirsch, *Pack Your Own Parachute*, Addison-Wesley, Reading, Mass., 1987, p. 23.

22. American Management Association Survey, *Personnel*, AMA, New York, October 1989.

23. Hirsch, p. 99.

24. William J. Morin, *Trust Me*, Drake Beam Morin, New York, 1990, p. 47.

25. Goodrich and Sherwood Company Survey.

26. Robert Levering, Milton Moskowitz, and Michael Katz, *The 100 Best Companies to Work for in America*, Addison-Wesley, Reading, Mass., 1984.

2
Toward
a New Theory

Few would argue with the fact that the most powerful way to ensure that the work of the firm gets done right is to synchronize the firm's goals with those of its employees—to ensure, in other words, that the two sets of goals are essentially the same, so that by pursuing his or her own goals, the employee pursues the company's goals as well. Creating commitment means forging such a synthesis.

Creating commitment has occupied thinkers, probably from the dawn of time: Plato, for instance, was concerned with securing the allegiance of citizens to the state.[1] Behavioral scientists have also spent much time studying the nature and consequence of employee commitment; the following sampling of their results provides an overview of the psychology of commitment—and of the practices that trigger it.

Commitment in Utopia

One of the most comprehensive investigations of commitment focused, not on businesses, but on utopian communities such as the Shakers and the Oneida. Most of those communities were formed in the United States in the 1800s, usually with the aim of having their people live together cooperatively, create their own governance, and operate according to a "higher order" of natural and spiritual laws.

Communities like these, says Rosabeth Moss Kanter, are held together not by coercion but by commitment: In Utopia what people *want* to do is the same as what they *have* to do. The interests of the individuals are congruent with those of the group, and personal growth and freedom entail responsibility for others.[2] Group life in these successful communities was therefore organized so as to support what Kanter calls "commitment building processes." These included sacrifice, investment, communion, and transcendence. All of these processes, as we'll see, are used by modern-day high-commitment organizations.

Sacrifice

Sacrifice meant community members had to give up something as a price of membership. Once the new members made their sacrifices—paid their dues—"membership [became] more valuable and meaningful."[3] Sacrifice, says Kanter, operates on the basis of a simple psychological principle: The more it costs someone to do something, the more valuable he or she will consider it, in order to justify the psychic expense. Signing over one's worldly goods, taking a vow of poverty, and pledging abstinence in one form or another constituted sacrifice in these nineteenth-century communes; we'll see later that extensive applicant testing and screening processes that border on initiation rites often constitute such "sacrifice" today.

Investment

All successful communes also demanded *investment* from their members, so as to ensure they had a stake in the fate of the community. If one commits his or her profit to the group, then leaving the group becomes more costly, and to that extent commitment tends to be enhanced. One implication is that commitment tends to be a function of the irreversibility of the person's investment: If you can't get it back, you're more committed to stay. Nineteenth-century communes thus demanded that members commit their profits to the group; modern-day high-commitment firms are more likely to create golden handcuffs with their pension plans.

Communion

The dictionary defines *communion* as a sharing or possession in common; as Kanter says, "Connectedness, belonging, participation in a whole, mingling of the self and the group, equal opportunity to contribute and to benefit—all are part of communion."[4] And communion, in turn, helps create commitment.

Kanter found that utopian communities used several practices to foster feelings of communion. She points out, for example, that "A certain amount of homogeneity of background facilitated communion in successful 19th century communities, for members shared a fund of common experiences to ease mutual role taking and identification with one another and the collectivity." Members often had a common religious background, similar social or educational status, or a common national or ethnic origin. In addition, "members of every successful community had some prior acquaintance with one another before coming together to form the community."[5]

This sense of communion was further heightened by communal sharing; joint ownership of property helped to create a "we" feeling and to implement the kindred spirit central to the forming of utopian communities.[6] Furthermore, there was communal work, "with all members, as far as possible, performing all tasks for equal rewards."[7] As Kanter found,

> [Job] rotation can be extremely effective as a commune mechanism, for it increases the area of the individual's responsibility to the group rather than limiting it to one task, and it emphasizes that the member is ready to perform any service the community may require of him, regardless of personal preference.[8]

Transcendence

Commitment in utopian communes was also fostered by what Kanter calls *transcendence*, in other words, the feeling among members that they were part of something bigger than themselves, something all-embracing. These communities, after all, were more than merely social clubs whose members banned together to enjoy each other's company. All the successful communities had a mission—often a spiritual one—as well as shared values and beliefs and a comprehensive ideology that all members could commit to. Orientation and socialization activities aided in the ideological conversion of new recruits, while an elaborate system of legends and ceremonial meetings served to constantly remind members of the community's ideological traditions.

Commitment at Work

What are the practices that trigger commitment at work? One study involved 279 managers for eight large U.S. organizations; researcher Bruce Buchanan's aim was to identify the "experiences that fostered commitment among all 279 managers."[9] Buchanan found that certain "organizational experiences" seemed to play a role in creating employee commitment:

Personal importance.   The experience of being treated as a productive and valuable member of the organization was far and away the most influential of the [organizational experiences].

Work-group experiences.   In general, the more cohesive (that is, friendly and close-knit) the manager's work group (the colleagues he or she had to interact with during the day), the more positive was both the group's overall feeling toward the organization and the manager's commitment to the organization.

Realization of expectations.   Managers were asked to evaluate their organizations in terms of questions such as "Has my organization fulfilled its promises to me and otherwise met my expectations in areas I care about?" Those that answered "yes" were much more likely to also be committed to the organization.

First-year job challenge.   Managers that had challenging job assignments during their first year or so at work were much more likely to be committed to the organization.[10]

Overall, the results here underscored the role of career satisfaction and success in winning commitment. The best route to employee commitment, concludes Buchanan, is "for the organization to take the time and the trouble to provide each manager with the experience he or she needs—even craves—at each stage of his or her career."[11]

An analysis of employee commitment among 382 hospital employees (including administrators, nurses, service workers, and clerical employees) and 119 scientists and engineers from a research lab led to a similar conclusion: The organization's ability to fulfill the employee's personal career aspirations had a marked effect on his or her commitment. As Richard Steers sums up his findings,

Individuals come to organizations with certain needs, desires, skills, and so forth and expect to find a work environment where they can utilize their abilities and satisfy many of their basic needs. When the organization provides such a vehicle [for example, where it makes effective use of its employees, is dependable, and so forth], the likelihood of increasing commitment is apparently enhanced. When the organization is not dependable, however, or where it fails to provide employees with challenging and meaningful tasks, commitment levels tend to diminish.[12]

Helping employees achieve their personal career aspirations is a recurring theme in other commitment studies, although other factors—organizational communication and a sense of communion, for instance—are obviously important as well. For example, in one study of some 500 employees of a manufacturing plant, the researchers defined commitment as "identification with company goals and values and even internalization of these values."[13] Here career-related practices—internal mobility and promotion from within, company-sponsored training and development, and job security—were all correlated with employee commitment. As these researchers concluded,

> ...commitment is higher among employees who believe they are being treated as resources to be developed rather than commodities to buy and sell. Even controlling for other known antecedents, employees are committed to the extent that they believe the company is providing a long-term developmental employment opportunity.[14]

After studying 367 managers, two other researchers similarly concluded that commitment is created when employees find a work environment where they can utilize their abilities and satisfy their needs. They found that such a high-commitment work environment was characterized by participative decision making; clear communications about the firm's intentions, activities, and performance; job autonomy (as opposed to close supervision); and a sense of cohesion and communion among employees. For example, it was "standard practice for the top management of the company to meet monthly with all lower level managerial employees in order to keep them informed about corporate performance and plans, and to gain their reactions to these plans."[15]

Creating Commitment

How does a firm create commitment? What are the management practices that foster it? Any study needs a starting point, and research findings like these were the starting point for mine. Several practices surfaced repeatedly in various studies—fostering communion, building cohesive work teams, helping employees self-actualize, providing jobs that challenged employees' minds, and hiring people with some similarity of values, for instance.

Yet as I studied the top 10 firms, my list of practices had to be both pruned and expanded. I found, for example, that all the top firms also emphasized people-first values: They trusted and respected their employees and were deeply committed to their employees' welfare. In fact, I found that where such values were not in place the other keys to commitment were seen as merely empty gestures. Similarly, two-way communication, job security, above-average rewards, and guaranteed fair treatment of employees showed up again and again. My final list of keys—people-first values, double-talk, communion, transcendental mediation, value-based hiring, securitizing, hard-side rewards, and actualizing—represent, I believe, the bundle of management practices that together create commitment.

Will employee commitment guarantee your firm's success? I think not. IBM is a good example. Historically, "commitment" and "IBM" have gone hand in hand, and yet IBM's sales, profits, and market share began sliding as they lost some of their competitiveness in the 1980s. Their employees, I think, were as committed in the '80s as they'd been in earlier years. But high commitment won't compensate for a strategy that has gone astray, nor will it overcome the inherent inefficiencies of overstaffing or the retarding effects of a slow-moving product-approval process.

Committed employees will help you to compete more effectively in good times and react to adverse conditions when things turn bad. They will help you gain a responsiveness and achieve quality and productivity levels your competitors will envy; they will do their jobs as if they own the company. More than anything, though, committed employees will do their best for you even when you're not looking, and many, many more jobs today are done far from the watchful eyes of a supervisory staff.[16] This book can start you on the road to creating commitment, but translating commitment into corporate success depends on you.

References

1. See Bruce Buchanan, "To Walk an Extra Mile: The What's, When's, and Why's of Organizational Commitment," *Organizational Dynamics*, Spring 1975, pp. 67–80; in Jerome Schnee, Harold Lazarus, and E. Kirby Warren, *The Progress of Management*, Prentice-Hall, Englewood Cliffs, N.J., 1977.

2. Reprinted by permission of the publisher from Rosabeth Moss Kanter, *Commitment and Community: Communes and Utopias in Sociological Perspective*, Harvard University Press, Cambridge, Mass., p. 1. Copyright 1972 by the Presidents and Fellows of Harvard College.

3. Ibid., p. 76.

4. Ibid., p. 93.

5. Ibid., p. 94.

6. Ibid.

7. Ibid., p. 95.

8. Ibid., p. 96.

9. Buchanan, p. 72.

10. Ibid., p. 73.

11. Ibid., p. 75.

12. Richard M. Steers, "Antecedents and Outcomes of Organizational Commitment," *Administrative Science Quarterly*, vol. 22 (March 1977), p. 53. See also Lyman Porter, Richard Steers, Richard Mowday, and Paul Boulian, "Organizational Commitment, Job Satisfaction, and Turnover among Psychiatric Technicians," *Journal of Applied Psychology*, vol. 59 (November 1974), pp. 603–609.

13. Karen Gaertner and Stanley Nollen, "Career Experiences, Perceptions of Employment Practices, and Psychological Commitment in the Organization," *Human Relations*, vol. 42, no. 11, 1989, p. 976.

14. Ibid., p. 987.

15. Thomas DeCotiis and Timothy Summers, "A Path Analysis of a Model of the Antecedents and Consequences of Organizational Commitment," *Human Relations*, vol. 40, no. 7 (1987), p. 466.

16. Charles O'Reilly III and Jennifer Chatman, "Organizational Commitment and Psychological Attachment: The Effect of Compliance, Identification, and Internalization on Pro-social Behavior," *Journal of Applied Psychology*, vol. 71 (1986), p. 493.

Additional Readings

Cathy Kline and Lawrence Peters, "Behavioral Commitment and Tenure of New Employees: A Replication and Extension," *Academy of Management Journal*, vol. 34, no. 1, March 1991, pp. 194–204.

Charles Glisson and Mark Durick, "Predictors of Job Satisfaction and Organizational Commitment in Human Service Organizations," *Administrative Science Quarterly*, vol. 33, no. 2, March 1988, pp. 61–81.

James P. Curry et al., "On the Causal Ordering of Job Satisfaction and Organizational Commitment," *Academy of Management Journal*, vol. 29, no. 4, Winter 1986, pp. 847–858.

Paul Brooke, Daniel Russel, and James Price, "Discriminant Validation of Measures of Job Satisfaction, Job Involvement, and Organizational Commitment," *Journal of Applied Psychology*, vol. 73, no. 2, April 1988, pp. 139–145.

Fred Luthans, Donald Baack, and Lew Taylor, "Organizational Commitment: Analysis of Antecedents," *Human Relations*, vol. 40, no. 4, 1987, pp. 219–236.

Richard Mowday, Lyman Porter, and Richard Steers, *Employee-Organization Linkages: The Psychology of Commitment, Absenteeism, and Turnover*, Academic Press, New York, 1982.

PART 2

The Keys to Commitment

3

People-First Values

Actions are the products of values. Values like duty, honor, country; respect for the individual; hard work, honesty, neighborliness, and thrift; and quality, service, and price all silently channel how we act, as we consciously or subconsciously compare our prospective actions with these guideposts in our minds.

You can usually infer a firm's values from the actions it takes. As I studied the high-commitment firms, several practices seemed always in evidence: These firms were given to fostering two-way communication, to creating feelings of community and "oneness," to hiring employees who could be developed for the long haul and providing them with full employment, to guaranteeing fair treatment, and to helping their employees become all they could be.

Actions like these, I found, all reflected what I've called "people-first values." All of the firms I've singled out—Goldman, Sachs; IBM; Ben & Jerry's; J. C. Penney; Federal Express; and all the rest—were founded and are run on the assumption that their employees are their most important assets; that they must respect their employees as individuals and treat them all fairly; that they must give all their people every chance to succeed and trust them; and that they must be committed to the welfare of their employees. People-first values like these are the bedrock of employee commitment: They drive the actions that are the keys to commitment. Employees become committed because they know these firms are committed to them.

And yet, as the chairman of Fed Ex, Fred Smith, has said,

> ...consistently keeping people first is hard work....Putting people first in every action, every planning process, every business decision, requires an extraordinary commitment from every manager and every employee...Every company says it's a people company.... Putting that somewhat ideal philosophy into practice means we must look for a multitude of ways to replace talk with action.[1]

Doing so begins with instituting people-first values throughout your firm, and this involves four steps: Know what you want, put it in writing, hire and indoctrinate, and "walk the talk."

Know What You Want

Few things are as corrosive to morale as an autocrat on a participative management binge. First you have to genuinely believe in people—that they can be trusted, that they should be treated with respect, that they deserve to be involved in making decisions on the job, that they should be encouraged to grow. Only if and when you truly believe this is it time to start your commitment program.

At Fed Ex, a top personnel officer told me that "You start the process of boosting employee commitment by making sure you know how you and your top managers really feel about people." Trying to institute commitment-creating practices that aren't solidly based in people-first values will only expose your program as a sham. First you have to commit firmly to putting your people first, to doing what's best for them.

However, managers don't adopt people-first values out of the pure goodness of their hearts. They do so because they also believe it is the best for their firms. That's true at Federal Express; Chairman Fred Smith sums it up this way: "When people are placed first, they will provide the highest possible service, and profits will follow."[2] The same is true at J. C. Penney. When James Cash Penney and his partners called their first store in Kemmerer, Wyoming, "The Golden Rule" back in 1902, they weren't just paying lip service to the value of fair and equitable treatment. Customer service was a top priority to Penney long before it became a 1990s phenomenon; he always said that "associates are what makes good customer service happen," and for over 90 years, the company he founded has adhered to the value that "every associate will be treated with respect, dignity, and consideration."[3] Similarly, "Where Shopping Is a Pleasure" is the motto on the signs all over Publix stores, but a Publix manager says, "Our customers come second; our people come first."

At Toyota, U.S.A., the top executives' dedication to people-first values is both sincere and pragmatic. Fujio Cho, the U.S. president of Toyota Motor Manufacturing, summed up the need for people-first values this way:

> The three main factors for plant operation in a manufacturing company are often expressed with 3 M's. They are man, machinery, and material....[However,] in any manufacturing industry, a new technology becomes common knowledge in a very short time, and all companies will certainly incorporate the new technology in their operation. The same is true with newly developed material. In terms of machinery too, as long as the money is available, anyone can buy state-of-the-art automated machines. Mass media is still paying a great deal of attention to robotics and to automation in a plant. But I suspect that the extent of automation and the use of robots in any automobile plant in North America is more or less the same. In other words, I do not think automation and robots are the deciding factors in the difference of quality or productivity among various auto plants. Machines and material, then, are no longer decisive factors in determining success of the present day manufacturing operation....The key factor that makes the difference among various plants is the workers.[4]

People-first values and the trust and respect they imply are thus the basis of Toyota's Kaizen system. *Kaizen* is a Japanese word meaning improvements or search for a better way. At Toyota, Kaizen means having the firm depend on its workers to find and eliminate all forms of waste. Toyota team members work together to plan their own jobs and make the work process smoother and their efforts more efficient. But such a process demands trust and respect.

Perhaps the best description of the need for people-first values came from Kenny Duncan, the UAW's partner to Saturn Corp.'s head of personnel:

> Our philosophy is, we care about people—and it shows. We involve people in decisions that affect them. I came from the Messena, New York, GM foundry and managers there, like a lot of the other managers you'll come across, take the position that "I'll tell you what to do, and that's what you'll do." In fact, some of those managers from the foundry are here now. But on the whole those who are here now are different, and the basic difference is wrapped up in the question, "Do you really believe in people?" Saturn's commitment really comes down to how you feel about people—your attitudes—more

than anything, because all the other Saturn programs—the work teams, the extensive training, the way people are paid—all flow from these people attitudes.[5]

Put It in Writing

Fed Ex's Fred Smith says that at some point you must "replace talk with action." The first step in doing so is to codify your people-first values and distribute them. That's why all of our 10 firms make frequent mention of their people-first values in company brochures and handbooks. For example, one Fed Ex personnel officer says that the company's most basic people-first value is codified, from the employee's point of view, in unmistakable terms in its *Manager's Guide:* "I have an inherent right to be treated with respect and dignity and that right should never be violated."

At Saturn, employees carry a card that lists the firm's values, one of which is set forth in these words:

> Trust and respect for the individual: We have nothing of greater value than our people. We believe that demonstrating respect for the uniqueness of every individual builds a team of confident, creative members possessing a high degree of initiative, self-respect, and self-discipline.

The firm's union contract also stresses the point:

> We believe that all people want to be involved in decisions that affect them, care about their job, take pride in themselves and in their contributions, and want to share in the success of their efforts.
>   By creating an atmosphere of mutual trust and respect, recognizing and utilizing individual expertise and knowledge in innovative ways, providing the technologies and education for each individual, we will enjoy a successful relationship and a sense of belonging to an integrated business system capable of achieving our common goals which ensures security for our people and success for our business and communities.[6]

The story is the same at other high-commitment firms. For example, Toyota's team-member handbook states that "People are our most important resource and are the most important factor in the success of the organization....The very basis of the [Toyota] production system is the respect and dignity of team members."[7] The first of IBM's three business principles, as stated in their handbook, is "Respect for the dignity and the rights of each person in the organization."[8]

Hire and Indoctrinate

Kenny Duncan's comment—"Commitment really comes down to what you feel about people"—underscores another of his firm's people-first practices: Saturn hires people who have people-first values from the start.

But we can find this philosophy in any of our 10 firms. Take Mike Da Prile, general manager of Toyota's assembly plant. After 30 years with General Motors, he was one of about 150 people who responded to Toyota's *Wall Street Journal* recruiting ad. (It was actually his wife who sent in his application.) The list was cut to 50, and finally to 15, as Toyota, according to Mike, asked the applicants questions such as "Do you feel good about yourself?" "Are you willing to learn?" and "What is your feeling about people in general?" It was his people-first values, not just his technical skills, that got him the job, Mike says.[9]

At J. C. Penney, their "certified interviewing" program helps screen out applicants who lack the people skills and values to do the job. As will be explained in Chapter 7, certified interviewing involves using a series of questions to identify and hire high-potential employees, those with values that "fit" the firm. One store manager put it this way:

> Mr. Penney's golden rule means do right by your people, and all of us work hard to maintain that philosophy. All Penney's people are therefore nice people—they have a heart and you would relate to them. If they're not nice, they'll be filtered out in the hiring and evaluation process. For example, we have a process called certified interviewing in which candidates are evaluated on, amongst other things, their leadership qualities and...their sensitivity to the needs of others and on how they influence and deal with people and work with people to get the work done.

Like all of these other high-commitment firms, Federal Express is very careful about the people it promotes to managerial positions. All Fed Ex supervisory candidates must enroll in the firm's multistage LEAP program to prove they have the values and skills to be Fed Ex managers. About 20 percent of these candidates fall out after the first phase of the program—"Is Management for Me?"—a one-day session that familiarizes them with the manager's job. This session is followed by about three months of both self-evaluations and supervisory assessments of the candidates' values and skills. Next comes a series of peer assessments and panel interviews with senior managers; this phase takes several days. Management training sessions in the firm's Leadership Institute then reinforce Fed Ex's people-first values and indoctrinate the new managers in the principles and values of the firm.

"Walk the Talk"

Above all, people-first values permeate everything these firms' managers say and do. As one Fed Ex manager said, "Most firms have their values posted, but at Federal Express these are real values that actually govern the business....You don't see managers here saying one thing and doing another." One Fed Ex vice president agrees: "I was with Flying Tiger and United and several other firms, but I've never been at a firm that works as hard as Fed Ex at treating people fairly."

Not far away, at Toyota, the comments are actually much the same. Russ Scaffede, head of power-train manufacturing, affirms that people-first values touch every decision:

> In all our meetings and in every way, all Toyota top managers continually express their trust in human nature. Mr. Cho continually reminds us that the team members must come first and that every other action we take and decision we make must be adapted to that basic idea; I must manage around that core idea.[10]

Says Mike Da Prile, the assembly plant's general manager:

> In all my 30 years in this business, I've never seen anything like the sort of total commitment to its people that Toyota top managers live every day. That is probably the single biggest difference between Toyota and GM: Here our people *are* the company—Toyota makes you feel that you are part of the company and virtually every one of us sees Toyota's long-term success as inseparable from ours.[11]

This basic notion that the people-first values should be applied to every decision the firm makes was summed up by Bob Gill, Penney's vice chairman and chief operating officer:

> Our people's high commitment stems from our commitment to them, and that commitment boils down to the fundamental "respect for the individual" that we all share. That respect goes back to the Penney Idea—"to test our every act in this wise: Does it square with what is right and just?" As a result, the value of respect for the individual is brought into our management process on a regular basis and is a standard against which we measure each and every decision that we make. We will always ask, "Does that square with what is right and just?" No one moves into management without first proving his or her commitment to Mr. Penney's ideals. Mr. Penney used to say, "You've demonstrated your honesty and value system and we now think you're ready to manage your own store."[12]

The bottom line is that the personal practices in these firms all reflect this commitment to putting their people first. At Federal Express, for instance, their new-employee orientation manuals stress that "PSP, People-Service-Profit, is the foundation of Federal Express' entire philosophy. We build on that idea by putting our *people first*." Specific examples of PSP in action are found in the manual:

> Survey Feedback Action: Using this opinion survey management responds to and in many cases makes changes as a result of your suggestions....
>
> We consider employees first when developing corporate programs and policies....
>
> We involve employees as valuable team members....
>
> We promote from within whenever the needed skills can be found in existing ranks....
>
> We invest in personnel through education and training....
>
> We strive to maintain open communications and be totally candid about every subject....
>
> We provide a fair procedure for handling employee complaints, problems, or concerns regarding unreasonable or inconsistent treatment....
>
> We are committed to a philosophy of avoiding layoffs and maintaining our outstanding wages, benefits, and compensation package....[13]

Similarly, the trick to implementing people-first values, says Toyota's Fujio Cho, is to "translate your people-first values into concrete actions." One example is the seven miles of "Andon cord" stretched throughout Toyota's plant in Georgetown, Kentucky. When a Toyota employee has an assembly problem, he or she pulls on the cord, which lights a board, called an Andon, and signals to all Toyota workers the specific location of the problem. Thus every employee has the power to shut down the assembly line, to stop production at a plant where 4000 people build 900 cars per day. Says Mr. Cho:

> To me, this length of rope says more about our philosophy of building cars than anything else at our plant. The Andon cord is part of a very simple, common sense process of building cars called the Toyota production system. The system is applied by a team of individuals who are intelligent and continually trained, and who take advantage of a system to help them do their jobs better.[14]

The Andon cord is just one symbol of Toyota's faith in and respect for its people. Gary Thompson, a general maintenance worker, talks about the importance of the day-to-day decisions he's allowed to make in programming the robots he maintains.[15] Assembler Kelvin Young stresses the firm's commitment to job security: "They always say they'd never lay someone off, and in lean times we'd be kept on to analyze and make the process more efficient."[16] To assembler Tammy Amburgey, Toyota's people-first values mean that "work here is hard work, but we don't mind because we believe the company is committed to us."[17] To Jeri Johnson, it's because "we know we have an input."[18] To Kim Graves and Dawn King it's because we know that "even if you make a mistake, they make a positive out of it—there's no pointing fingers."[19]

Toyota's people-first values manifest themselves in other ways, says Fujio Cho. Fair treatment in disciplinary situations is guaranteed by a rigid grievance procedure, and by a warning system that includes a day of paid leave to give an employee time to think about rehabilitating his or her performance. Termination recommendations are generally only finalized after they've been reviewed and approved by a peer review committee consisting of three of the employee's peers and two managers. Toyota encourages team members to say what's on their minds and uses several methods, including periodic opinion surveys and quarterly round-table meetings with management, to facilitate that. There's a hot line through which team members can voice questions and concerns anonymously by telephone to a recorder: A written response appears on the bulletin board. No closed offices (even the president doesn't have one), no reserved parking spots, no executive dining room, and extensive benefits—including an $8.5 million family center and childcare facility—are other examples.

Saturn Corporation similarly translates their people-first values into practice every day. Extensive two-way communication systems (frequent meetings, open-door policies, and so forth), job security, team-centered work groups, and an emphasis on employee self-actualization—giving each employee an opportunity to be all he or she can be through involvement in most job-related decisions, plus promotion from within and extensive career assessment, training, and development programs—all reflect Saturn's people-first values.

For a door-finishing team that I met with, Saturn's people-first values came down to a matter of trust. Finisher Sean Graham said, for instance, "Other companies talk a lot about ownership and trust but never really carry through." Bob Laura emphasized, "Here we're trusted with a lot of confidential information such as the financials on how Saturn is doing. And they'll tell you, Here is the problem; what would you do about it?" Greg Arthur told me, "You can tell how they really feel about you from all the training we receive. You know that they're really investing in you." "And here," Sean added, "we're all salaried, not hourly, and there are no time clocks and no security guards." Rick Stemple, Jr., insisted that the company's respect for its employees is also shown by how payrolls are done; even though employees are salaried, they get paid for overtime hours: "You go into the keyboard and punch in the number of hours you worked, and that's how your payroll checks are produced," Stemple said. Joe Caldwell said,

> What it comes down to is that they trust us, and it shows. In one GM plant that I used to be with they used to have a chain-link fence around the plant with the barbed wire leaning in to keep their own people from stealing. There's nothing like that here. No checks to see if you're stealing, no time clocks, no chain-link fences. They treat you like adults.

Sean Graham summed it up for the team: "They teach us how to manage and we teach them how to build cars," he said.[20]

I also met with Steve Ochab and Cliff Cantrell, the crew coordinators—department heads—for the vehicle interior systems unit at Saturn. Steve is the Saturn manager, and Cliff his union partner. To them, the most concrete manifestation of Saturn's people-first values is the company's extensive involvement system: "Involving people, opportunities for career growth and development, and extensive training all show that Saturn is really committed to its people and [has] respect and...faith in them," Steve said.[21]

Bob Boruff, Saturn's vice president for manufacturing, told me that the key to Saturn's success in igniting employee commitment stemmed from

> ...creating a value system that encourages the kind of behavior we knew we wanted. We knew we had to put in an actionable value system that changed how managers thought and how people built cars. If you start with the premise that you trust people and they they will do a good job, it takes you in a whole new direction. But if you really want to trust people, you have to show that you do and you start by eliminating all those things that say, "I don't trust you." That includes time clocks, gates, and hourly pay, for example.[22]

A Summary: People-First Values as Key to Commitment

1. Start the process of creating commitment by making sure you know how you and your top management really feel about people. To create commitment, you must be willing to put your people first in every action, every planning process, and every business decision you make. You must be willing to trust them.

2. Put your people-first values in writing. Let your employees *see* your creed, expressed in words such as:

   We care about people and it shows.

   We value trust and respect for the individual; we hold nothing of greater value than our people.

   We believe that all people want to be involved in decisions that affect them, that they care about their jobs, and that they take pride in themselves and in their contributions.

   We believe that all people have an inherent right to be treated with respect and dignity and that that right should never be violated.

   We believe that people are our most important resource.

3. Hire people who have people-first values from the start. Establish rigorous interviewing procedures to screen out those without the people skills and values to do the job.

4. Translate your people-first values into actions every day:

   Continually remind your supervisors that employees come first and that every action they take must be based on that standard.

   Eliminate symbols like time clocks that say, "I don't trust you."

   Monitor each group's reactions to its supervisor's actions.

   Maintain open communications; be candid with your people.

   Invest in your people through training and education.

   Provide your people with job security.

   Promote from within.

   Work hard to make sure that each employee has the most successful career he or she can, that each employee is able to use personal skills to the fullest.

   Get your employees more involved in making job-related decisions and give them the training and the information that they need to make those decisions.

References

1. *Blueprints for Service Quality: The Federal Express Approach,* AMA Membership Publications, New York, 1991, p. 13.
2. *Blueprints for Service Quality,* p. 12.
3. J. C. Penney Employee Manual, p. 2.
4. Fujio Cho, "Employee Motivation by Applying the Toyota Production

System," address to the Asian Business Club of Harvard Business School, March 4, 1991.

5. Personal interview with Kenny Duncan, March 1992.

6. Saturn Corporation, Memorandum of Agreement, 1988, p. 2.

7. *Team Member Handbook*, Toyota Motor Manufacturing, U.S.A., February 1988, p. 3.

8. *All About Your Company*, IBM employee handbook, p. 6.

9. Personal interview with Mike Da Prile, March 1992.

10. Personal interview with Russ Scaffede, March 1992.

11. Personal interview with Mike Da Prile, March 1992.

12. Personal interview with Bob Gill, March 1992.

13. *Federal Express New Hire Employee Orientation Workbook*, #136352, pp. 2–4, 2–5.

14. Fujio Cho, "Employee Motivation by Applying the Toyota Production System."

15. Personal interview with Gary Thompson, March 1992.

16. Personal interview with Kelvin Young, March 1992.

17. Personal interview with Tammy Amburgey, March 1992.

18. Personal interview with Jeri Johnson, March 1992.

19. Personal interviews with Kim Graves and Dawn King, March 1992.

20. Personal interview with team members Greg Arthur, Joe Caldwell, Sean Graham, Bob Laura, and Rick Stemple, Jr., March 1992.

21. Personal interviews with Steve Ochab and Cliff Cantrell, March 1992.

22. Personal interview with Bob Boruff, March 1992.

4

Double-Talk

When I asked a Saturn work team, "What's the first thing you would tell a boss to do in order to get employee commitment?" the response was, in unison, "Tell them to listen."

Unfortunately, most firms don't seem to be listening. Hay Research conducted a survey of 750,000 middle managers and compared data from 1985–1987 with data from 1988–1990. The percent of middle managers who expressed a favorable attitude on "information given to employees" fell from 85 percent in 1985–1987 to 69 percent in the later survey. "Top management listening to their problems and complaints" elicited favorable attitudes from 42 percent in the earlier survey and 35 percent in 1988–1990.[1] Louis Harris & Associates polled office workers and their managers on behalf of the Steelcase Office Furniture Company; they concluded that what top management thinks their workers want is much different from what the workers themselves say they want. For example, workers ranked "more honest communications between employees and senior management" higher than management's choice, "job security."[2] Opinion Research Corporation surveyed 100,000 middle managers, supervisors, professionals, salespeople, and technical, clerical, and hourly workers of Fortune 500 companies a few years ago. Except for the sales group, all employees believed that at that point top management was less willing to listen to their problems than they had been five years earlier.[3]

This is not the case in our high-commitment firms, where managers know that commitment is built on trust, and that trust requires a flood of two-way communication. Indeed, you'll find an enormous quantity of two-way communication in these firms, two-way communication that, for brevity, I've called "double-talk." Executives in these firms do more than express a willingness to hear and be heard. They've also set up programs that *guarantee* two-way talk. I found basically four types of programs employed: "guaranteed fair treatment" programs for filing grievances and complaints; "speak up" programs for voicing concerns and making inquiries; "periodic survey" programs for expressing opinions; and various "top-down" programs for keeping employees informed.

Guaranteed Fair Treatment Programs

The potential for grievances and discontent is always present in any firm. Just about any factor involving wages, hours, or conditions of employment has and will be used as the basis for grievance in most firms. Discipline cases and seniority problems (including promotions, transfers, and layoffs) probably top the list. Other grievances grow out of such issues as job evaluations and work assignments, overtime, vacations and holidays, and incentive plans.

Whatever the source of discontent, today most firms give their people channels through which to air grievances. Unionized firms don't hold a monopoly on such fair treatment practices. Many nonunionized firms also have formal grievance procedures.[4] In one study, 24 out of 41 companies responding reported that they had grievance procedures for nonunionized employees. In 10 of these firms the grievance procedures covered all employees (including executives), while in most of the others the procedures were reserved for rank-and-file workers and (in some firms) first-line supervisors. Another survey showed that two-thirds of the 62 nonunion respondents had grievance policies. Several of these used either an open-door policy or a step procedure with arbitration. The steps typically involve discussion of the matter with a supervisor, then with a department head, then with the head of personnel, and then perhaps with a vice president before the matter is turned over to an inside arbitrator.[5] In most of these firms the grievance process is codified in the personnel handbook.

Federal Express's Guaranteed Fair Treatment Procedure

Programs such as Federal Express's Guaranteed Fair Treatment Procedure (GFTP) go far beyond this. I say this because special, readily available forms make filing the grievance easy; employees are encouraged to use the system; and the highest levels of Fed Ex's management are routinely involved in reviewing complaints. As their employee handbook says,

> Perhaps the cornerstone of Federal Express' "people" philosophy is the guaranteed fair treatment procedure (GFTP). This policy affirms your right to appeal any eligible issue through this process of systematic review by progressively higher levels of management. Although the outcome is not assured to be in your favor, your right to participate within the guidelines of the procedure is guaranteed. At Federal Express, where we have a "people-first" philosophy, you have a right to discuss your complaints with management without fear of retaliation.[6]

The net effect is twofold: Complaints don't get a chance to accumulate and managers think twice before doing anything unfair, since their actions will likely be brought to their bosses' attention. In fact, each Tuesday morning, a group of five Federal Express executives gathers to review and rule on employee complaints and grievances filed through the program. They include CEO Fred Smith, Chief Operating Officer James Barksdale, the firm's chief personnel officer, and two other senior vice presidents.[7]

Eligible Concerns.   GFTP is available to all permanent Fed Ex employees. It covers all concerns regarding matters such as job promotion, compensation policies, and discipline affecting the individual complainant. Basically, as the firm's handbook points out, "If for any reason you are a recipient of discipline, you will have access to the GFTP."[8]

Steps.   The Fed Ex Guaranteed Fair Treatment Procedure contains three steps. In step 1, *management review*, the complainant submits a written complaint to a member of management (manager, senior manager, or managing director) within seven calendar days of the occurrence of the eligible issue. Then the manager, senior manager, and managing director of the employee's group review all relevant information; hold a telephone conference and/or meeting with the complainant; make a decision to either uphold, modify, or overturn management's action; and communicate their decision in writing to the complainant and the department's personnel representative. All of this occurs within 10 calendar days of receipt of the complaint.

In step 2, *officer review*, the complainant can submit a written complaint to an officer (vice president or senior vice president) of the division within seven calendar days of the step 1 decision. The vice president and senior vice president then review all relevant information; conduct an additional investigation when necessary; make a decision to uphold, overturn, or modify management's action or to initiate a board of review; and communicate their decision in writing to the complainant with a copy to the department's personnel representative and the complainant's management. As in step 1, the step 2 review generally occurs within 10 calendar days of receipt of the complaint.

Finally, in step 3, *executive appeals review*, the complainant can submit a written complaint within seven calendar days of the step 2 decision to the employee relations department. This department then investigates and prepared a GFTP case file for the appeals board executive review. The appeals board—CEO Smith, COO Barksdale, Chief Personnel Officer Jim Perkins, and two other senior vice presidents—then reviews all relevant information; makes a decision to uphold, overturn, or initiate a board of review or to take other appropriate action; and generally does this within 14 calendar days of receipt of the complaint. Barring the formation of a separate board of review, the decision of the appeals board is final.

A board of review is used when there is a question of fact. It's actually a five-member jury of Federal Express employees.[9] Two are chosen by the complaining employee from a list of names submitted by the board chair. Three are selected by the board chair from a list of names submitted by the employee. Board chairpersons are chosen from the ranks of management at the director level or above and receive special training for this responsibility.

Documentation. Packets of forms in folders entitled "Guaranteed Fair Treatment Procedure" are used to file GFTP-registered complaints; these packets are available from the personnel office. They include a fact sheet listing the complainant's name and work history; a GFTP tracking sheet to keep track of the complaint at each step; and instructions and space for a write-up of management's rationale (for instance, in terms of applicable policies and procedures), a write-up from the personnel department, and key documents (termination letters and so on). There is also space for backup material, including witness statements, medical statements, and training records. These packets are widely available and easily accessible.

Remember, for a process like this to work, it must be founded on people-first values. As one Fed Ex manager told me:

Our guaranteed fair treatment program is based on the idea that you have to foster feelings of individual significance and importance amongst your employees. And that all stems from our core people-first values. There's no way to generate this from the bottom—you must espouse it from the top down, and so it's Fred Smith's values, his people-first values—he fosters it and we've institutionalized it.

Toyota's Concern Resolution System

Like Fed Ex, Toyota has a formal Concern Resolution System, which also allows for multistep review, but with several twists. While disciplinary procedures have historically been punitive in most firms, Toyota's program addresses employee performance problems more positively. It is aimed at emphasizing the correction or improvement of the person's performance through a progressive procedure, one that lets employees maintain their dignity throughout the process. It is based on five steps.

Oral Reminder. An oral reminder, consisting of a conversation between the group leader-supervisor and the team member, takes place when a team member experiences a relatively minor performance problem, one that can usually be corrected by being brought to the team member's attention.

Written Reminder. If the team member fails to correct a performance problem after receiving an oral reminder (or if it is determined that the team member's performance problem is serious enough), he or she gets a written reminder. Here, after a formal conversation between the supervisor and team member, the supervisor prepares, with the personnel department's assistance, a written memo summarizing the conversation. The employee relations manager then includes the document in the employee's personnel record. If the problem is corrected (and no more problems arise during the following 12 months), the memo is removed from the file and returned to the employee.

Corrective Action Conference. This step is taken if the employee fails to correct the performance problem, or if his or her behavior is serious enough to warrant further action. Here a meeting takes place between the team member, supervisor, area personnel representative, employee relations manager, and section manager. The aim is to pinpoint what aspects of the employee's performance are unacceptable, why they are unacceptable, and what action must be taken to resolve the problem. Information regarding this conference stays in the team member's personnel file for 24 months. It is then removed if the problem is corrected.

Decision-Making Leave.   This step is taken if an employee fails to correct the performance problem after the correction action conference. In a decision-making leave, the employee is told to stay home the following day and to use the time to make a final decision regarding whether he or she wants to stay with the company. If the decision is yes, the team member commits to correcting the problem; he or she then receives eight hours' pay for the one day's leave. Information regarding the decision-making leave stays in the personnel file for 48 months and is then removed if the problem is corrected and no more problems have developed.

Termination.   If the employee doesn't respond to the steps outlined above (or if a team member's actions are such that the company feels his or her employment cannot be continued), the team member will be dismissed. However, even at this stage, dismissal is generally subject to *peer review.*

The firm has a voluntary review board composed of three employee "peers" and two managers. Three of the board members are selected from the same job classification as the team member. These members serve on a voluntary basis and rotate by their length of service, which could eventually provide all Toyota Motor Manufacturing team members with an opportunity to participate in this process. The other two board members are managers selected by the employee relations department.

The peer review board is authorized to call anyone in and to review all documents related to the infraction. The board then gives the personnel department a recommendation, which the company has always (as of 1992) followed. Virtually all ("99 percent") terminations go through peer review, according to Sam Heltman, the firm's head of human resources.[10] However, some activities such as selling drugs might be subject to summary dismissal.

IBM's Open-Door Program

IBM's fair treatment program is called the Open Door. It gives every employee the right to appeal their supervisors' actions. Employees are told to first discuss the problem with their immediate manager, their manager's manager, their personnel manager, or their branch or site manager. If that doesn't solve the problem, they are instructed to go to the senior management in their business unit.

There are two other avenues available at IBM for openly expressing fairness concerns. First, if employees don't get satisfactory answers via the normal process, they may discuss the matter with IBM's chairman by mail—or personally, if the chairman finds it appropriate. An *executive interview* is the second avenue of appeal. This is sometimes referred to as the *skip-level interview, cross-talk,* or *second-level interview.* Here, employees are periodically invited (participation is voluntary) to speak to a manager one or more levels above that of their own manager. Employees may also initiate a request for such an interview.

Programs like those at IBM and Toyota haven't the structure and formality of Fed Ex's Guaranteed Fair Treatment Procedure. However, they do help ensure healthy communications regarding disciplinary matters.

Speak Up Programs

Disciplinary matters represent the tip of the iceberg when it comes to the concerns that employees care about. These concerns run the gamut from malfunctioning vending machines to unlit parking lots to one's manager spending too much of the department's money traveling.

IBM's Speak Up!

About 30 years ago an IBM facility in San Jose, California, launched a program called "What's On Your Mind?" At the time, the site general manager said in the employee newspaper that "We want to make it easy for our people to learn more about their company and how it's run. We invite any and all questions—even tough or touchy ones."[11] Several years later the program's name was changed to Speak Up! and the program went worldwide. Since then, according to Michael Zimet, IBM's Speak Up! administrator, the program has been used more than 450,000 times by employees in more than 40 countries. Its basic aim is to give employees a confidential channel for speaking their minds.

What makes the program unique, says Zimet, is the anonymity it provides. Employees may ask questions or make comments and receive a reply without revealing their identity to anyone except the Speak Up! administrator. The program works to protect the employee's identity as soon as a Speak Up! form is filed. The form itself is a combination letter-envelope, is easily available to all employees, and is self-addressed to the Speak Up! administrator. On the top is a detachable stub where employees print their names, home addresses, and IBM locations and indicate if they prefer to discuss the matter with a qualified person (usually by phone). There is also a space for the handwritten concerns, along with a note to the effect that the Speak Up! entry will be typed so that the "handwriting cannot be identified." The form can be completed, folded, and mailed.

When the form is received, a Speak Up! administrator removes the name stub and assigns the form a file number. The stub itself is then secured in a locked box and no one, except the Speak Up! administrator, ever sees the writer's name. All information that could possibly identify the writer or a third party is deleted from the Speak Up! comments. The Speak Up! is then typed and assigned to an investigator for an answer.

The investigator is usually the highest-level manager familiar with the Speak Up! concern. Answers are usually provided within 10 working days.

All nonanonymous Speak Up! inquiries get written replies in the form of individual letters signed by the investigating manager. The Speak Up! administrator first checks all responses for accuracy and completeness. He or she then personally addresses an envelope and mails the answer to the employee's home. The letters are mailed through U.S. mail—never along with internal company mail—to further assure anonymity. The program is managed by IBM's communication organization through 80 Speak Up! administrators around the world.

Employees are encouraged to file a Speak Up! at any time but are told that they might first consider talking to their own managers, reviewing the employee handbook, or calling the department involved to get a direct answer. Similarly, the IBM Suggestion Program is generally used to propose ideas that could save the company time or money. What the Speak Up! program does is let employees jump the normal chain of command. It lets them express their comments, concerns, or suggestions directly to someone responsible for the activity in question.[12]

Informal Open-Door Concepts

In some firms the open-door concept isn't formal but is built into the management process. At Delta, for instance, Maurice Worth, senior vice president for personnel, says, "I always reserve enough time to be visible and speak with employees when I travel; and I get eight to ten calls per week with suggestions, etc., and see about three people per week who want to meet with me."[13] One Mary Kay manager told me, "We have a very explicit open-door policy here. Employees know they can always go to Mary Kay and to the other top executives; they can go right to them." At Federal Express—which also has its own formal open-door practice (see below)—managers describe the firm as having an open, informal culture. Anyone can walk into Fred Smith's office without an appointment, and that's true throughout the chain of command. "Employees here are encouraged to interact with managers, and managers are encouraged to go out to the field to speak with our people," one personnel officer says. "We care about them and we're very accessible....People do not hesitate to come to the manager. We rarely have to use the Guaranteed Fair Treatment process because of this open-door philosophy."

Federal Express's Open-Door Policy

Federal Express also has a formal Open-Door process that serves about the same purpose as does Speak Up! at IBM: Its purpose is to encourage all Fed Ex employees to express any concern or address any issue of a systemic nature, one in which the remedy might affect not just an individual but the firm as a whole. However, Fed Ex's Open-Door is *not* anonymous: Senders must sign their name, and their name stays with the form. The sorts of issues addressed—seniority, vacation schedules, company benefits, area maintenance, and so on—are similar to those raised in the IBM Speak Up! program.

As at IBM, Fed Ex employees are urged to contact their own managers first if they want to voice a concern, although Fed Ex emphasizes that this is not required. It's widely understood that any employee can just submit a one-page Open-Door multipart form directly to employee relations. A sender indicates his or her name, employee number, and division and then explains the issue involved. Those responding to an Open-Door inquiry are advised on the form to respond directly to the employee "on the above issue in memo form within 14 calendar days of your receipt."

As an example, several years ago CEO Smith (who reviews all Open-Doors on a monthly basis) reportedly noticed part-time employees were questioning the fairness of the firm's seniority and job promotion policies. Upon investigating, he found that part-time employees working at "desirable" locations were often bumped from their jobs by full-time employees wanting to relocate from other, less desirable locations. Alerted by the Open-Door complaints, Federal Express revised its seniority policies. Part-time employees now accrue seniority points. This helps them qualify for full-time jobs and also makes it less likely that long-term part-time employees will be bumped to less desirable jobs or locations by shorter-term full-time employees.[14]

Toyota's Hotline

Toyota Motor Manufacturing tells its employees, "Don't spend time worrying about something...speak up!" At Toyota, the primary double-talk communication channel is called "Hotline." Its purpose is to give their team members an additional channel for bringing questions or problems to the company's attention.

Here's how it works. Hotline is available 24 hours a day. Employees are instructed to pick up any phone, dial the Hotline extension (the number is posted on the plant bulletin boards), and deliver their message to the recorder. *All* inquiries received on Hotline are guaranteed to be reviewed by the human resources manager and to be thoroughly investigated. If it's decided that a particular question would be of interest to other Toyota team members, then the question, along with the firm's response, is typed up and posted on plant bulletin boards. If a personal response is desired, employees have to leave their name when they call. In general though, employees know that their identity will remain confidential and that there will be no attempt to identify a particular Hotline caller.[15] Toyota is not the only "Hotline" firm, by the way. Publix has a 24-hour 800-number WOW line for employees' suggestions, complaints, and ideas.

Periodic Survey Programs

Most high-commitment firms also administer periodic—and anonymous—opinion surveys. At IBM the survey regularly asks employees their opinions about the company, management, and work life. Its stated purpose is "to aid management at all levels in identifying and solving problems."[16] At IBM and other high-commitment firms such as J. C. Penney and Toyota, the standard practice is to have department heads conduct feedback sessions after the survey results are compiled, in order to share the results and to work on solutions.

Federal Express's Survey Feedback Action Program

The Federal Express program is typical of survey programs. Called Survey Feedback Action (SFA), it is the cornerstone of the free-flowing communications at Federal Express, along with the Guaranteed Fair Treatment program and the Open-Door process.

The SFA program involves an anonymous survey that lets employees express feelings about the company and their managers—and to some extent about service, pay, and benefits. Each work group's manager then uses the results to help design a blueprint for improving work-group commitment. As one manager told me, "The heart of our system is respect for the individual, our justice system, and our survey process. We put our people first. We have the guaranteed fair treatment process that helps guarantee all grievances are dealt with. And we use the SFA survey process to continuously monitor our employees as a sort of manager's report card. With SFA, when people are fair they come out OK. The trick is to treat your people right."

The program has three phases. First, the survey itself—a standard, anonymous questionnaire—is administered each year to every employee. Sample items include:

I can tell my manager what I think.

My manager tells me what is expected.

My manager listens to my concerns.

My manager keeps me informed.

Upper management listens to ideas from my level.

Fed Ex does a good job for our customers.

In my environment we use safe work practices.

I am paid fairly for this kind of work.

Results of the survey for a work group are compiled and returned to the group's manager. (To ensure anonymity, the smaller units do *not* receive their own results. Instead, their results are combined with those of similar work units until a department of 20 or 25 people obtains the overall group's results.)

The second phase of SFA involves a feedback session that brings together the manager and his or her work group. The goal here is to identify specific concerns or problems, examine specific causes for these problems, and devise action plans to correct the problems. The managers are trained to ask probing questions. For example, suppose the low-scoring survey question was "I feel free to tell my manager what I think." Managers are trained to ask their groups questions such as "What restrains you from expressing your opinions?" and "What do I do that makes you feel that I'm not interested?"

The feedback meeting should result in a third, "action plan," SFA phase. Managers use an action-planning worksheet containing four columns: What is the concern? What's your analysis? What's the cause? What should be done? The aim is to resolve problems and boost results.

Top-Down Programs

It's hard to feel like a partner when your boss won't tell you what's going on. High-commitment firms give their people extensive data on the performance of, and the prospects for, their operations. "You've got to create an environment where people trust you" is how Jim Rhodes, a Publix personnel officer, puts it, and to do that "you've got to always tell the truth, and keep the lines of communication open."[17]

At Saturn the employees consider this mostly a matter of trust. "They must trust you to do the job," says one worker, "and they therefore trust you with a lot of confidential information, for instance, on the financials of our firm. They tell you, 'Here is the problem; what would you do about it?'" Consider one example of Saturn's policy in action. It became apparent after the plant had been running for a while that (as one assembler told me) "We couldn't make enough cars in four days to match demand. They gave us options—such as working 50 hours per week—and the information to make the decision, which we did; they gave us the choice."

The firm uses several channels to get data down to the troops. "The communication is excellent," says assembler Greg Arthur. "We get information continuously via the internal television network and from financial documents."[18] "And the hierarchy is pretty flat here," says another worker, "so the point people on the teams, including the team leaders, can quickly find the information and the resources that you need." Kenny Duncan, with the UAW, says "We have 'town hall' meetings once per month, and usually have at least 500 to 700 people attending. That, plus the broadcasts, usually makes sure that everyone's knowledge base is up. [And] you better know the facts if you want to work here."[19]

Toyota's Sam Heltman stresses that the old saying about knowledge being power doesn't apply at his plant: Management works too hard to share all it knows with every team member. There are twice-a-day five-minute team information meetings at job sites, where employees get the latest news on the plant. There's also a TV in each work-site break area. The TV runs continuously, presenting plantwide information from the in-house Toyota broadcasting center. There are quarterly round-table discussions between top management and selected nonsupervisory staff, and there's an in-house newsletter. The Hotline described earlier in this chapter is another channel of top-down information, one that gives management a chance to answer, publicly, any anonymous (or nonanonymous) questions team members might have. Mike Dodge, the plant's general manager, points out that Mr. Cho himself is often in the plant, fielding questions, providing performance information, and ensuring that his general managers, managers, and team members—in fact, all in the company—are "aware of Toyota's goals and where we are heading."[20]

One Fed Ex station manager praised the daily Fed Ex TV broadcasts—seen by about 70 percent of employees each day—for their role in disseminating real-time company information. The broadcasts cover "what the company is up to and what we're trying to do about things." And Fed Ex's monthly call-in broadcast shows (which Fred Smith calls "one-on-one") give the firm a chance to answer questions about important matters. For instance, a recent show fielded questions about a reorganization, and a compensation manager answered questions about the firm's pay and bonus plans.

At Publix, too, the emphasis is on getting data to—and from—the troops. As Jim Rhodes summed it up:

> Communications are very important here. Management always tells us the truth, there's no deception even when the news is unpleasant. There's always a line of communication because we feel everyone must always know what's going on, why we're doing what we're doing. We send video tapes out all the time, have meetings and just talk with all the employees. We always want to know what we can do better, or more.
>
> When I talk with people it's amazing what they tell me. The important thing is you have to create an environment where people trust you to tell you what they think. The company understands from the bottom of its heart that only by being honest and open will it grow.[21]

Double-Talk and Commitment

Double-talk practices—Guaranteed Fair Treatment, Speak Up!, periodic surveys, and top-down programs—are crucial for winning your people's commitment. These practices give employees the data they need to make them feel like partners, and they give managers the data they need to respond to employee concerns. Double-talk helps prove that management trusts its people and in turn can be trusted. That's not enough, by itself, to ensure commitment, but it's a crucial start.

A Summary: Double-Talk as a Key to Commitment

1. Use open and candid two-way communication to help build trust.

2. Institute procedures that guarantee the fair treatment of all employees in all grievance and disciplinary matters; make sure those procedures are easy to use and are supported by top management; make sure that employees are encouraged to use the procedures when needed.

3. Audit your disciplinary procedures. Make sure they contain an appeals process and that the process is clearly fair.

4. Install formal, easy-to-use channels that employees can use to express concerns and gripes and get answers to matters that concern them. Speak Up!, Open-Door, and Hotline are three examples of formal channels.

5. Administer periodic opinion polls such as Fed Ex's Survey Feedback Action to aid management at all levels in identifying and solving problems.

6. Use every opportunity to tell employees what's going on in their organization. Such opportunities include daily and other periodic meetings, in-house TV networks, monthly "town halls," frequent round-table question-answer periods, and various written materials.

References

1. Anne B. Fisher, "Morale Crisis," *Fortune*, November 18, 1991, p. 70.
2. Allan Farnham, "The Trust Gap," *Fortune*, December 4, 1989, p. 57.
3. Ibid.
4. Thomasine Rendero, "Grievance Procedures for Nonunionized Employees," *Personnel*, vol. 57, no. 1 (January–February 1980), pp. 4–10.

5. Mary Ellen LoBosco, "Non-union Grievance Procedures," *Personnel*, vol. 62, no. 1 (January 1985), pp. 61–64.

6. *The Federal Express Employee Handbook*, August 7, 1989, p. 89.

7. *Blueprints for Service Quality: The Federal Express Approach*, AMA Membership Publications, New York, 1991, p. 42.

8. *Federal Express Employee Handbook*, p. 89.

9. *Blueprints for Service Quality*, p. 45; *Federal Express Employee Handbook*, pp. 89–91.

10. Personal interview with Sam Heltman, March 1992.

11. Reprint from *Think Magazine*, vol. 55, no. 6, 1989, p. 37.

12. Ibid.

13. Personal interview with Maurice Worth, January 1992.

14. *Blueprints for Service Quality*, pp. 49–50.

15. *Team Member Handbook*, Toyota Motor Manufacturing, U.S.A., February 1988, pp. 52–53.

16. *All About Your Company*, IBM employee handbook, p. 184.

17. Personal interview with Jim Rhodes, April 1992.

18. Personal interview with Greg Arthur, March 1992.

19. Personal interview with Kenny Duncan, March 1992.

20. Personal interview with Mike Dodge, March 1992.

21. Personal interview with Jim Rhodes, April 1992.

5

Communion

Letting managers get the gravy while the workers get the crumbs is no way to win commitment. Yet that's exactly what many firms do.

Pay disparities are probably the biggest examples here. Much attention has been focused recently on the fact that in Japan top executives earn only about six times workers' pay, while America's top executives often earn hundreds or thousands of times more than their employees. Many top managers earn over a million dollars a year, and blockbuster-size examples like the $78 million earned several years ago by Time Warner's chief symbolize, for many, the system's problems. During the 1980s, in fact, CEO compensation increased about twice as fast as that of hourly production workers.[1]

Managers have also traditionally received perks ranging from executive dining rooms and private bathrooms to cars and country club memberships. More subtle are some workers' growing feelings that those running their firms aren't privileged just in the sense of traditional perks. With the downsizings and cutbacks of the past few years has come a growing feeling among many workers that their firms' heads are, like Marie Antoinette, largely insulated from the vagaries of the market. Observes David Sirota, the chairman of an opinion polling firm:

> CEOs say, "We're a team, we're all in this together, rah, rah." But employees look at the difference between their pay and the CEOs. They see top management's perks—oak dining rooms and heated garages, versus cafeterias for the hourly guys and parking spaces half a mile from the plant. And they wonder: "Is this togetherness?" As the disparity in pay widens, the wonder grows.[2]

In companies across this land employees—whether they're supervisors, assemblers, nurses, firefighters, or professors—are asking why their top officers continue to get big raises, unlimited travel, and other perks while the workers' livelihoods are increasingly constricted. It is not a happy situation.

Rosabeth Moss Kanter, whose study of utopian communities was discussed in Chapter 2, has made some interesting observations about how the communities she looked at encouraged commitment. Applying conclusions like hers—based, as they are, on a special type of organization—to a corporate setting is always risky. However, I think there are some lessons to be learned in what she found. For one thing, she found in all successful communities (like those formed by the Shakers and like the Oneida Community and the Amana Society) a sense of communion, one in which "connectedness, belonging, participation in a whole, mingling of the self and the group, and an equal opportunity to contribute and to benefit all are part."[3]

Kanter found that this sense of communion—this sense of "connectedness, belonging, participation in a whole,..."—contributed to creating commitment among the communities' members. In turn, the community itself developed a strong "we-feeling." They felt, in other words, like they were a family. The result was a "cohesive, emotionally involving, and effectively satisfying community."[4]

Kanter identified several practices through which the communities encouraged communion, and thereby commitment. There was, first, usually some *homogeneity* of background among members. This made it easier for them to share common experiences and identify with one another and with the community. There was an element of *communal sharing* of both property and work—in other words, a feeling that its members shared (to some extent) the assets of the community and the output of its efforts. *Communal work* meant an emphasis on joint effort, with all members, as far as possible, performing all tasks for equal rewards. There was *regularized group contact*, continuing activities that brought the individual into periodic contact with the group as a whole. As Kanter says:

> Frequent group meetings and member attendance at a large number of community events also serve a communion function simply because they bring together the entire collectivity and reinforce its existence and meaning, regardless of the purpose of the gathering. Participation in such events makes a member more involved in the group, keeps him more informed of events, gives him a greater sense of belonging, and increases his opportunity to help influence day-to-day decisions.[5]

Kanter's high-commitment communities also depended on *ritual*, rites involving "collective participation in recurring events of symbolic importance to enhance communion....Through ritual, members affirm their oneness and pay homage to the ties that bind them."[6]

As it turns out, one of the most striking similarities among our high-commitment firms is the effort they all make to encourage this same sense of communion and shared fate. Given the wide disparity between the types of companies I studied, it's not surprising that Kanter's practices—homogeneity, communal sharing, communal work, regularized group contact, ritual—went through a metamorphosis in their transfer to these industrial firms. Yet the similarities are there. What I've called value-based hiring helps ensure some homogeneity and commonality among the members of high-commitment firms, for instance, and dress codes (in some cases, uniforms) help underscore the commonalities. There is always evidence of communal sharing, often symbolized by common lunch areas, the absence of executive parking spaces, profit-sharing programs, and common memberships in exercise and country clubs. There is an emphasis on communal work, as evidenced by a widespread use of team membership, teamwork, and job rotation. Regularized group contact is assured in these firms through practices such as regularly scheduled group meetings and internal TV conferencing. And rituals abound, from the "partnership pledges" taken by J. C. Penney's new managers to the award ceremonies at Mary Kay. Let's look more closely at these practices.

Homogeneity: We've Got So Much in Common

How do you go about hiring a "homogeneous" workforce in these days of cultural diversity and equal employment opportunity? We'll devote Chapter 7 to answering this. However, given the relevance of homogeneity to building a sense of communion, a few words are required here.

First, I should stress that high-commitment firms do not aim for homogeneity in terms of discriminatory traits such as ethnic background or race, of course. Instead, they seek homogeneity in terms of values, aspirations, and skills.

This manifests itself in three ways. First, the high-commitment firms I studied seek to hire, as the head of personnel at Goldman, Sachs put it, "people who will be good team players." This theme came up again and again in my research. J. C. Penney looks for people with "good interpersonal skills who are willing to take direction—we're not looking for mavericks." Toyota and Delta both look for "team players." Preferring to hire team players is certainly not exclusively a high-commitment firm practice, of course, although (as we'll see in Chapter 7) the *care* these firms take to screen out mavericks is probably unusual.

Second, creating homogeneity in terms of values means that these firms all require an explicit set of values. At Goldman, Sachs & Company the values sought include excellence, creativity and imagination, the ability to assume responsibility rapidly, teamwork and dedication to the firm, intense effort in work, and integrity and honesty. At Toyota, interpersonal skills, reasoning skills, flexibility, and willingness to be team players characterize successful employees (who are, in fact, referred to as "team members").

Third, these firms work hard to create a sense of homogeneity by screening out those who might not "fit" in other ways. They use what I've called value-based hiring practices: The screening process is exhaustive and is keyed to hiring people whose values fit the firm's. Thus Ben & Jerry's depends partly on their policy of not paying executives more than seven times the firm's lowest entry-level wage to attract managers whose values and social philosophies fit the firm's. As one Ben & Jerry's manager told me, "What this company *feels* like to me is more important than things like salary or benefits. What I personally value here is a definite culture that I'm comfortable with, one that's politically and socially progressive." Adds Jim Miller, another Ben & Jerry's manager, "If you're motivated by money, this is not the place for you. You come here for the firm's social side, and because you believe in the values of the firm."[7]

The end result at all these firms—including Delta, Mary Kay, Federal Express, and the rest—is that the people who are hired are already well on their way to fitting in. They are homogeneous, but not in the sense of all-white, or all-male, or all–Ivy League. They are homogeneous in their potential fit with their new firms' values. They are team players who by aspirations, values, and skills should fit right in.

Seeking common values sometimes translates into seeking common backgrounds. For example, given the high achievement levels sought by Goldman, Sachs, their college recruiters tend to stress Ivy League and other top schools, although non-top-tier schools are represented and their hiring is actively nondiscriminatory. J. C. Penney, seeking managers who tend to mirror their middle-America roots, tends to avoid the academic superstars and the top-tier schools.

In many of these firms, dress codes reinforce the resulting homogeneity. IBM was known for its gray suits and white shirts. At Toyota, says Sam Heltman, the in-plant "Toyota store" sells upwards of $20,000 per month of the firm's standard blue Toyota polo shirt and similar supplies.[8] Although the blue shirt/tan pants "uniform" is strictly voluntary, about 80 percent of team members (including Mr. Cho) were so attired when I was there. Team-member shirts were also widely in use when I was at Saturn. And when I called ahead to ask my Ben & Jerry's coordinator if I needed a suit, my question was met by laughter: The uniform of the day there is eclectic rustic: in winter, it is layered, eclectic rustic.

Communal Sharing: I Own a Piece of the Rock

Most of these firms also work hard to foster a sense of sharing. You see this first in a firm's attempts to establish a sense of equality throughout the company. In part, this is reflected in the fact that top managers are easily accessible via the double-talk channels described in Chapter 4.

In addition, there is usually a deliberate emphasis on avoiding the status differences that often set top management apart from employees. For example, when you visit the Toyota plant in Georgetown, Kentucky, you'll pass a receptionist and walk up one flight of stairs. Turn right, and you're in a huge room. Here the entire office staff works, without offices, without walls, and without partitions. President Fujio Cho is there along with secretaries, public relations people, data entry clerks, and all the other employees needed to support the firm. Executives at Ben & Jerry's have private offices, but they are spartan compared with those that you'll find in most firms; the company's founders worked in a trailer at the foot of a hill on which the plant is situated until a few years ago.

You'll find few firms here with executive parking spots: Fujio Cho, Toyota's president, often has to park the equivalent of a block or two away from the plant because the graveyard shift employees get there before he does. At Fed Ex, Fred Smith has no assigned parking spot and there are no company cars. There is no executive lunchroom and the executives' offices are nice but not spectacular. "We do as much as we can to minimize differences between nonexecutive levels and ourselves" is how one top Fed Ex manager put it. Similarly, at Saturn, the sense of sharing is enhanced by shared facilities: For instance, assembly workers eat in the same lunchrooms as the president, Skip LeFauve, and there are no assigned parking spaces. At Ben & Jerry's the cap on executives' salaries, the informal dress code, the spartan offices, and the accessibility of the management team leads, as one employee put it, to a "very egalitarian feeling on the part of employees regarding management; they're not isolated in glass towers."

But these firms do more than evoke the sense of sharing: They put their money where their mouths are. As we'll describe in more detail in Chapter 9 all of these firms provide profit-and-risk-sharing plans. These generally put some portion—typically 5 to 20 percent—of each employee's annual pay "at risk," subject to the firm's performance, with the possibility of earning a substantial bonus above one's salary if the company does well. The result is that employees of firms such as Saturn, Publix, Toyota, Federal Express, Mary Kay, J. C. Penney, and Ben & Jerry's are in a real sense financial "partners" in their firm's success. For example, about 20 percent of the annual salary of each Toyota employee is "at risk" each year, and could be lost if Toyota America doesn't do well. At Federal Express the board of directors sets the amount paid in a profit-sharing distribution, and allocations are usually made semiannually in June and December. At Goldman, Sachs, substantial payouts in the form of discretionary bonuses are paid at the end of the fiscal year to all eligible employees.

The Penney Policy

When Thomas Callahan and William Guy Johnson tapped James Cash Penney to open their "Golden Rule" store in Kemmerer, Wyoming, in 1902, they invited their young colleague to become one-third partner in the new store. In later years, Mr. Penney would say that this one simple act was the key to his success. Becoming a partner, he said, fired his ambition to succeed.

James Cash Penney, in turn, made financial partnership a key part of the company he built. Each new store manager was invited to become a partner in the store he managed and in any stores managed by associates that manager had trained. The compensation practices of the firm have since changed, but sharing in the store's profits is still the policy at Penney's. As Don Finn, the company's compensation director told me, the firm pays modest salaries but very high incentive payments—as much as 80 percent—based on store profits and sales.[9] It's a notion that harkens back to that original Golden Rule store in Wyoming. And it builds a sense of sharing and thus commitment.

Ben & Jerry's Communal Sharing

In some ways Ben & Jerry's does the most to use compensation as a symbol of communal sharing. The keys here are their compressed compensation ratio, and their annual profit-sharing bonus plan. We'll return to this in Chapter 9, but to make the point we'll cite here, in brief, the Ben & Jerry's compressed compensation ratio: "The highest paid employee at Ben & Jerry's [including corporate officers] may earn no more than seven times what the lowest paid employee could earn for an equivalent work week, excluding overtime."[10] The "1" in the 7-to-1 ratio is based on both cash compensation and the cash value of benefits received by the lowest-paid, full-time employee in good standing who has worked for the company at least one year. The minimum total compensation was recently $16,339. Thus the maximum *total compensation* for a Ben & Jerry's employee, based on those 1990 figures, is 7 times $16,339, or $114,373. Now *that* is communal sharing!

The Mary Kay System

Few firms emphasize communal sharing to the extent that Mary Kay Cosmetics does. According to executive vice president Barbara Beasley, "Everything we do at Mary Kay is aimed at encouraging our sales force to share tips and techniques. As Mary Kay has said, `If we share ideas we have two ideas; otherwise, each of us has one idea.'"[11]

The firm's policies and award system reinforce these "sharing" values, says Mary Kay:

> Because we don't have territories at Mary Kay Cosmetics, a director who lives in Chicago can be vacationing in Florida, or visiting a friend in Pittsburgh, and recruit someone while there. It doesn't matter where she lives in the United States; she will always draw a commission from the company on the wholesale purchases made by that recruit. The director in Pittsburgh will take the visiting director's new recruit under her wing and train her, the recruit will attend the Pittsburgh sales meetings and participate in the local sales contests. Although the Pittsburgh director will devote a lot of time and effort to the new recruit, the Chicago director will be paid the commissions. The Pittsburgh recruit may go on to recruit new people on her own. No matter where she lives, she becomes the nucleus for bringing in additional people for the director who brought her into the business.[12]

Similarly, according to Barbara Beasley, "The highest award a sales director can get is the Miss Go-Give Award. This goes to the individual who has shared the most with the most people. This person is nominated by her peers and must reflect the giving spirit at Mary Kay Cosmetics."[13] Consider some of these excerpts from recent nominations for Go-Give Award recipients:

Executive Senior Director Sue Kirkpatrick about nominee Cindy Grimaldi: "Cindy has gone above and beyond helping my people in her area. I have two star recruiters because of her positive go-give leadership."

Consultant San Peveler about Director Marlinda Licon: "Marlinda is a wonderful director and always willing to help in any area. She gives freely of her time, knowledge and love."

Consultant Sandy Burpo about Director Naomi Lawson Swan: "Naomi always welcomes adoptees, treats all consultants equally and takes the time to encourage everyone."[14]

There are many ways to foster the feeling that your people share the assets and the outputs of their labors!

Communal Work: Get on the Team

The feeling of community created by homogeneity and communal sharing is further enhanced by encouraging joint effort and communal work. In practical terms our 10 firms accomplish this in three ways: by organizing around small work teams, by encouraging job rotation, and by establishing a tradition of encouraging everyone—top managers included—to share in even the most mundane tasks when the going gets rough.

Small Work Teams

Back in the 1950s psychologist Rensis Likert formulated what, for later generations of organizational experts, would become the classic explanation of cohesive work teams. He said, first, that the leadership and other processes of the organization must be such as to ensure that each employee will view the experience as one that builds and maintains his or her sense of personal worth and importance.[15] Furthermore, said Likert,

> The most important source of satisfaction for this desire is the response we get from the people we are close to, in whom we are interested, and whose approval and support we are eager to have. The face-to-face groups with whom we spend the bulk of our time are, consequently, the most important to us....[Therefore] management will make full use of the potential capacities of its human resources only when each person in an organization is a member of

one or more effectively functioning work groups that have a high degree of group loyalty.[16]

From a practical point of view, Likert might have added, employees probably tend to develop their first and perhaps most intense commitment to the people in their work groups and to their group's norms and ideals. To many people at work the company itself—what it is, where it's going, what its values are—is often little more than an abstraction. But the people with whom they work every day—the door-trim team at Saturn, the menswear group in the Penney's store, the securities group at Goldman, Sachs—these are real, and worthy of their commitment. You can't let your teammates down.

For many firms the ideal situation, as Likert saw, is thus to organize work around small, close-knit teams whose goals are high and whose aims are the same as the firm's. And this is generally what firms such as Saturn; Toyota; Goldman, Sachs; Mary Kay; J. C. Penney; and Federal Express do. As a result, intense group loyalties are fostered as members develop a deep sense of responsibility to their colleagues in the group.

The practices used at Toyota illustrate the basic approach. Team building here begins with the firm's commitment to the teamwork principle. For example, their team-member handbook states their commitment "to work as a team with mutual respect and equal opportunities for all: our abilities are maximized when we work together in a cooperative manner toward common goals. Mutual trust and respect for each other are the basis on which team spirit is developed."[17]

The factory work itself is thus organized around work teams. For example, there are teams of about five to ten people in charge of door installations, assembly trim, power-train conveyance, stamping tool and die, and body weld. There are no individuals on the plant floor; every Toyota production worker belongs to a work team.

The firm then uses several practices to assure smoothly functioning work teams. They use value-based hiring to select prospective team members who have the skills to work amicably on teams. Once hired, employees are steeped in the terminology and techniques of teamwork. As mentioned, there are no employees in the plant, only team members. There is no employee handbook, there's a team-member handbook. There is no employee activities association, there's a team-member activities association, and so on. Teamwork training begins during initial orientation, as new members meet their teams and are trained in the interpersonal techniques that make for good teamwork. The closeness is enhanced by letting work teams recruit and select their own new members.

The monthly *Toyota Topics* magazine continually publicizes the accomplishments of "teamwork heroes." For example, an article in the June 1990 *Toyota Topics* describes the accomplishments of a body-weld maintenance group this way:

> Because production goes on around the clock, each maintenance shift plays an important role in making sure everything on the line is running smoothly when the next shift takes over. One example of how this group pulls together in a difficult situation was evident when a wiring harness inside a robot went bad one night in late April. Several team members removed the bad harness while several others removed the good wiring harness from a robot not in use and reinstalled it in the other robot. "The problem occurred at about 3:30 A.M.," Dennis Waltz explained. "By the time first shift came on at 6:30 we had the counter measure in place." That took a lot of teamwork and hard work.[18]

The article goes on to explain that Dennis and the group were especially grateful to Bob Morrow, an earlier-shift group leader in body weld, who often stayed after his own shift to assist in technical training and problem solving.

The feeling that they're all there to share the group's work comes across when you speak with team members themselves. For example, Kelvin Young, a body-shop team member told me that one of the things he liked about Toyota was the "Toyota teamwork—on every other job I've had people wouldn't contribute or help each other out, but it's the complete opposite here. Here everyone depends on someone else."[19]

Team assignments are also emphasized at J. C. Penney. Under Penney's team concept, the regions and divisions and support departments "join together at various levels in management teams to ensure focus on consumers and to ensure they are offered the service and merchandise they expect, at the right time, and at the right price. These teams are critical to the success of the management process of J. C. Penney's stores."[20]

What we have in the Penney store structure is thus essentially a hierarchy of linked work teams all aimed at coordinating buying and merchandising decisions at successively higher levels. Within the store, for instance, might be a woman's wear team, a menswear team, a home and leisure clothing team, and a children's wear team. They in turn send representatives to a storewide management team, which in turn provides input regionally and nationally. Buying decisions are thereby coordinated nationally, while each store's teams get to share the work of choosing next season's fashions.

Job Rotation

The feeling that work is shared is enhanced by the use of job rotation (letting employees rotate from job to job) in most of these firms. Job rotation actually serves several purposes. It creates cross-trained, flexible employees. It creates more interesting (at least, less boring) work experiences. It gives employees a better appreciation for the jobs of their colleagues down the line—be it at Saturn or Delta. And, last but not least, it assures a very real sharing of all the work.

Most of the firms use job rotation on both a companywide basis and within work groups. At Delta, airport work teams routinely rotate jobs; reservations clerks fill in at the check-in ramp or in baggage handling if the need arises. The Delta *Policy Manual* puts it this way:

> Cross-utilization is also routinely employed in the work environment as a means of growing and developing our people. Personnel at all levels serve in rotating special assignment positions, in some staff positions, and participate in cross-divisional task forces and special projects.[21]

At J. C. Penney employees are encouraged to move between the firm's four divisions (operations, merchandising, purchasing, and general management) as they plan their careers. At Saturn, Toyota, and Ben & Jerry's, team members themselves decide on the schedules that they'll use to rotate their short-cycle jobs: The average Toyota assembly task takes less than 10 minutes, for example, and rotating the jobs breaks the monotony while creating a feeling of sharing the work.

Top-Down Involvement

But perhaps the classic example of work sharing occurs when, at firms such as Ben & Jerry's, executives routinely get down to pitch in with the troops. For example, one of Ben & Jerry's manufacturing executives spoke to me in awe when he described one recent incident.

> Last week...we didn't have enough people for our midnight shift. We all volunteered—at 2:00 a.m.—Jerry, me, and others, we were all down in the plant. "I never would have believed that," one employee told me. The fact is, this place is not hung up on titles, and everyone from Ben and Jerry down will do whatever it takes to make the company successful, everyone will pitch in and do.

At Goldman, Sachs one manager expressed much the same sentiment: "At the end of the day everyone shares in the process. Everyone here is working long hours—no one hands you work and walks out the door."

Regularized Group Contact: Let's Get Together

The sense of sharing and communion that comes from homogeneity, communal work, and communal sharing is further nurtured by scheduling activities that bring individual employees into regular contact with the group as a whole.[22] Frequent group meetings, member attendance at a great many community events, and other regularized contacts like these bring the entire collectivity together, says Kanter,

> and reinforce its existence and meaning, regardless of the purpose of the gathering. Participating in such events makes a member more involved in the group, keeps him more informed of events, gives him a greater sense of belonging, and increases his opportunity to help influence day-to-day decisions.[23]

High-commitment firms are filled with opportunities for firmwide contact. At Ben & Jerry's there are monthly staff meetings in the receiving bay of the Waterbury, Vermont, plant. Production stops and all employees attend. One such meeting took place at 8 a.m. on a Friday. Coffee and fresh donuts abounded as Jerry Greenfield reported on Ben Cohen's effort to open an ice cream parlor in Moscow. Other updates from Jerry concerned the firm's efforts to refurbish and maintain a New York City subway station for one year. At one point everyone joined in to sing "Happy Birthday" to an employee.[24] Ben & Jerry's Joy Gang organizes regular "joy events," including Cajun parties, Ping-Pong contests, and "Manufacturing Appreciation Day," all aimed at getting everyone together.

At Federal Express daily teleconferenced meetings described the prior day's accomplishments. Toyota has a similar TV system, called *Toyota Network News.* Toyota also spends about $250,000 annually on a "perfect attendance" meeting to which all high-attendance employees are invited. There's also an annual picnic. The Toyota team-member activities association also organizes regularly scheduled events such as magic shows. Weekly meetings of Mary Kay directors and their sales consultants similarly serve to reinforce the sense of communion and togetherness that characterize high-commitment firms.

Ritual: It's a Tradition

Finally, "collective participation in recurring events of symbolic importance"—in other words, ritual—also fosters a sense of communion.

Through rituals, "members affirm their oneness and pay homage to the ties that bind them." In all these companies, rituals provide constant reminders of the firm's values and traditions and raise employee commitment to "the level of the universal and abiding."[25]

These rituals tend to be very symbolic affairs. For example, consider the Penney "HCSC" inauguration meetings. Remember that from the firm's inception, Penney's managers were encouraged to view themselves as partners in the business. And also from the beginning, all new managers have attended a ritual HCSC inauguration meeting, to pledge themselves to the same principles of honesty, confidence, service, and cooperation that their predecessors affirmed back in the early 1900s. "Today," as company documents tell new partners,

> the J. C. Penney partnership is many times the size of the small group that first took the HCSC pledge in 1913. But the distinction of partnership is no less significant. It defines the heritage left to us by men like Mr. Penney...who made moral values and individual character the foundation on which to build a great enterprise.[26]

The highlight of these meetings is a ceremony in which the partners pledge their loyalty to the Penney principles of honor, confidence, service, and cooperation and receive a lapel pin with the raised letters "HCSC."

But when it comes to collective participation in recurring events of symbolic importance—rituals—the annual Mary Kay "Spotlight on Success Seminar" may be in a class by itself. Take the 1990 seminar, held at the Dallas Convention Center. The participants at this "Hollywood spectacular"—beauty consultants, sales directors, senior sales directors, executive senior directors, and national sales directors—entered through an arch that proclaimed their arrival at "Mary Kay Studios." They walked along the Mary Kay Walk of Fame carpet, featuring inlaid stars emblazoned with the names of the national sales directors; they were greeted by screen-legend look-alikes Marilyn Monroe, Charlie Chaplin, and the Marx Brothers. The lobby was converted into "a magical movie set reminiscent of Hollywood's golden era."[27] Looking out on the audience you were struck by a sea of women in blue suits, red suits, and deep pink suits, denoting the various levels of directors in the Mary Kay sales organization. (National sales directors, the highest rung, wear deep-pink suits.)

It's at these ritualistic meetings that the awards and prizes are given, ranging from the Go-Give Award described above, to Mary Kay's famous fur coats, pink Cadillacs, and diamond rings. But more than that, it is at these meetings that the bonds are cemented between Mary

Kay Ash and her salespeople. When the curtain parts and Mary Kay herself emerges, flanked by chorus girls in flowing gowns, thousands of her people in the convention center stand with tears in their eyes to applaud her—and you know that something big is in the air. As the blue-suited, red-suited, and pink-suited directors march across the stage to accept their awards to thundering applause, it's not hard to see how rituals like these enhance the feelings of "oneness," the ties between the organization and the individual that are the basis of communion and commitment.

A Summary: Communion as a Key to Commitment

1. To create commitment you must foster a sense of communion among your employees—a sense of connectedness, belonging, and participation in a whole that makes employees see that they are part of a cohesive, satisfying community, one that has a shared fate.

2. Foster this sense of communion in part through "selective homogeneity." Use value-based hiring to select people whose values (excellence, quality, thrift, for instance) fit your firm's value system. Hire team players, and encourage dress codes that reinforce a sense of commonality and homogeneity.

3. Foster a sense of communal sharing by eliminating unnecessary status differences. Examples of practices that have proved effective here include eliminating offices or minimizing status differences between offices; banning executive parking spots, company cars, executive lunchrooms and bathrooms; capping executives' salaries; and encouraging dress codes or informal dress.

4. Use profit-and-risk-sharing plans to put a portion of each employee's annual pay at risk to further evoke the sense of sharing by making all employees financial "partners" in the profits of the firm. Facilitate accessibility via double-talk channels.

5. Reward acts of sharing by employees to underscore your commitment to building a sense of communion.

6. Encourage joint effort and communal work: Organize around small work teams; utilize job rotation; establish a tradition of encouraging everyone—top managers included—to share in even the most mundane tasks.

7. Specific communal work practices include the following:

- Work teams—hire team players; stress teamwork in company documents; organize work around teams; steep the firm in the terminology of teamwork; use teamwork training.
- *Job rotation*—facilitate and encourage firmwide and team-based job rotation.
- *Top-down involvement*—get *all* managers to pitch in when the pressure is on; when it comes to working late or coming in early, make sure it's the management of the firm that sets the right example.

8. Continually publicize the accomplishment of "teamwork heroes."

9. Schedule activities that bring individual employees into regular contact with the group as a whole. These can include daily, weekly, or monthly meetings; daily teleconferences; annual get-togethers; and so on.

10. Encourage collective participation in recurring events of symbolic importance—in other words, rituals. Establish traditions such as new-manager inauguration meetings that include a solemn pledge of loyalty.

References

1. Allan Farnham, "The Trust Gap," *Fortune*, December 4, 1989, p. 56.
2. Ibid.
3. Rosabeth Moss Kanter, *Commitment and Community: Communes and Utopias in Sociological Perspective*, Harvard University Press, Cambridge, Mass., 1972, p. 93. You should note that the next line in her quote is "The principle is 'from each according to his abilities, to each according to his needs.'" Thus we have to be quite choosy about which practices might be applicable in a corporate setting.
4. Ibid.
5. Ibid., p. 99.
6. Ibid., pp. 99–100.
7. Personal interview with Jim Miller, March 1992.
8. Personal interview with Sam Heltman, March 1992.
9. Personal interview with Don Finn, October 1991.
10. *Ben & Jerry's Homemade, Inc., Employee Handbook*, pp. A2 and A3.
11. Interview with Barbara Beasley, March 1992.

12. Mary Kay Ash, *Mary Kay on People Management*, Warner Books, New York, 1984, pp. 2–3.

13. Interview with Barbara Beasley, March 1992.

14. *Applause*, May 1992, p. 18.

15. Rensis Likert, *New Patterns of Management*, McGraw-Hill, New York, 1961, p. 103.

16. Ibid., p. 104.

17. *Team Member Handbook*, Toyota Motor Manufacturing, U.S.A., February 1988, p. 11.

18. *Toyota Topics*, IW 870–Body Weld: Maintaining Excellence," June 1990, p. 8.

19. Personal interview with Kelvin Young, March 1992.

20. *Penney Store Management Team (PSMT)*, company document, p. 1. Students of organizational behavior will notice the similarity between the Penney's team management philosophy and the concept of Rensis Likert's "linking pin" which he formulated back in 1960. As Likert said at that time, "An organization will function best when its personnel function not as individuals but as members of highly effective work groups with high performance goals. Consequently, management should deliberately endeavor to build these effective groups, linking them into an overall organization by means of people who hold overlapping group membership. The superior in one group is a subordinate in the next group, and so on through the organization." (Likert, p. 105.)

21. Delta's *Personnel Policy Manual*, p. 18.

22. Kanter, pp. 98–99.

23. Kanter, p. 89.

24. "The Bad Boys of American Business," *Inc.*, July 1988, p. 5.

25. Kanter, pp. 99–100.

26. *The Tradition Continues: The 1989 HCSC Inauguration Meetings*, p. 3.

27. *Spotlight on Success: Mary Kay Seminar 1990*, p. 3.

6

Transcendental
Mediation

We're generally loyal to things but committed to ideas. Countries, leaders, schools, and employers may win our loyalties. But it's usually ideas—to make the best quality car, to feed the homeless, or to improve the environment—that ignite and earn our commitment.

Committed employees, in other words, need missions and values to be committed to. That's why high-commitment firms excel at formulating shared transcendental ideologies, missions, and values—and mechanisms for communicating these to their employees. Shared missions and values are the focal points for the efforts of committed employees: Having commitment without a mission is impossible, while having a mission but no commitment is useless.

Workers at firms like Saturn are thus not just workers, but soldiers in a crusade that allows them to redefine—and transcend—themselves in terms of an ideology and a mission. Saturn people burn their GM bridges when they come to Spring Hill, Tennessee, in part for a better life, but also to join a crusade, to show that they can build a car to compete with the best of the Japanese products. Rosabeth Moss Kanter says that transcendence—a process whereby someone "attaches his decision-making perspective to a power greater than himself, surrendering to the higher meaning contained by the group and submitting to something beyond himself"—permits the person "to find himself anew in something larger and greater."[1] The commitment in high-commitment firms derives in part, in other words, from the power of the firm's mission, and from the willingness of the employees not just to accept the company's aims as their own but to acquiesce to the needs of the firm for the good of achieving its mission. They are crusaders.

High-commitment firms use three sets of practices to achieve this feeling among employees that they're part of something "larger and greater" than themselves. First, they create an ideology that lays out a basic way of thinking and doing things, which all employees are expected to share. Second, they often create "institutional charisma" by linking their firms' missions and values to a higher calling or to ultimate moral values. Finally, they promote the ideological conversion of their employees to the missions and values of their firms, in part through value-based hiring, orientation, and training, and in part through symbols and stories and rites and ceremonials.

Creating the Ideology

We've seen that values guide behavior. High-commitment firms therefore create an ideology that lays out their basic way of thinking and doing things, an ideology which all employees are expected to share. This ideology can take the form of a statement of mission or vision, a statement of basic values or philosophy, or a code of ethics. In any event, the ideology specifies the guideposts employees are to use as they go about their jobs, as well as the vision they are to share and commit to.

Consider Mary Kay's ideology. According to Vice Chairman Richard C. Bartlett,

> Our vision of our company is: to be preeminent in the manufacturing, distribution, and marketing of personal care products through our independent sales force. To provide our sales force an unparalleled opportunity for financial independence, career achievement, and personal fulfillment. To achieve total customer satisfaction worldwide by focusing on quality, value, convenience, innovation, and personal service."[2]

The firm's "company philosophy" then lays out its basic values:

> Every person associated with the Company, from the Chairman Emeritus [Mary Kay Ash] to the newest recruit, lives by the golden rule, *Do unto others as you would have them do unto you,* and the priorities of God first, family second, and career third. The *go-give* sharing spirit and the adoptee program form the foundation [of our firm].[3]

(Recall that the firm doesn't assign exclusive territories to its consultants. Thus, if a new consultant is recruited by a director who lives, say, in another city, the director in the recruit's area will "adopt" her into her unit and, in the "go-give sharing spirit," she will provide the recruit with training, education, and motivation.[4])

The beauty consultant's code of ethics then rounds out Mary Kay's ideology. In summary, it holds that

1. The golden rule and the true go-give spirit are to be practiced every day in all facets of the Mary Kay business.

2. The Mary Kay skin care program, other Mary Kay products, and all facts concerning a Mary Kay career are to be presented to customers and the prospective consultants in a truthful, sincere, and honest manner.

3. The customer's needs are always to be kept in mind. The personal and professional approach to serving customers must set the Mary Kay beauty consultant apart from someone who just sells cosmetics.

4. Every Mary Kay beauty consultant must reflect the highest professional standards of integrity, honesty, and responsibility in dealing with customers or fellow consultants and the company. The consultant must act as a professional and must set fair prices, avoiding the temptation to set prices too high or too low, which risks the loss of customers.[5]

Ideologies such as Mary Kay's are composed of the missions, principles, values, and beliefs that guide the firm. They therefore play two roles in gaining commitment. First, a shared ideology fosters commitment by enhancing the sense of commonality, communion, and "oneness" among employees that is itself a precursor to commitment. Second, a firm's ideology—like that of a church—fosters commitment by giving employees something to be committed *to*. The ideology is something they can believe in, something that transcends them, permitting each person, as Kanter says, "to find himself anew in something larger and greater than himself."

Formulating clear, well-documented ideologies is crucial to commitment. Not surprisingly, all 10 of our high-commitment firms have formulated such a statement. In some cases—Toyota; Saturn; Goldman, Sachs; J. C. Penney; and Mary Kay—the statement of ideology is sufficiently comprehensive to provide fairly detailed daily guidance. This is evidenced, for instance, in the 14 "business principles" of Goldman, Sachs presented in their entirety in Figure 6-1. This comprehensive list of principles, along with the explanation of each principle, provides an ideology that helps define the essence of Goldman, Sachs.

1. Our clients' interests always come first. Our experience shows that if we serve our clients well, our own success will follow.

2. Our assets are people, capital and reputation. If any of these are ever lost, the last is the most difficult to regain.

3. We take great pride in the professional quality of our work. We have an uncompromising determination to achieve excellence in everything we undertake. Though we may be involved in a wide variety and heavy volume of activity, we would, if it came to a choice, rather be best than biggest.

4. We stress creativity and imagination in everything we do. While recognizing that the old way may still be the best way, we strive always to find a better solution to a client's problems and pride ourselves in having pioneered many of the practices and techniques which have become standard in the industry.

5. We make an unusual effort to identify and recruit the very best person for every job. Although our activities are measured in billions of dollars, we select our people one by one. In a service business, we know that without the best people, we cannot be the best firm.

6. We offer our people the opportunity to move ahead more rapidly than is possible at most other places. We have yet to find the limits of responsibility which our best people are able to assume. Advancement depends solely on ability, performance, and contribution to the firm's success, without regard to race, color, age, creed, sex, or national origin.

7. We stress teamwork in everything we do. While individual creativity is always encouraged, we have found that the results of a team effort are often better than the sum of the parts. We have no room for those who put their personal interests ahead of the interests of the firm and its clients.

8. Our profits are a key to our success. They replenish our capital and attract and keep our best people. It is our practice to share our profits generously with all who helped create them. Profitability is critical to our future.

9. The dedication of our people to the firm and the intensity of their effort to their jobs are greater than one finds in most other organizations. We think it is an important part of our success.

Figure 6-1. The business principles of Goldman, Sachs. (*Reprinted with permission from Goldman, Sachs'* Our Business Principles.)

10. We consider our size an asset which we try hard to preserve. We want to be big enough to undertake the largest project that any of our clients could contemplate, yet small enough to maintain the loyalty, the intimacy, and the esprit de corps which we all treasure and which is an important part of our success.

11. We strive constantly to anticipate the rapidly changing needs of our clients and to develop new services to meet those needs. We know that the world of finance will not stand still and that complacency can lead to extinction.

12. We regularly receive confidential information as part of our normal client relationships. To breach a confidence or to use confidential information improperly or carelessly would be unthinkable.

13. Our business is highly competitive, and we aggressively seek to expand our client relationships. However, we are always fair competitors and must never denigrate other firms.

14. Integrity and honesty are at the heart of our business. We expect our people to maintain high ethical standards in everything they do, both in their work for the firm and in their personal lives.

Figure 6-1. (Continued).

Similarly, consider the Saturn ideology, as presented in the company documents shown in Figure 6-2. The Saturn mission ("[To] market vehicles developed and manufactured in the United States that are world leaders in quality, cost and customer satisfaction") is buttressed by the more detailed Saturn philosophy—how, for example, Saturn will meet its customers' and workers' needs. Finally, each team member receives the small card of Saturn values (also shown in Figure 6-2) that lists and explains Saturn's basic values. Such documents present a comprehensive ideology that a team member can "get into" and be committed to.

Toyota Motor Manufacturing has by far the most comprehensive ideological statement. It comprises the first 13 pages of its 105-page team-member handbook and provides a detailed explanation of the firm's mission, philosophy, and values and how they are to be pursued. The first page of the statement, which is presented in Figure 6-3, illustrates the comprehensive, doctrinal nature of Toyota's ideology. As you can see, the complete ideology has three elements: a basic philosophy, operating principles, and company objectives.

K SATURN

MISSION

Market vehicles developed
and manufactured in
the United States that are
world leaders in quality,
cost and customer
satisfaction through
the integration of
people, technology and
business systems and
to transfer knowledge,
technology and
experience throughout
General Motors.

K SATURN

PHILOSOPHY

We, the Saturn Team, in concert with
the UAW and General Motors, believe that
meeting the needs of Customers,
Saturn Members, Suppliers, Dealers and
Neighbors is fundamental to fulfilling
our mission.

To meet our customers' needs:
• Our products and services must be world leaders in value and
  satisfaction.

To meet our members' needs:
• We will create a sense of belonging in an environment of mutual trust.
  respect and dignity.
• We believe that all people want to be involved in decisions that affect
  them, care about their jobs and each other, take pride in themselves
  and in their contributions and want to share in the success of their
  efforts.
• We will develop the tools, training and education for each member.
  recognizing individual skills and knowledge.
• We believe that creative, motivated, responsible team members who
  understand that change is critical to success are Saturn's most
  important asset.

To meet our suppliers' and dealers' needs:
• We will strive to create real partnerships with them.
• We will be open and fair in our dealings. reflecting trust, respect and
  their importance to Saturn
• We want dealers and suppliers to feel ownership in Saturn's mission
  and philosophy as their own.

To meet the needs of our neighbors, the communities in which we live and
operate:
• We will be good citizens, protect the environment and conserve
  natural resources.
• We will seek to cooperate with government at all levels and strive to
  be sensitive, open and candid in all our public statements.

By continuously operating according to this
philosophy, we will fulfill our mission.

Figure 6-2. Saturn Corporation values statement and pocket card. (*Reprinted with permission of Saturn Corporation.*)

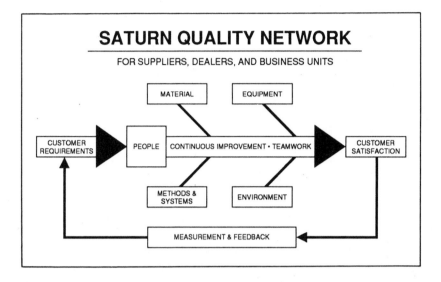

SATURN QUALITY NETWORK

FOR SUPPLIERS, DEALERS, AND BUSINESS UNITS

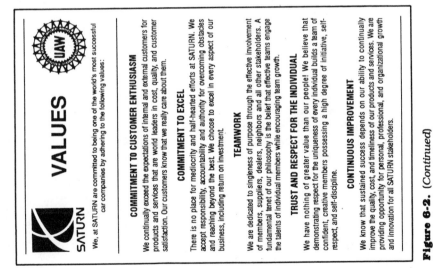

VALUES

We, at SATURN are committed to being one of the world's most successful car companies by adhering to the following values:

COMMITMENT TO CUSTOMER ENTHUSIASM

We continually exceed the expectations of internal and external customers for products and services that are world leaders in cost, quality, and customer satisfaction. Our customers know that we really care about them.

COMMITMENT TO EXCEL

There is no place for mediocrity and half-hearted efforts at SATURN. We accept responsibility, accountability and authority for overcoming obstacles and reaching beyond the best. We choose to excel in every aspect of our business, including return on investment.

TEAMWORK

We are dedicated to singleness of purpose through the effective involvement of members, suppliers, dealers, neighbors and all other stakeholders. A fundamental tenet of our philosophy is the belief that effective teams engage the talents of individual members while encouraging team growth.

TRUST AND RESPECT FOR THE INDIVIDUAL

We have nothing of greater value than our people! We believe that demonstrating respect for the uniqueness of every individual builds a team of confident, creative members possessing a high degree of initiative, self-respect, and self-discipline.

CONTINUOUS IMPROVEMENT

We know that sustained success depends on our ability to continually improve the quality, cost, and timeliness of our products and services. We are providing opportunity for personal, professional, and organizational growth and innovation for all SATURN stakeholders.

Figure 6-2. (*Continued*)

TOYOTA MOTOR MANUFACTURING, U.S.A., INC.
COMPANY POLICY AND OBJECTIVES

The Company Policy, as set forth below, will serve as an overall guide for all actions and decisions by Toyota Motor Manufacturing, U.S.A., Inc. The Policy consists of two parts: (a) <u>Basic Philosophy</u> and (b) <u>Operating Principles</u>. Each team member, section, and department should strive to act in accordance with the philosophy and principles expressed in this policy.

Our immediate objectives are contained in part (c) <u>Company Objectives</u>. We should move toward achieving these objectives as soon as possible in order to maintain our Basic Philosophy.

BASIC PHILOSOPHY

- Produce American's Number 1 quality car based on "customer first" philosophy.
  We will produce quality cars which our customers feel are America's best. To achieve this goal, everyone at TMM, as a proud member of the Toyota team, needs to participate in Kaizen* and our cost savings efforts. By producing the Number 1 quality car in the United States, our Company will surely grow and provide benefits to our team members and community.

  We should never forget that our policy is very personal and special to our customers. To produce a car which satisfies our customers is very important. We should always listen carefully to the opinions and/or complaints of customers and dealers. We should establish systems by which we can receive and consider information in our daily jobs and utilize this information to improve our product. In summary, our customer must always come first.

(*see discussion Kaizen page 19)

Issued: February 1988
Edition I

8

Figure 6-3. Toyota's basic philosophy. (*Reprinted with permission from* Team Member Handbook, *Toyota Motor Manufacturing, U.S.A., Inc.*)

Toyota's *basic philosophy* is itself composed of four elements (the first of which is shown in its entirety in Figure 6-3): to produce America's number 1 quality car based on a customer-first philosophy; to contribute to the quality of life as well as the economic growth in the communities it shares; to promote stable employment and improved well being of employees through steady growth of the company; and to develop unique, innovative production and management systems by combining the best ideas of two countries.

The firm's *operating principles* (each fully explained in a paragraph or two in the handbook) are, in brief:

- To promote cost-savings effort
- To promote Kaizen and team-member participation
- To promote the personal development of team members
- To promote open communication and encourage a free-flowing exchange of information
- To encourage teamwork, with mutual respect and equal opportunities for all
- To establish effective work practices and principles
- To promote pride of workmanship
- To maintain a safe work environment
- To develop a close working relationship with Toyota Motor Sales
- To join other Toyota organizations in endeavoring to grow as a team
- To develop a friendly relationship with the community

Toyota's *company objectives* (each also described in full in the handbook) are, basically,

- To exceed Toyota plants in Japan in quality and cost of products
- To nurture suppliers and establish good relations
- To become profitable as soon as possible
- To build a flexible organization to respond to various changes[6]

In summary, Toyota and other high-commitment firms formulate comprehensive ideologies, ideologies composed of the missions, principles, values, and beliefs that guide the firms. The ideology in each case provides a comprehensive set of principles and a common set of guidelines that all employees can share and adhere to. Converting employees to "believers" then helps foster a sense of commonality and communion by providing employees with a transcendent and mutual ideology.

Creating the Charisma

Many company ideologies evoke "higher callings" or ultimate moral values like "improve the quality of life of all the people in the world." The result is the creation of a sort of corporate charisma in which the firm and what it achieves becomes to employees a source of enormous pride and awe. Like medieval crusaders, employees do what they do not just because they've joined the firm, but because it is "right" in terms of these ultimate values. These higher values or principles, such as Ben & Jerry's social and political aims, can then be used to legitimize the firm's demands, such as capping executives' pay at seven times what the lowest-paid Ben & Jerry's worker is paid.

In fact, Ben & Jerry's is a good example of charisma building. Their mission symbolizes the founders' unique idea of what a business should be and provides the firm and its employees with an ideology that represents a higher, transcendent calling to which one can commit:

> Ben & Jerry's is dedicated to the creation and demonstration of a new corporate concept of linked prosperity. Our mission consists of three interrelated parts:
>
> Product Mission: To make, distribute and sell the finest quality all-natural ice cream and related products in a wide variety of innovative flavors made from Vermont dairy products.
>
> Social Mission: To operate the company in a way that actively recognizes the central role that business plays in the structure of a society by initiating innovative ways to improve the quality of life of a broad community: local, national and international.
>
> Economic Mission: To operate the company on a sound financial basis of profitable growth, increasing value for our shareholders and creating career opportunities and financial rewards for our employees.
>
> Underlying the mission of Ben & Jerry's is the determination to seek new and creative ways of addressing all three parts, while holding a deep respect for individuals, inside and outside the company, and for the communities of which they are part.[7]

Ben & Jerry's makes it clear to its employees that such values form the ultimate justification for its business decisions. In other words, the feeling that employees are part of a higher calling is fostered by actions, not just words. This in turn contributes to the charisma the firm has for its employees and the commitment to its aims that they all share.

For example, Ben & Jerry's has "green teams," who are responsible for assessing the firm's environmental impact in all areas of operation and for developing and implementing programs to ameliorate or compensate for any negative impact. Ben & Jerry's also donates 7.5 percent of its pretax earnings to the Ben & Jerry's Foundation, a nonprofit institution established in 1985 by personal contributions from founders Ben Cohen and Jerry Greenfield. The foundation awards monies to nonprofit and charitable organizations. It also supports

> projects which are models for social change; projects infused with a spirit of generosity and hopefulness; projects which enhance people's quality of life, and projects which exhibit creative problem solving. Proposals related to children and families, disadvantaged groups, and the environment are some of those to be reviewed.[8]

The foundation is just one way the firm answers founder Ben Cohen's question, "Should a business exist for the exploitation of society, or should it exist for the benefit of society?" The firm's answer has been to integrate the company's profits with society's needs.[9] For example, in explaining Ben & Jerry's choice of suppliers for some of their ice cream production, Cohen says,

> Wild Maine Blueberry is another step in how we're defining what caring capitalism is all about. Our goal is to integrate a concern for the community in every business decision we make. We're trying to develop a system that improves the quality of life through socially conscious purchasing of our ingredients. The brownies in Chocolate Fudge Brownie benefit the employment of underskilled persons, the nuts in Rainforest Crunch benefit the preservation of the rain forest, the peaches in Fresh Georgia Peach support family farms, and the blueberries in Wild Maine Blueberry support traditional native American economy.[10]

For essential ingredients in the firm's Chocolate Fudge Brownie ice cream, Ben & Jerry's chose Greyston Bakery of Yonkers, New York, to supply it with 30,000 pounds of brownies a month. That produces an annual income of about $750,000 a year for Greyston, whose programs provide homeless people with housing, job training, childcare, and counseling. The blueberries for the Wild Maine Blueberry ice cream are bought from the Passamaquoddy Indians of Maine, thus supporting the economy of that indigenous people. To make its Rainforest Crunch ice cream, Ben & Jerry's buys from suppliers in the Brazilian rainforest and distributes 40 percent of its profits from Rainforest Crunch purchases to rainforest preservation groups and international environmental projects. One percent of the profits from some Ben & Jerry's products goes to "One Percent for Peace." This is a nonprofit organization advocating legislation to reallocate 1 percent of the U.S. defense budget to fund programs promoting peace through understanding.

Actions like these help turn Ben & Jerry's employees into more than employees; they become crusaders. There's Alan Parker who likes the firm because it is "politically and socially progressive" and because of incidents like this:

> When we saw milk prices falling in 1991, we went to suppliers and told them they were not charging enough. We felt that the effect of the lower prices on the farmers and on the whole social fabric would be devastating. We paid a premium based on the average price we'd paid for milk in the previous few years. The point is we did the right thing. We took about $500,000 right off the bottom line, but we put our money where our mouths are.[11]

There is one production official who says "every day I come to work I feel I make a difference in people's lives. That's what people believe in here. For me this has been the greatest time of my life." And there's Jim Miller who puts it this way: "If you're motivated by money, this is not the place for you. You come here for the firm's social side and for the values of the organization."[12] Liz Lonerghan, the firm's acting head of personnel, cites the "pride factor":

> Employees know that when they tell others they work for Ben & Jerry's the reaction is often "Wow!" I still don't know exactly what accounts for the cache Ben & Jerry's has; but I know people work here because they think they can make a difference—in the environment and social aims, for instance—and because of how we treat people, and because it's fun to work here.[13]

Sometimes, as at Toyota and Saturn, the goal is more modest, but the effort is still to link the firm with a "higher calling." Saturn aims to "market vehicles developed and manufactured in the United States that are world leaders in quality, cost, and customer service." It's always clear that a transcendent aim of these former GM employees is to show that "we can beat them." Similarly, Toyota seeks not just to be good but "to produce America's number 1 quality car," an awesome mission for a plant just three years old.

To help cultivate corporate charisma, Saturn and Toyota, like Ben & Jerry's, take steps to hammer home the company's greatness. Toyota's in-house bulletin, *Toyota Topics*, frequently runs articles quoting the comments of satisfied customers and the results of industry surveys—

like the J. C. Power survey that ranked Toyota's Lexington plant number 1. And Ben & Jerry's continously talks up its accomplishments—raising money for peace, feeding the homeless, and so on—in company documents and in-house speeches and on the firm's bulletin boards.

Achieving Ideological Conversion

Having an ideology, even a charismatic one, isn't enough: You also have to promote the conversion of your employees to the ideology—the missions and values of your firm. In her study of utopian communities, Rosabeth Moss Kanter found that successful communities achieved this in several ways: by requiring commitment to the ideology, by expecting recruits to take vows, by enforcing fairly exhaustive procedures for choosing members, by frequently rejecting prospective members, and by emphasizing tradition. I found modern-day equivalents to these practices in high-commitment firms in terms of extensive, value-based hiring, orientation, and training programs. These practices all bond employees to the missions and values espoused by their firms, mediating and closing the gap between the employee and the firm's ultimate aims.

Value-Based Hiring

The process of linking employees to ideology begins before the worker is even hired. High-commitment firms use what I've called "value-based hiring" practices. They first clarify what their basic values are. Then they enforce procedures for screening new employees; require evidence of commitment to the firm's values by selected candidates; and reject large numbers of prospective employees. The net effect (as we'll see in more detail in Chapter 7) is to select employees whose values and skills match the firm's ideology and who are thus well on the road to becoming "believers." Value-based hiring thus screens out those who might not "fit." Ben & Jerry's screens out managers who don't share the firm's social goals, Toyota screens out nonteam players, and Goldman, Sachs puts great emphasis on integrity. Elaborate screening procedures—tests, interviews, background checks—enable the firms to carry out this concept of value-based hiring.

Consider Toyota's hiring practices. According to Sam Heltman, the firm's head of personnel,

Most firms take selection too lightly. Each assembly worker here is a million-dollar decision. Ours is the most extensive [selection] system I've ever seen. Applicants also learn much about us. There's some self-selection taking place during the simulations, videos (when they see the hard work and listen to the group discussions), and individual problem solving session. That itself requires commitment, "I want to work there and am willing to put up with these tests."[14]

The process helps to ensure that Toyota hires people who are ideologically in step with its own values and aims. For example (as we'll see again in Chapter 7), the interviewing process is exhaustive, and it is specifically aimed at screening out those who might not be committed to basic Toyota values such as teamwork and quality. Its effect—as in all high-commitment firms—is to reject large numbers of prospective employees: Toyota hires only about 1 of every 40 recruits. But those who are hired are well on their way to being "believers."

Similarly, at Delta Air Lines:

We don't have to do much recruiting; we get about 4000 applications per day. Who are we looking for? We're looking for people who can work in our team environment, who have a strong work ethic, who have the basic education required, and who are well-rounded and who we think can deal well with the customers. Some of our applicants say, 'We won't start at the bottom' (for instance, cleaning aircraft), and we generally end up not hiring these, of course. What we get, therefore, are employees who are willing to go along with and work in our team environment."

Value-Based Orientation

The next step in ideological conversion is to orient and indoctrinate the new employees. Social psychologists Daniel Katz and Robert Kahn have said that "The adult socialization process in the organization can build upon the personal values of its members and integrate them around attractive organizational models. People can thus identify with the organizational mission."[15] The new-hire orientation program in high-commitment firms is always extensive and always value-based.

The orientation (or, as they call it "assimilation") program at Toyota Motor Manufacturing, U.S.A., is typical. While it covers traditional topics such as company benefits, it's mostly intended to convert Toyota team members to the firm's ideology of quality, teamwork, personal development, open communication, and mutual respect. The program covers four days.

Day 1. Day 1 begins at 6:30 a.m. with an overview of the program, a welcome to the company, and a discussion of the firm's organizational structure and human resource department by Sam Heltman, vice president for human resources. About an hour and a half is devoted to discussing Toyota's history and culture, and about two hours to employee benefits. Another two hours is devoted to discussions of Toyota Motor Manufacturing policies (including quality and teamwork).

Plant Manager Mike Dodge told me the Toyota new-employee assimilation process stresses "quality from day 1," a fact that's also evident from the documents new employees receive. For example, *Toyota Quality* notes that "Toyota's commitment to a world class, quality automobile is entrenched in the entire manufacturing philosophy. Through every development stage, the quest for superior quality is evident."[16]

Day 2. Day 2 starts with about two hours devoted to "communication training, the TMM way of listening," and then covers Japanese culture and work customs. The rest of the day is devoted to general issues, including safety, environmental affairs, the Toyota production system, and the firm's learning resource center—a library Toyota team members can use to boost their skills in a wide range of subjects from engineering to leadership.

Day 3. Again, the first two-and-a-half or three hours of the day is devoted to communication training, in this case the "TMM way of making requests and giving feedback." The assimilation program then covers Toyota problem solving, quality assurance, hazard communications, hearing conversation, and an introduction to the firm's method by which work teams develop and fine-tune standardized work procedures.

Day 4. The morning here is devoted mostly to teamwork-related topics such as teamwork training, Toyota's suggestion system, and the Toyota team-member activities association. It also covers basic team-member issues such as team responsibilities and team cooperation. The afternoon focuses on safety issues, in particular, fire prevention and fire extinguisher training.

Employees completing the four-day process are steeped in—and hopefully converted to—Toyota's ideology, its mission of quality, and its values of teamwork, Kaizen, and problem solving.

Saturn has a similar indoctrination program, where the first two days are devoted to discussions of benefits, safety and security, and the company's production process—just-in-time delivery, materials management, and so forth. However, in days 3 and 4 the focus shifts to the Saturn ideology and to discussions of the company's mission, philosophy, and values. According to People Systems team member Mariellen Freeland, Saturn's top managers—including President Skip LeFauve if he's in town—spend about an hour and a half explaining the firm's philosophy and its importance. It's also at this point, she says, that all new employees get their copy of Saturn's mission card (see Figure 6-2) and go through each point—teamwork, trust and respect for the individual, etc.—to emphasize its meaning. Short exercises are used here: The new employees might be asked, "If you saw a team member do this, what would you do?" "If you saw a team member 'living' this value, what would you see?"[17]

Value-Based Training

In all of our high-commitment firms the ideological conversion of these newly assimilated employees then continues with value-based training, training aimed not just at technical skills but at hammering home the basic values and missions of the firm. At Saturn, for example, "new people spend anywhere from 250 to 750 hours in training, just to get job-ready."[18] And these "new people" are not just learning the business; most are UAW veterans with years of experience at other GM plants.

Such extensive training is needed because "Just as we started Saturn with a clean-sheet approach—to relearn the business—so must our team members. This extends from basic concepts to innovative processes."[19] Most of the Saturn training is thus aimed not at basic skills, but at value-based issues such as conflict management, team building, and consensus decision making. Each course is designed to make believers of employees, believers in Saturn's ideological foundations: teamwork, quality self-direction, self-initiative, and worker empowerment.

For their part, Saturn supervisors get their ideological conversion largely through a special two-day leadership seminar called "Values and Beliefs." It's taught by Saturn's senior vice president for manufacturing, Bill Boruff, and by his UAW partner, Dick Jones. The program's basic aim is to familiarize supervisors with Saturn's core values and illustrate how to translate them from words into actions. Part 1, for instance, explains how values influence behavior, and cautions managers to beware of any disparities between stated and operative values: "It's what you *do*, not what you say, that sends the real signal to workers about what your department's *operative* values are," Boruff and

Jones reiterate. Thus talking "trust" while insisting on time clocks is a contradiction; the time clock seems to say, "We don't trust you."[20] (There are no time clocks at Saturn.)

Succeeding sessions use lectures and exercises to explain and illustrate each of Saturn's basic values. Core Saturn values such as respect for people, making employees full partners, building customer satisfaction through teamwork, and putting quality in every product are presented here, with the aim of making believers of Saturn leaders through the use of concrete examples of what these values mean.

Symbols and Stories, Rites and Ceremonials

"Creating a value system that encourages the kind of behavior you want," says Saturn's Bob Boruff, "is not enough. The challenge is then to engage in those practices that symbolize those values, and tell people what it's really OK to do—and what not [to do]. Actions, in other words, speak much more loudly than words."[21] High-commitment firms continuously engage in deeds that exemplify the values and ethics they want their employees to espouse. This is often called "culture building" and is achieved through symbols and stories, rites and ceremonials.[22]

Symbols, for example, are used throughout these firms to exemplify the values each firm wants to stress. For example, in a company where having fun is both a basic value and an inalienable right, what else could you expect but a Ben & Jerry "Joy Gang"? The Joy Gang is a concrete symbol of Ben & Jerry's ideology, which emphasizes charity, fun, and goodwill toward fellow workers. Legend has it that the then-named "Joy Committee" was born when cofounder Jerry Greenfield returned from a sabbatical to find the company a bit too traditional. Subsequently, says Peter Lind, the group's "grand pooh-bah" and full-time R&D director, the name Joy Committee was dropped as "much too formal."[23]

The Joy Gang is a voluntary group that meets once or twice a week to create new ways to inject fun into what the B&J people do. For instance, they once hired a masseur to give every worker a 15-minute massage. They periodically give "joy grants": "500 quick, easy, no-strings-attached dollars for long-term improvements to your work area, given to those groups or departments that give the Joy Gang a few good reasons why their "Joy" idea will enhance 'joy on the job.'"[24] Joy grants have thus far been awarded for flowers for the patio, a barbecue grill for the marketing offices, a hot chocolate machine, hi-fi speakers for the freezer room, and a basketball court.

The Joy Gang also routinely distributes Joy T-shirts and tickets to the haunted forest (wherever that is). It often schedules events that would cause consternation at stuffier companies. There was a Barry Manilow Appreciation Day, for instance, during which the singer's music blared continuously from the company's Muzak system. They held a Slinky relay to inaugurate a new set of stairs, and one year everyone dressed up as Elvis Presley to commemorate the anniversary of the singer's death. A random list of other Joy Gang projects would include a Ping-Pong contest, a tacky dress-up day, a Santa Claus visitation, a trip to a fine arts museum, a canoe trip, and a Disfigure Fred's Head contest (I didn't ask). The Joy Gang has given away tickets to a stock-car race, distributed Joy Ninja buttons, and, of course, sponsored the world's largest Vermont-made milkshake. Goofy perhaps. But the Ben & Jerry's Joy Gang reminds every employee every day of the firm's values, particularly its emphasis on fun, collegiality, and informality.

It's easy to find examples of rites and ceremonials in other high-commitment firms. For example, we've seen that both J. C. Penney and Mary Kay have elaborate ceremonials that symbolize their values and convert employees to the values. The annual J. C. Penney HCSC inauguration meetings are an example of this. Here new management associates are inducted into the Penney Partnership, vowing to commit to the firm's ideology as embodied in the Penney Idea. Each inductee solemnly swears allegiance to the Penney Idea and then receives his or her HCSC lapel pin, symbolizing Penney's basic values of honor, confidence, service, and cooperation.

The in-house newsletters at high-commitment firms are usually filled with stories of company heroes who symbolize company ideology. *Toyota Topics* talks about the second-shift crew who, during a snowstorm, voluntarily stayed on after their shift because they feared their third-shift colleagues wouldn't be able to get to work on time.

A Summary: Transcendental Mediation as a Key to Commitment

1. Formulate shared transcendental ideologies, missions, and values, and mechanisms for communicating these values to your employees. You want your employees to be crusaders.

2. Create a written ideology that lays out your organization's basic way of thinking and doing things. Components may include a statement of mission or vision, a statement of basic values or philosophy, and/or a code of ethics. The important thing is that the ideology specify the guideposts employees are to use as they go about their jobs and embody a vision for them to share and to commit to.

3. Try to lend a charismatic element to your firm and its ideology. Make the ideology a source of pride for your employees by having it evoke "higher callings" such as ultimate moral values like "help your fellow human beings." Then take steps to hammer home the company's greatness—the people your firm has helped, the number 1 quality of its products, and so on.

4. Promote the conversion of your employees to the mission and values of your firm: Require commitment to the ideology; expect new employees to take "vows"; enforce exhaustive procedures for choosing new employees; reject a good number of prospective employees; emphasize your traditions.

5. Institute formal and extensive new-employee orientation/indoctrination/assimilation programs wherein the ideology of your firm is stressed.

6. Continually engage in deeds—symbols and stories, rites and ceremonials—that exemplify the values and ethics you want your employees to espouse.

References

1. Rosabeth Moss Kanter, *Commitment and Community: Communes and Utopias in Sociological Perspective*, Harvard University Press, Cambridge, Mass., 1972, p. 74.
2. *Mary Kay's Cosmetics Consultant's Guide*, p. I.
3. Ibid., p. 2.
4. Ibid.
5. Ibid., pp. 3–4.
6. *Team Member Handbook*, Toyota Motor Manufacturing, U.S.A., February 1988, pp. 10–12.
7. *Ben & Jerry's 1990 Annual Report*, p. 5.
8. Ibid.

9. Joan Stableford, "Ben and Jerry's Sweetens Its Success by Helping Others," *Westchester County Business Journal*, March 4, 1991, p. 13.

10. Ben & Jerry's public relations release, October 5, 1990.

11. Personal interview with Alan Parker, April 1992.

12. Personal interview with Jim Miller, April 1992.

13. Personal interview with Liz Lonerghan, April 1992.

14. Personal interview with Sam Heltman, March 1992.

15. Daniel Katz and Robert Kahn, *The Social Psychology of Organizations*, John Wiley, New York, 1966, p. 366.

16. Personal interview with Mike Dodge, March 1992.

17. Personal interview with Mariellen Freeland, March 1992.

18. Jacob M. Schlesinger and Paul Ingrassia, "GM Woos Employees by Listening To and Talking Up Its 'Team,'" *The Wall Street Journal*, January 12, 1989, p. 1, as discussed in Kathryn M. Bartol and David Martin, *Management*, McGraw-Hill, New York, 1991, p. 104.

19. Ibid.

20. Personal interview with Bill Boruff, March 1992.

21. Ibid.

22. For fuller discussion, see Linda Smircich, "Concepts of Culture and Organizational Analysis," *Administrative Science Quarterly*, vol. 28 (1983), pp. 339–358.

23. Personal interview with Peter Lind, April 1992.

24. Ibid.; *Joy Grant*, company document.

7

Value-Based Hiring

We've seen that the time to start building commitment is before—not after—employees are hired. Thus high-commitment firms use value-based hiring practices. They don't just look at an applicant's job-related skills. They try to get a sense of the person and his or her personal qualities and values; they identify common experiences and values that may flag the applicant's fit with the firm. They give their applicants realistic previews of what to expect; and they usually end up rejecting large numbers of applicants. In short, they put enormous effort into interviewing and screening to find the best people. Toyota, U.S.A., Vice President Alex Warren put it:

> You might be surprised, but our selection or hiring process is an exhaustive, painstaking system designed not to fill positions quickly, but to find the right people for those positions. What are we looking for? First, these people must be able to think for themselves...be problem solvers...and second, work in a team atmosphere. Simply put, we need strong minds, not strong backs....We consider the selection of a team member as a long-term investment decision. Why go to the trouble of hiring a questionable employee only to have to fire him later?[1]

We've seen that value-based hiring also plays an indirect role in creating commitment through its effect on most of the other high-commitment practices, such as communion, transcendental mediation, securitizing, and actualizing. It may be unwise, for instance, to promise job security to employees who haven't the values or skills to achieve the company's ends. Fostering a sense of communion is facilitated by sacrifice and by a rigorous hiring process that screens out those without the common, coveted values. Similarly, it's useless to preach people-first values if the people you hire don't trust or respect other people.

Let's look at several examples of how high-commitment firms hire employees and then review some common themes.

Quality, Kaizen, and Commitment: The Toyota Story

At Toyota, hiring top-quality people is vital. The Toyota mission states that the interests of the firm and its employees are best served by producing high-quality cars as efficiently as possible. This kind of production depends on employee commitment to Kaizen, the firm's philosophy of continuous improvement. This kind of production depends, in turn, on a workforce of highly qualified people who are capable of cooperative teamwork, flexibility, problem solving, and continual learning. As the Toyota *Team Member Handbook* says, "People are our most important resource and are the most important factor in the success of our organization."[2] The firm is well aware that "hiring a 30-year employee who will earn $30,000 to $40,000 a year is really a million dollar plus decision for us. That's why Toyota puts as much or more time and effort into hiring as it does into buying machinery."[3]

Past and Present

By way of background, Toyota Motor Manufacturing, U.S.A., is located in Georgetown, Kentucky (not far from Lexington), and they recruit almost exclusively from within Kentucky. Since the Kentucky workforce has virtually no auto manufacturing experience (in fact, little manufacturing experience of any kind), this has meant that most of the people Toyota has hired have come with no background skills in car building. From the day it was announced in 1985 that Toyota would build an automobile manufacturing plant, the Kentucky Department of Employment Services has recorded inquiries from over 200,000 people. First-shift hiring was completed in December 1988. Hiring for the second shift was completed in May 1989. Employment will reach approximately 5000 people when the expansion facility begins operation in late 1993. Annual payroll, as of November 1991, was over $150 million.

Group leaders and their subordinate team leaders (first-line supervisors) are promoted from within. Outside applicants are typically not considered for these positions.

The Hiring Process

Given that background, Toyota's hiring process has two distinguishing features: its exhaustiveness and the extent to which it identifies, not just candidates with technical skills (such as manufacturing know-how), but rather candidates whose intelligence, interpersonal skills, flexibility, desire to learn, and problem-solving skills are compatible with the basic values of the firm.

Toyota's head of personnel has said that the firm's hiring process is "the most exhaustive I've ever seen."

> If we can find someone with potential, we can teach them the technical skills. A candidate for a production job at Toyota will undergo our 20 hours of testing and interviewing before selection. We seek team members who have the aptitude to absorb the considerable training an inexperienced person will need to absorb to do their job, and especially to analyze their work and suggest improvements.[4]

The exhaustiveness of the screening process has three effects. First, it allows the firm to use a much more comprehensive package of selection interviews, exercises, and tests than would normally be the case. Second, the process, entailing as it does 20 hours of tests, exercises, and interviews over five or more days, gives candidates a realistic preview of what working in Toyota will be like. As a result, considerable self-selection takes place: This is not everyone's cup of tea, in other words. Last but not least, candidates who do get hired often view themselves as part of a special, chosen few. To that extent, the hiring process is not unlike the initiation rites of a private social club. Like the fraternity pledge who staggers through four months of trials, new Toyota employees start their jobs already immersed in the traditions and ideology of the firm and with a deep sense of commonality, communion, and awe that they, like their colleagues, have all traveled the same difficult road.

As summarized in Figure 7-1, Toyota's hiring process involves about 20 hours and six phases, spread over five or six days. The Kentucky Department of Employment Services conducts phase I. Here applicants fill out application blanks summarizing their work experience and skills and view a one-hour video describing Toyota's work environment and selection system. The video gives applicants a realistic preview of work

Phase I	Orientation/Application
	■ Fill out an application and view a video of the Toyota work environment and selection process (1 hour).
	Objective: To explain the job and collect information about work experiences and skills
	Conducted by: Kentucky Department of Employment Services
Phase II	Technical Skills Assessment
	Pencil/Paper tests
	■ Take a general knowledge test* (2 hours).
	■ Take a tool-&-die or general maintenance test* (6 hours).
	Objective: To assess technical knowledge and potential
	Conducted by: Kentucky Department of Employment Services
Phase III	Interpersonal Skills Assessment
	■ Engage in group and individual problem-solving activities* (4 hours).
	■ Participate in production assembly simulation** (5 hours).
	Objective: To assess interpersonal and decision-making skills
	Conducted by: Toyota Motor Manufacturing
Phase IV	Toyota Assessment
	■ Undergo group interview and evaluation (1 hour).
	Objective: To discuss achievements and accomplishments
	Conducted by: Toyota Motor Manufacturing
Phase V	Health Assessment
	■ Undergo physical exam and drug/alcohol tests ($2\frac{1}{2}$ hours).
	Objective: To determine physical fitness
	Conducted by: Scott County General Hospital and University of Kentucky Medical Center
Phase VI	On-the-Job Observation
	■ Undergo observation and coaching on the job after being hired (6 months).
	Objective: To assess job performance and develop skills
	Conducted by: Toyota Motor Manufacturing

*Skilled-trades workers only
**Production workers only

Figure 7-1. Summary of Toyota's hiring process. (*Adapted with permission from Toyota Motor Manufacturing, U.S.A., training and orientation documents.*)

at Toyota and of the extensiveness of the hiring process. Many applicants simply drop out at this stage.

Phase II is aimed at assessing the applicant's technical knowledge and potential and is also conducted by the Kentucky Department of Employment Services. Here applicants take the U.S. Employment Services' General Aptitude Test Battery (GATB), which helps identify problem-solving skills, learning potential, and occupational preferences. Skilled-trades applicants (experienced mechanics and so forth) also take a six-hour tool-and-die or general maintenance test. Kentucky Employment Services scores all tests and submits the files to Toyota. (Many state employment offices will arrange similar prescreening services for firms doing heavy recruiting in their areas; many will also administer GATB tests for firms in their areas.)

Toyota takes over the screening process in phase III. The aim here is to assess the applicant's interpersonal and decision-making skills. All applicants participate in four hours of group and individual problem-solving and discussion activities in the firm's assessment center. This is a separate location where applicants engage in exercises under the observation of Toyota screening experts.

The group discussion exercises help reveal how individual applicants interact with others in their group. In a typical exercise participants playing roles as company employees constitute a team responsible for choosing new features for next year's car. Team members first individually rank 12 features, based upon market appeal, and then suggest one feature not included on the list. They must then come to a consensus on the best rank ordering.

The problem-solving exercises are usually administered individually and are aimed at assessing each applicant's problem-solving ability, in terms of insight, flexibility, and creativity. In one typical exercise, for example, an applicant is given a brief description of a production problem and is asked to formulate questions that will help him or her understand the causes of the problem. The candidate then gets a chance to ask questions of a resource person, one with considerable information about the problem's cause. At the end of this question-and-answer period, the candidate fills out a form, listing the problem's causes, recommended solutions, and reasons for suggesting these solutions.

Also in phase III, production-line assembly candidates participate in a five-hour assembly simulation. In one of these scenarios, candidates play the roles of the management and workforce of a firm that makes electrical circuits. During a series of planning and manufacturing periods, the team decides which circuits to manufacture and how to effectively assign people, materials, and money to produce them.

A one-hour group interview constitutes phase IV. Here groups of candidates discuss their accomplishments with Toyota interviewers. This phase helps give Toyota a more complete picture of what drives each candidate, in terms of what sorts of things each is proudest of and most interested in. Phase IV also gives Toyota another opportunity to watch their candidates interact with each other in groups. Those who successfully complete phase IV (and are tentatively tapped as Toyota employees) then undergo two-and-a-half hours of physical and drug/alcohol tests at area hospitals (phase V). Finally, phase VI involves closely monitoring, observing, and coaching the new employees on the job, to assess their job performance and to develop their skills during their first six months at work.

Traits and Skills Sought

If you think back to our discussion of Toyota's mission and values in Chapter 6, you'll see why I call this hiring process "value-based." It is value-based in that it aims to select people not just on the basis of technical skills or work history, but on human traits and values such as cooperativeness, learning ability, and quality-orientation that fit best with Toyota's basic ideology—its missions, aims, and values. As Sam Heltman, the firm's personnel chief, says, the first thing you have to do in designing a hiring process like Toyota's is "to know what you want." At Toyota this objective is clear. They are looking, first, Heltman says, for interpersonal skills because of the firm's emphasis on team interaction.[5] (Heltman told me that about 100,000 people had gone through the firm's group discussion exercises as of mid-1992. Here trained observers assessed candidates' interpersonal skills such as willingness to communicate and diplomacy. Those scoring low here, said Heltman, "should work somewhere else," given his firm's stress on team-based values.)

Similarly, because the entire thrust of Toyota's Kaizen process is to improve work processes through worker commitment, reasoning and problem-solving skills are also crucial human requirements. For example, in speaking with assembly workers and team leaders when I visited the plant, I saw how the employees have redesigned the standard worksheets, which specify how each of the group's jobs must be done. They began with the standard job sheets from Japan, then continuously changed and improved them through Kaizen, a process which demands strong reasoning and problem-solving skills.

This emphasis on Kaizen—on having the employees themselves improve the system—helps explain Toyota's emphasis on hiring intelligent, educated workers. The GATB and problem-solving simulations have in fact helped produce such a workforce. "Those who did the best in their education did the best in the simulations," Heltman told me. One hundred percent of Toyota workers have at least a high school degree or equivalent, and many plant employees (including assemblers) are college-educated.[6]

Quality is one of Toyota's central values, and so the firm also seeks a history of quality commitment in the people it hires. This is one reason for the group interview, the one that focuses on accomplishments. By asking candidates about the things they are proudest of, Toyota gets a better insight into the person's values regarding quality. This is very important in a firm devoted to having employees build quality into its cars each step of the way.

Toyota is also looking, says Heltman, for employees "who have an eagerness to learn and a willingness to try it not only their way, but our way and the group's way."[7] After all, Toyota's production system is based on consensus decision making, job rotation, and flexible career paths, and these require open-minded, flexible team players. The firm's group decision-making and problem-solving exercises help identify such people.

As we saw in Chapter 3, which dealt with people-first values, value-based hiring has a special meaning when it comes to hiring managers. Here a great emphasis is placed on hiring or promoting only people-oriented applicants. As with General Manager Mike Da Prile, Toyota was looking for men and women who share the people-first values of mutual trust and respect for the individual, which are the foundations of Toyota's production.

Unions and Team Selection: The Saturn Story

The philosophies of Toyota and Saturn are similar, stressing as they do consensus, quality, people-first values, teamwork, and continuous improvement. However, Saturn's operating partnership with the UAW means that its hiring process differs from nonunion Toyota's in several ways.

Past and Present

First, some background. To begin with, under the memorandum of agreement between Saturn and the UAW, active and inactive GM-UAW employees are "the primary source for the initial complement, up to full capacity, of operating and skilled trades technicians."[8] While it's acknowledged that "Saturn membership is conditional on meeting established recruitment and selection criteria," this has meant that in practice all plant employees have come (and will continue to come) from active or laid-off GM workers. (Of the 2700 Saturn plant employees in 1988, about 55 percent came from the UAW's "inactive," or laid-off, rolls.) Furthermore, also by agreement, GM-UAW workers going to work at Saturn can't go back to GM. Since there were no GM plants anywhere near Spring Hill, Tennessee, that has meant that every Saturn employee has had to resettle his or her family in a brand-new area. The result, as one Saturn manager told me, is a production workforce composed entirely of former GM-UAW members, coming from about 130 different GM plants in 30 different states. And because they had to burn their bridges to get there, Saturn's is a workforce composed of risk takers, people who were willing to strike off and try something entirely new. The first contingent of Saturn employees moved on to the Spring Hill site February 1, 1986; the total workforce numbered about 4000 in 1992.

Saturn also didn't have the home-field advantage that Toyota did when it came to recruiting applicants. Toyota was and is one of the most attractive employment opportunities in western Kentucky, and they continue to be flooded with applicants—over 200,000 applicants for 4000 jobs, as of 1992.

On the other hand, Saturn people began recruiting the first of 3000 workers in February 1988 at 136 GM-UAW plants and union halls throughout the United States. They told candidates they would have to shed old habits and work as a team. And they explained that technical skills would be less important than interpersonal ones in a plant where small groups of highly committed employees had to work on their own. Even before the actual screening began, in other words, these realistic previews meant that the screening was already under way. It was hoped that applicants who were willing to shed old habits and join a team-based production system while moving far from old friends might already have the flexibility and desire to learn that Saturn was seeking.

The Hiring Process

Beyond that, Saturn's hiring process is similar to Toyota's both in its exhaustiveness and in the fact that it's value-based. Active and inactive GM-UAW applicants are first prescreened and then undergo three-and-a-half hours of paper-and-pencil testing. This involves a four-part test battery covering mathematics, reading, mechanical comprehension, and spatial relationships for skilled-trades workers. Standardized tests similar to the GATB are taken by other applicants. (Unlike Toyota, by the way, where every production employee has at least a high school equivalency degree and many have college experience, Saturn's testing program has resulted in the hiring of fewer high school grads and relatively few with college degrees. Saturn workers also tend to be older, in their thirties.)

At this point the surviving candidates undergo about two-and-a-half hours of group-exercise assessment. Here, as at Toyota, they work in teams to complete problem-solving and team-interaction exercises. Viable candidates are then made available as "recruits" to Saturn work teams, who are trained to interview and evaluate candidates using a special, structured interview form. Thus it is the individual work teams that actually make the final hiring decisions. As a result, as one Saturn manager told me, "Once a person is hired by a team there's a feeling of great ownership created about who's there and about the sharing of work." It fosters, in other words, a feeling of communion within the team.

The team members I spoke with were enthusiastic about recruiting and hiring their own team members. What actually happens, said one in explaining the process to me, is that Saturn's People Systems (personnel department) compiles a file on applicants, including references, work history, and test results. When an opening occurs, the team is given access to the relevant files; the team also conducts an initial phone interview. The basic objective here is to let the team get a feel for whether the applicant has an orientation toward the team concept and whether the person is open to change. The team (or team representative) conducting the phone interview asks a series of questions from a structured form. These are then rated by the Saturn rating system. On the basis of the candidate's interview and file materials, the team decides if he or she has what it takes to do the job and join the team. The team then has to decide whether to bring the candidate in for a personal interview. If they decide to do that, the trip is paid for with funds from the team's budget. After the team has conducted the in-person interviews, a final decision is made.

The Certified Interview: The J. C. Penney Process

Most high-commitment firms, including J. C. Penney, don't use paper-and-pencil tests or structured exercises to select employees. Most use a combination of background checks (education, work history, and so on) plus comprehensive interviews; we'll look more closely at these interviews in the following paragraphs.

The Hiring Process

Hiring entry-level merchandising-manager trainees at J. C. Penney involves what the firm calls "Certified Interviewing." An initial screening interview takes about a half-hour and is usually conducted on college campuses or at career day conferences. Interviewers are told to spend about 15 to 20 minutes interviewing the applicant and to allow at least 10 minutes for the candidate in turn to ask questions about J. C. Penney. The basic aims of this first interview are to assess the person's interest in retailing and to assess his or her problem-handling, initiative, and leadership skills and score them on a one-page form. If a decision is made at this point to pursue the person's candidacy, he or she is invited to complete the application form and to meet with the local store personnel manager for a more detailed interview.

If this hurdle is passed, the candidate next meets with three levels of store managers: a current merchandising-manager trainee who has been "on the floor" for perhaps a year; an "associate" such as a merchandising manager; and the store manager. The candidate will spend about an hour with the trainee, two to three hours with the merchandising manager, and about three hours with the store manager.

The exhaustiveness of the Certified Interview form used by all three interviewers standardizes the process and sets it apart from the interviewing processes of most firms. The form contains about four questions (one on each of four pages) for each of the basic skills being evaluated (planning and organizing, judgment, and so on). An interview question might be "Tell me about a recent major decision that you had to make." There is a space on the page for the interviewer to summarize the situation described by the candidate, what the candidate said he or she did in response to the situation, how he or she did it, and what the outcome was. The interviewer then assesses the candidate's skills as demonstrated by the response—for instance, "Gathers appropriate information before reaching decisions"; "Bases decisions on relevant information and sound reasoning"; and so on.

In addition to being exhaustive, the Penney hiring process (like those at Toyota and Saturn) is also value-based. This is the company, you will recall, whose first store was called "The Golden Rule," and which still adheres to the Penney Idea:

To serve the public as nearly as we can to its complete satisfaction, to expect for the service we render a fair remuneration, and not all the profit the traffic will bear, to do all in our power to pack the customer's dollar full of value, quality, and satisfaction, and to test our every policy, method and act in this wise: Does it square with what is right and just?[9]

Given such values, what sorts of people do you think Penney's wants to hire—over and above those having basic skills such as judgment, initiative, and leadership? Here is a sampling of what some managers told me they're looking for:

"Good solid citizens."

"Solid grades, but not magna cum laude grades."

"Generalists, not quantitative types."

"A Penney-type person, someone who likes people, has good interpersonal skills, and is willing to take direction; we're not looking for mavericks."

"Hard-working, loyal, honest, fair, team players."

"A lot like our customers, good middle-of-the-road people."

"People who come looking for a job where they can stay a while."

"All Penney's people are nice people. They have a heart; you would relate to them."

"Someone who's willing to get his hands dirty and has a high focus on working with people."

In summary, Penney's people work hard to find candidates who will fit in, ones whose values seem compatible with those of the firm.

The hiring process at Penney's, as at Saturn and Toyota, is aimed at giving candidates realistic previews of what a Penney's job is like. For example, in the candidate's first interview, the merchandising-manager trainee will emphasize that the job will entail one or two nights per week, perhaps 50 hours per week of work, and that the pay (at this entry level) won't be much (about $20,000 to $25,000 annually). Similarly, as one personnel officer told me, "When we recruit, we tell people what we're looking for. The main question we want these people to ask is `Do I like this?'" A store manager put it this way: "We do a lot of interviewing because we want the input of our managers, of course; but we also want the candidate to understand what the job really is. We therefore encourage managers to tell candidates what the job entails as frankly and as candidly as possible."

The Best and the Brightest:
The Goldman, Sachs Story

In the rough-and-tumble world of investment banking, Goldman, Sachs stands out. They stand out as Wall Street's biggest deal makers (in terms of dollar volume of transactions completed in 1990, $50.8 billion). They stand out as the last big private-partnership investment bank on Wall Street. They stand out with their record pretax profits of $600 million, or roughly $5 million per partner.[10] And many believe that they stand out for their pride in the professional quality of their work and in their principle: "Our clients' interests always come first." You may recall several other of the firm's business principles (see Figure 6-1 for a complete listing):

Our assets are people, capital, and reputation.

We take great pride in the professional quality of our work.

We stress creativity and imagination in everything we do.

We stress teamwork in everything we do.

The dedication of our people to the firm and the intensity of their effort to their jobs are greater than one finds in most other organizations.

To breach a confidence or to use confidential information improperly or carelessly would be unthinkable.

We offer our people the opportunity to move ahead more rapidly than is possible at most other places.

Integrity and honesty are at the heart of our business.[11]

Given these values, it is not surprising that Goldman, Sachs' principles also include this one:

We make an unusual effort to identify and recruit the very best person for every job. Although our activities are measured in billions of dollars, we select our people one by one. In a service business, we know that without the best people, we cannot be the best firm.[12]

Goldman, Sachs goes after the cream of the crop, and not just in terms of intelligence or financial skills. They are looking for values, values like a commitment to excellence as evidenced by a pattern of success in a candidate's background, as well as honesty, integrity, and a preference for working as a member of a team.

As a result, as Jeffrey Sanderson, the firm's vice president and director of employment and employee relations, told me,

As with all of our human resource activities, we take our responsibility for selecting new hires very seriously. Every year, the firm nominates team captains, an appointment which is considered an honor, to help us build a positive relationship with each school at which we recruit. Each campus visit includes time set aside for getting to know the professors, having dinner with students and faculty members, in addition to extensive interviewing both on and off campus. After passing an initial interview, a candidate typically goes on to meet with 10 to 15 other people before he or she is hired. Although this requires a great deal of time and energy, we believe it is well worth the extra effort. And everyone is more than happy to get involved in the process, including our most senior-level personnel. Ask 10 partners to attend a meeting to discuss recruiting, and all 10 will do whatever they have to do to be there. Why? Because they really do believe that Goldman, Sachs can only be as good as its people.

Self-Selection: The Process at Delta, Ben & Jerry's, and Mary Kay

There is always a heavy dose of self-selection in the hiring practices of high-commitment firms: For one thing, the exhaustiveness of the hiring process alone ensures it. From the realistic previews at J. C. Penney to the five-day testing ritual at Toyota, U.S.A., all of these firms rely to some extent on having "nonfit" candidates pull themselves out of the running. While all firms rely on self-selection to some extent, several depend on it more than do others.

Delta Air Lines

Delta is one example. Perhaps the nation's premier airline, Delta can afford to be selective: They get about 4000 applications per day. At Delta, self-selection results in part from the types of entry-level jobs most new operations employees are offered. Maurice Worth, the firm's senior vice president of personnel, says that most of Delta's operations employees "come in as 'cleaners'; 40 percent have college degrees and 5 percent have masters'. Within two to three years they can move up to a ticket agent's position and eventually to supervisory positions."[14] Jobs cleaning aircraft may not be what most college grads covet, of course. But those who do tend to be the sort of team players that Delta is seeking.

Ben & Jerry's Homemade

The "7-times" pay policy for managers plays a similar role at Ben & Jerry's. As one of their managers told me, "This place is staffed by people who wouldn't survive in most other business cultures." Another said, "If you're looking to get rich, this isn't the place. As a result, we get competent people who fit in." Another put it this way: "If you're motivated by money, this is not the place for you. You come here for the firm's social side and for the values of the organization." "People," said another, "come here because they think they can make a difference—in the environment, for instance—and because they're proud of how we treat people, and because it's fun to work here."

Mary Kay Cosmetics

At close to 80 percent, the annual turnover of Mary Kay beauty consultants is below average for other direct sales firms, but still very high. As a result, it's safe to say that those who remain and work up the sales hierarchy go through a self-selection process not unlike those at other high-commitment firms. In fact, at Mary Kay, it's only the very top rung of the sales positions—the national sales directors—who have to undergo formal screening before taking their jobs. For all the other levels—beauty consultant, star recruiter, team leader, team manager, and director-in-qualification—the decision to move up is entirely the person's own. It's thus not the company but the job itself *and* the company's values—customer service, the "go-give" attitude, the continual recruiting and goal setting, and above all, the industriousness and commitment to the product/service mission of the firm—that screen out those who do not fit. The voices you hear shouting at the annual Mary Kay meetings are the voices of highly committed people.

Common Themes

High-commitment firms use value-based hiring to select employees whose values are compatible with those of the firm. While we've seen that firms go about this in various ways, five common themes are apparent. First, value-based hiring requires that you've clarified your firm's own values—whether they're excellence, Kaizen/continuous improvement, integrity, people-first values, or some other ideal. "You must first know what you want," as one manager said at Toyota.

Second, high-commitment firms devote time and effort to an exhaustive screening process. Eight to ten hours of interviewing, even for entry-level employees, is not unusual, and firms like Goldman, Sachs, Saturn, and Toyota will spend 20 hours or more with someone before deciding whether to hire or not.

Third, the screening process does not just identify knowledge and technical skills. Instead, the candidates' values and skills are matched with the needs of the firm. Teamwork, Kaizen, and flexibility are central values at Toyota; therefore problem-solving skills, interpersonal skills, and commitment to quality are crucial human requirements here. Integrity, honesty, intelligence, hard work, and teamwork are emphasized at Goldman, Sachs.

Fourth, value-based hiring always includes realistic job previews. High-commitment firms are certainly interested in "selling" good candidates. In fact, firms like Goldman, Sachs will wine and dine their chosen stars to get them to join the firm. But to all of these firms it's more important to make sure that the candidates know what working in the firm is going to be like and, more importantly, what sorts of values the company cherishes. The last thing a high-commitment firm wants is to hire an employee whose values are inconsistent with those of the firm. You should find no financial wizards who cut ethical corners at Goldman, Sachs, no abrasive personalities at J. C. Penney.

Finally, self-selection is an integral part of the screening at most of these firms. In some this just means realistic previews. At others, practices such as long "probationary" periods in entry-level jobs (Delta), unusually low salary ceilings (Ben & Jerry's), and rigorous sink-or-swim job assignments (Mary Kay) help screen out those who do not fit. In *all* of these firms the screening process demands sacrifice for prospective employees: The time and effort asked is always extensive, and one firm (Saturn) even requires that employees sacrifice any chance of returning to one's former employer (General Motors) and that they uproot their families. Sacrifice and value-based hiring in turn contribute to the sense of communion and awe and shared values that help foster commitment in all of these firms.

A Summary: Value-Based Hiring as a Key to Commitment

1. Use value-based hiring to select employees whose values are compatible with those of the firm. Start by clarifying your firm's own ideol-

ogy so that its elements can be translated into concrete questions, tests, and exercises and thus be made part of your firm's screening process.

2. Design an exhaustive screening process. Even with entry-level employees you should involve middle- and higher-level managers in the interviewing; design screening tools like structured interviews to help ensure that applicants are exhaustively screened. Recruit actively so that those who are hired see that many were rejected and that they have become part of an "elite."

3. Don't just look for job knowledge or technical skills. Instead, use questions, tests, and exercises to match the candidate's values and skills with the needs of the firm and with its ideology.

4. Always provide candid, realistic previews of what working at your firm will be like and what the entry job entails. Make it clear what sorts of values your firm cherishes.

5. Self-selection is important. This can involve long probationary periods in entry-level jobs, low salary ceilings, or merely a very exhaustive hiring process. Require a spirit of sacrifice in employees.

References

1. Alex Warren, speech to the City Club, Cleveland, Ohio, November 15, 1991.
2. *Team Member Handbook*, Toyota Motor Manufacturing, U.S.A., February 1988, p. 15.
3. Alex Warren, speech to the City Club, p. 7.
4. Ibid.
5. Personal interview with Sam Heltman, March 1992.
6. Ibid.
7. Ibid.
8. Saturn Corporation, Memorandum of Agreement, p. 10.
9. *The Penney Idea*, company document.
10. "Wall Street's Shining Maiden," *The Economist Newspaper Limited,* 1990; Randall Smith, "Wall Street's Long-time Stars Lead the Dealmakers' League," *The Wall Street Journal,* January 2, 1991.
11. *Goldman, Sachs Business Principles*, company document.
12. Ibid.
13. Personal interview with Jeffrey Sanderson, April 1992.
14. Personal interview with Maurice Worth, January 1992.

8
Securitizing

A story is told of how a large electronics firm in Houston dismissed 1200 employees over a six-week period several years ago. According to eyewitness accounts, many of the workers first discovered they'd been fired when armed guards appeared at their office doors. The guards showed up with more than 250 boxes, obviously stockpiled long in advance, and the workers were given 20 minutes to pack their belongings, empty their lockers, and get out of the building. Managers who had driven their company cars to work were given coupons for cab rides home, and a line of cabs had formed at the entrance to cart former employees away.[1]

While the apparent brutality of that layoff may be unusual, there's no doubt that employers are continuing to dismiss workers in record numbers. For example, the years 1985 through 1989 marked the third through seventh years of continuous economic expansion in the United States. Over that period, total employment—the total number of people employed—expanded by 11.7 million. But at the same time 4.3 million workers who had been with their employers for at least three years lost their jobs because their plants or businesses closed down or moved, their positions or shifts were abolished, or not enough work was available for them to stay on. Included in those dismissed—and remember that this precedes the bloodbath of the early 1990s—were 870,000 managers and professionals and 625,000 administrative support workers.[2] Eighty percent of these workers were between the ages of 25 and 54, and most of the others were 55 or older. The pace has increased in the 1990s: For instance, one report had large corporations alone announcing plans to cut 556,000 jobs permanently in 1991.[3] In June 1992 the U.S. unemployment rate hit an eight-year high of 7.8 percent.[4]

It might be comforting to think that these cuts were just a product of recession, but that's not the case. The period 1985 to 1989 was a period of rapid economic growth, not one of recession. Furthermore, a study by the American Management Association found that while about half the firms downsizing blamed "business downturn," the rest cited "improved staff utilization," "attempts to do the same work with fewer people," "mergers/acquisitions," "work transfers," "automation," "obsolescence," and "other." Almost 60 percent of the firms reporting reductions said the cuts had nothing to do with recessionary expectations.[5]

Security and Commitment

While the abruptness of a Houston-type dismissal will exacerbate the situation, anyone who's ever been fired knows the effects can be traumatic. We are what we do—we are sales managers, secretaries, professors, and door installers—and when our jobs are taken away we lose not just the income, but the power, the predictability, and in many cases, the identity and self-esteem that went with them. The effects of job insecurity on those left behind may be no less severe: The best people, concerned that the ax will fall again, resign as they look for greener pastures; morale drops as coworkers leave and uncertainties increase; and commitment evaporates with the growing realization that the firm is not committed to its employees. Consequences like these can be reduced, but not eliminated, by handling the dismissals with kid gloves.[6]

In fact, job security and employee commitment go hand in hand. For one thing, the cost involved in value-based hiring, and in extensively training, empowering, and actualizing employees presumes the firm is committed to keeping them around: Recall that "At Toyota we hire people who we hope will stick around for 30 or 40 years or the remainder of their working years. So we always try to remember that hiring a 30-year employee who will earn $30,000 to $40,000 a year is really a million dollar plus decision for us."[7] Furthermore, commitment is a two-way street: Employees are committed to companies that are committed to them, and few things express an employer's commitment like the goal of lifetime employment. It is an ultimate manifestation of the fact that the firm's destiny is inextricably intertwined with that of its staff. Toward the end of 1992, two of our high-commitment firms—Delta and IBM—announced that for the first time in years they might unilaterally dismiss employees. It remains to be seen what affect this will have on their workers' commitment.

Lifetime Employment Without Guarantees

While the phrase "lifetime employment without guarantees" may seem an oxymoron, it's the policy followed by our high-commitment firms.

Toyota's Policy

Take Toyota. On the one hand, the firm's documents and managers' comments continually refer to lifetime employment. The team-member handbook, for instance, states it this way:

> Lifetime employment is our goal—the ultimate result of you and the company working together to ensure TMM's success. We believe that job security is fundamental to the development of motivated employees. We also know that career employees have a significant stake in the company's success. If TMM is profitable, your job will be secure and you will receive a fair salary over the course of your career. We feel we have hired the best to make up our Toyota team. Job security demands that you must do everything possible to maximize the efficiency of the company in order to maintain its competitive edge in the marketplace. We count on you to help us search for a better way...to obtain success...[and] job security at TMM.[8]

Toyota also uses its lifetime employment policy to emphasize to employees that their destinies and the firm's are one:

> Stable employment and continual improvement of the well-being of our team members are essential and can be obtained through the smooth, steady growth of our company. We must fully understand that our team members' well-being can be accomplished as long as the company continues to grow and is successful. The success, therefore, of our team members and the company are inseparable.[9]

Toyota managers similarly emphasize the central role of lifetime employment. For example, several managers told me that they are trained to guarantee that if the suggestion system yields an idea that eliminates a process, jobs will not be eliminated. Instead, employees will be rewarded for contributing to the quality of the product and will be reassigned elsewhere in the plant.[10] Another manager emphasizes that job security reflects mutual trust,

> By which I mean that management and nonmanagement employees have confidence in one another, that they are working for the same thing, and that is the prosperity of the company. And that translates

to better and more secure employment for everyone. Job security is one of the ways we build mutual trust. Management does its long-term planning to assure that layoffs do not become a possibility. Imagine the gusto you'd have at your job knowing that management doesn't see layoffs as the answer to hard times.[11]

Another officer put it this way: "Other firms talk a lot about how important their employees are, but then lay them off when times get tough. We work hard to keep them here: The last thing we'd do is let people go."[12]

In reality, though, there are no guarantees. For example, the Toyota team-member handbook also prominently displays the usual "employ-ment-at-will" disclaimer found in most company handbooks today.

All employment relationships at TMM will be "employment-at-will" arrangements. This means that either the team member or TMM may terminate the employment relationship at any time and for any rea-son. No contract, implied or otherwise, will be considered to exist between TMM and any TMM team member.[13]

Yet Toyota employees are convinced—for good reason, I might add—that their jobs are secure as long as they do those jobs well. As one body-shop team member told me, "They always say they'd never lay someone off. In lean times, we'd be kept on to make the process more efficient."

That kind of confidence is probably not misplaced. While the plant hasn't been in operation long enough to test the "no-layoff" policy, Fujio Cho, Toyota's president, publicly takes the position that the firm would in fact redeploy, not dismiss, its people if times got tough:

At TMM we have not yet reached the point of making adjustments in production. However, should adjustments become necessary, TMM would use it as an opportunity for further training of our team mem-bers, as we call our employees. Team members would use this time to work on their Kaizen [continual improvement] ideas, which they have been too busy to pursue when production is in full swing.[14]

As we'll see in a moment, the firm's compensation policies would also kick in to absorb part of the slack.

Saturn's Contract

Employment security is more ironclad at the unionized Saturn than in the other firms I studied. Most Saturn employees are eligible for "job security," which means they will "not be laid off except in situations which the Saturn Automobile Corporation determines are due to unforeseen or catastrophic events or severe economic conditions." The employees with job security are those

> who had quit or been hired while on layoff with recall or rehire rights from a GM-UAW unit in the U.S. when they joined Saturn as part of the full initial complement of operating and skilled technicians, or who, at any point in time, are among the 80% of Saturn members with the longest length of service in their business unit.[15]

As at Toyota, the Saturn team members I spoke with were convinced, as one told me, that "job security is within my control. If we keep productivity up and quality up, we'll stay here."[16] Saturn accomplishes this job security in part by "hiring fewer people and running a tighter ship."[17]

Delta's Experience

As of 1992, Delta Air Lines had not laid off any permanent employees in 35 years, and their "no layoff" policy was among the firmest in American industry.[18] That is obviously quite an accomplishment, given the wholesale layoffs that have characterized the airlines industry the past few years, and it stems mostly from two practices. First, Delta relies heavily on its temporary part-time workers, or TPTs, who compose as much as 10 percent of its workforce. In the event of temporary downsizings or adverse economic conditions, the TPTs are the first (and only) ones to go. As a Delta personnel officer told me:

> To help protect our no-layoff policy, we keep a small temporary workforce of about 5900 people in airport operations and regional offices. Our business has many seasonal changes, of course, for example being heavy in summer. We also keep a lot of part-time people who are trained and in a "ready reserve" program who can work for a daily rate and are ready to step in if demand warrants.

Cross-utilization is the second practice contributing to Delta's job security. Personnel at all levels routinely serve in rotating special assignment positions, in some staff positions, and in cross-divisional task forces and special projects. Similarly, it's not unusual for employees to wear several hats even during the same day—for instance, moving from the reservations desk to passenger boarding if particular bottlenecks require such a switch. This holds down total staffing levels and helps Delta weather recessionary times. Delta also has used job sharing (temporarily having, say, two people share the job of one) and voluntary personal leaves to avoid layoffs.

In any case, Delta's no-furlough policy was unique among U.S. airlines. In a story that's become an airline legend, during the economic slump of 1982 Delta not only did not furlough anyone but gave employees a raise. Delta employees then embarked on Project 767. This voluntary program, begun and maintained by nonmanagement Delta employees, let employees use voluntary payroll deductions to purchase the firm's first Boeing 767, a $30 million aircraft.

Federal Express's Commitment

Federal Express is also dedicated "to providing the maximum job security for all of our employees."[19] But as one executive emphasized, "No-layoff is a commitment, not a policy. There are no guarantees but the firm is on record as having a strong commitment to make every effort not to lay off personnel except in the most extreme economic circumstances as determined by the chief executive officer."

In fact, the firm has avoided layoffs since its incorporation on June 24, 1971. For example, consider what happened when the firm discontinued its facsimile products (ZAP mail) in the early 1980s. Over 1000 employees assigned to that area were retained and reassigned without a loss in pay.

Publix Practices

"Publix," says Jim Rhodes, director of personnel, "hasn't laid off a full-time employee in over 62 years."[20] That fact reflects the people-first values of the firm and its continuing commitment to its workers' welfare. Two specific Publix practices help the firm avoid layoffs. As with most supermarket chains, a high percentage of Publix employees are part-time rather than full-time. Industry averages, according to Rhodes, are about 80 percent part-time and 20 percent full-time. Because Publix stresses promotion from within, a higher percentage of their workforce is full-time—about 40 percent—but the still-large 60 percent contingent of part-time and seasonal workers helps Publix to adjust to changes in demand. Second, while the firm tends to pay salaries that are "competitive or above" (the average store manager earns around $65,000), a large portion of this is in the form of "pay-for-performance" bonuses. For example, about 45 percent of the annual compensation for store management personnel is in the form of a bonus tied to store and company performance.

IBM's History

For many years IBM was synonymous with "job security." Thomas J. Watson, Jr., in his book *A Business and Its Beliefs* traces IBM's full-employment tradition to his father: "He had known hard times, hard work and unemployment himself, and he always had understanding for the problems of the working man....He recognized that the greatest of these problems was job security."[21]

Until recently, the firm's full-employment policy was unassailable. In the mid-1960s for instance, cutbacks in the space program eliminated the jobs of some IBM employees at Cape Canaveral, but they were all offered comparable jobs. In 1984 the firm closed its last punchcard plant in Washington, D. C., ended its biomedical business, and combined two service organizations into one; it reportedly did this without putting one employee out of work. When it closed a major distribution facility in Greencastle, Indiana, in 1986, IBM offered all 985 employees the chance to relocate, with special moving and living coverage, or, for those eligible, additional benefits under the retirement incentive program.[22] Attrition brought the number of IBM employees from a peak of about 400,000 in 1985 to about 385,000 in 1987.

As the firm faced harder times in the late 1980s, they turned to a practice called "resource balancing" to maintain full employment. Resource balancing involves, as the company puts it, "moving work to people and people to work." It generally meant taking IBMers whose jobs are being phased out and retraining them to assume new responsibilities in other areas. Because of resource balancing, IBM began pulling work back from subcontractors in 1986.

However, as became increasingly apparent from press stories, IBM's gradualist approach to controlling labor costs wasn't sufficient to keep the firm in the fighting trim it needed to confront faster-moving rivals. Its share of the world computer market dropped from 36 to 23 percent in the 1980s, and by the early 1990s, its share of the PC market had dropped from 27 to 16.5 percent.[23]

In response, IBM began a program of more aggressively eliminating jobs both through attrition and through costly early retirement programs. Between 1987 and 1991 this strategy led to the voluntary elimination of about 53,000 jobs. With the 1991–1992 recession, revenues declined for the first time since the 1940s, and profits remained weak by historical levels. In November 1991 and again in 1992, IBM announced that 20,000 more workers would be eliminated, possibly through involuntary dismissals, an announcement that reportedly caused consternation throughout IBM's ranks.

In early 1992 Walt Burdick, IBM's senior vice president for personnel, told me that his firm was still committed to job security and full employment, and that even during the firm's most recent downsizing they'd retrained 70,000 people to avoid layoffs.[24] Nevertheless, the firm's 1991 annual report indicated that IBM's worldwide workforce declined by about 29,000 in 1991—mostly through voluntary quits and early retirements—and was expected to continue to decline in 1992. In fact, it would appear from the firm's own estimates that an additional 20,000 jobs were pared in 1992. This required taking a charge of about $3 billion against earnings in the fourth quarter of 1991 "to cover the cost of the reductions and other actions."[25] In the summer of 1992 several articles appeared in *The Wall Street Journal* describing the anguish expressed by some IBMers whose new job assignments were viewed as steps down—from marketing manager to telephone customer service rep, for instance—and predicting further cuts of 32,000 employees in 1992.[26] The marketing manager complained of being "the highest paid telephone operator in the U.S." Forty thousand employees eventually left IBM in 1992.

This leaves IBM's full-employment policy without the sort of ironclad guarantee that most IBMers were used to. But as one IBM officer told me in early 1993, "we'll still be treating our employees more humanely, and trying harder than most firms to blunt the effects of layoffs if they do occur." Wholesale layoffs had not taken place as of 1992; early retirements are still encouraged; large-scale retraining and balancing continues. Innovative options called "alternative business arrangements"are being used to convert some IBM employees to free-lancers. For example, a new firm called Employment Solutions has signed up a dozen IBMers to perform the in-house personnel work—such as processing applications and checking resumes—that was formerly carried out by permanent staffers.[27] "Job security" may never mean the same to IBMers as it did in the past, but my guess is that it will still mean a lot more in IBM than in most other U.S. firms. In any event, IBM's recent travails underscore an important point about job security and worker commitment. Job security is valuable in part because it fosters commitment. Commitment, in turn, is valuable in part because it fosters quality, efficiency, and flexibility and enables the firm to stay "lean and mean"—as do Saturn and Toyota. However, when your strategy or other management actions let overstaffing breed, then much of the benefit of job security will be lost.

Strategies for Maintaining
Full Employment

In his book, *Theory Z*, William Ouchi says that lifetime employment in Japan is possible largely as a consequence of a "unique social and economic structure not replicated in the United States." This structure has three elements: bonus-paid compensation, large numbers of temporary employees, and use of satellite firms as suppliers.[28]

For example, in large lifetime-employment firms, workers are paid much of their compensation in the form of a bonus. This bonus may add up to five or six months' worth of salary for each employee annually. The consequent drop in labor costs that occurs during bad years thus helps buffer the firm from layoffs. Similarly, large cadres of temporary employees, primarily women, serve as a buffer to protect the job security of permanent employees, primarily men. Finally, major firms tend to contract out to smaller satellite vendors those products or services most susceptible to fluctuation. During recessions it's therefore the employees of these small vendors that take the brunt of the layoffs.

In the United States, achieving dramatic workforce reductions (say, 15 percent or more) within a year or two may leave no choice but deep, across-the-board dismissals or aggressive early retirement or buyout offers.[29] However, less dramatic reductions are increasingly achieved these days with other techniques. As in Japan, Delta, Publix, and Federal Express maintain large cadres of temporary part-time employees who are the first to go when cutbacks are required. A combination of attrition and retraining and redeploying of employees, as at IBM, is used as well. Toyota, as we've seen, would redeploy workers to special Kaizen teams, and devote extra time to retraining. When Ben & Jerry's found itself with surplus employees several years ago, they redeployed them to community work, painting fire hydrants and doing other things to spruce up Waterbury, Vermont. As we'll see in Chapter 9, most high-commitment firms—Delta, Toyota, Saturn, Federal Express, Penney's, Mary Kay, Publix, and Goldman, Sachs—also put a big portion of each employee's salary "at risk" with yearly bonuses that shrink in harsh economic times, thus reducing the need for layoffs.

But in the final analysis it is, ironically, worker commitment that helps high-commitment firms ensure full employment. With the possible exception of IBM, our high-commitment firms have always been "lean and mean." Whether it's a Delta reservations clerk racing down the ramp to fill in at boarding, Toyota workers spending their lunchtime improving work methods, Publix managers stocking shelves, or young Goldman, Sachs investment bankers working through the night, high-commitment firms derive a resilience and efficiency from their employees' commitment that help them skip relatively unscathed through bad times.

And that's as it should be. Employee commitment means that employees identify with the firm and its goals and that the interests of the firm and its employees are merged. In a very real sense these employees are not just working for the firm, they are working for themselves. As a result, their commitment drives the firm's efficiency and that efficiency helps assure their job security. That's what Toyota means when it says, "Job security demands that you must do everything possible to maximize the efficiency of the company in order to maintain its competitive edge in the marketplace. We count on you to help us search for a better way...to obtain success...[and] job security at TMM."[30]

A Summary: Securitizing as a Key to Commitment

1. Make it clear that you are committed to doing your best to provide your employees with job security. Practice "lifetime employment without guarantees."

2. Institute company practices that facilitate employee security: draft compensation plans that place a substantial portion of each employee's salary "at risk" with yearly bonuses that shrink in harsh economic times; use temporary and part-time employees; provide cross-training that permits and/or requires employees to wear several hats; plan to redeploy workers when volume turns down.

3. Formulate company policies that encourage the firm to stay "lean and mean," so that you have the ability to ride out recessions without resorting to layoffs.

References

1. This description is based on Robert Tomasko, "Downsizing: Layoffs and Alternatives to Layoffs," *Compensation and Benefits Review,* July–August 1991, p. 19.

2. Diane Herz, "Worker Displacement Still Common in the Later 1980s," *Monthly Labor Review,* May 1991, pp. 3 and 4.

3. Edmund Faltermayer, "Is This Layoff Necessary?" *Fortune,* June 1, 1991, p. 71.

4. "Selected Unemployment Indicators," *Monthly Labor Review*, December 1992, p. 64.

5. Eric Rolfe Greenberg, "Downsizing: AMA Survey Results," *Compensation and Benefits Review*, July–August 1991, pp. 33–34.

6. See, for example, Dan Rice and Craig Dreilinger, "After the Downsizing," *Training and Development Journal*, vol. 45, no. 5 (May 1991), pp. 41–45.

7. Alex Warren, speech to the City Club, Cleveland, Ohio, November 15, 1991, p. 7.

8. *Team Member Handbook*, Toyota Motor Manufacturing, U.S.A., February 1988, p. 102.

9. Ibid., p. 9.

10. Alex Warren speech, p. 12.

11. Ibid., p. 14.

12. Personal interview with Sam Heltman, March 1992.

13. *Team Member Handbook*, p. 103.

14. Fujio Cho, "Employee Motivation by Applying the Toyota Production System," speech to the Asian Business Club of Harvard Business School, Cambridge, Mass., March 4, 1991.

15. Saturn Corporation, Memorandum of Agreement, pp. 11–12.

16. Personal interview with Sean Graham, March 1992.

17. Personal interview with Reid Swafford, Jr., March 1992.

18. Interview with Maurice W. Worth, January 1992.

19. *The Federal Express Employee Handbook*, August 7, 1989, p. 21.

20. Personal interview with Jim Rhodes, April 1992.

21. *IBM: About Your Company*, p. 10.

22. Ibid., pp. 10–11.

23. John Verity, Thane Peterson, Diedre Depke, and Evan Schwartz, "The New IBM," *Business Week*, December 16, 1991, p. 114.

24. Personal interview with Walt Burdick, April 1992.

25. Don Schreiber, "Redefining IBM—A Spectrum of Businesses," *Think*, no. 1 (1992), p. 33.

26. Laurence Hooper, "IBM Expands '92 Forecast of Staffing Cuts to 32,000," *The Wall Street Journal*, July 29, 1992, p. A3.

27. Faltermayer, p. 76.

28. William Ouchi, *Theory Z*, Avon Books, New York, 1981, pp. 20–21.

29. Faltermayer, p. 80.

30. *Team Member Handbook*, p. 102.

9

Hard-Side Rewards

Can You Buy Commitment?

Considering the effort that commitment building requires, you could reasonably ask if it wouldn't be cheaper and more direct just to institute some kind of incentive plan to synchronize the employees' and the company's goals. In fact, that was the idea behind early incentive plans, like those popularized by Frederick Taylor in the late 1980s. As a supervisory employee of the Midvale Steel Company, Taylor had become concerned with what he called "systematic soldiering"—the tendency of employees to work at the slowest pace possible. What intrigued him was that some of these people still had the energy to run home and work on their cabins, even after a hard 12-hour day. Taylor knew that if he could find some way to harness this energy at work, huge productivity gains could be achieved.

At that time, primitive piecework systems were in use but were generally ineffective. Rate cutting by employers was flagrant, and workers knew that if their earnings became excessive, their pay per piece would be cut. Most workers therefore produced just enough to earn a decent wage, but little enough so that their rate per piece would not be cut. One of Taylor's great insights was in seeing the need for a standardized, acceptable view of a fair day's work. As he saw it, this "fair day's work" should depend not on the vague estimates of supervisors but on a careful scientific process of inspection and observation. It was this need to evaluate each job scientifically that led to what became known as the scientific management movement.

In turn, the ultimate aim of scientific management was to find a way to synthesize the goals of the firm and its employees. Scientific management, said Taylor, was "not just an efficiency device, or a new scheme of paying men, or a bonus system," but instead,

> ...involves a complete mental revolution on the part of working men engaged in any particular establishment or industry—a complete mental revolution on the part of these men as to their duties toward their work, toward their fellow men, and toward their employers. And it involves the equally complete mental revolution on the part of those on the management side—the foremen, the superintendent....
> The great revolution that takes place in the mental attitude in the two parties under scientific management is that both sides take their eyes off the division of the surplus as the all important matter, and together turn their attention toward increasing the size of the surplus until the surplus becomes so large that it is unnecessary to quarrel over how it shall be divided. They come to see that when they stop pulling against one another and instead both turn and push shoulder to shoulder in the same direction, the size of the surplus created by their joint effort is truly astonishing.[1]

Unfortunately, there was a flaw in Taylor's assumptions, which were the prevailing assumptions of the day. The concept of the human as a rational being, driven only by a desire for economic gain, allowed Taylor and his disciples to largely disregard the variables of human behavior in organizations. We know today that money, by itself, generally can't buy commitment.

In his classic explanation of why money can't buy commitment, Frederick Herzberg said that "hygiene" factors like pay result only in short-term motivation. With pay, Herzberg said, the motivation disappears as soon as the incentive is removed. Furthermore, firms that rely on financial incentive are caught in a vicious cycle, continually ratcheting up rewards as employees become used to their current rates of pay. Pay should be sufficient to get and keep good people, Herzberg said, but to win employee commitment you've got to appeal to other needs— to achieve, for instance, to affiliate, and to become all that we can be.[2]

In fact, some of the best known incentive plans depend on much more than money.[3] For example, a plan in effect for years at the Lincoln Electric Company reportedly produces for this welding products firm the lowest labor cost per sales dollar in the industry, and sales of over $150,000 per factory worker.[4] This occurs in spite of a bonus plan that pays employees twice the take-home of similar workers, due to a yearly incentive bonus that often equals the worker's regular year pay.[5] But it's not just the money: A focus on employees, extensive two-way communications, job security,[6] exhaustive hiring, and worker empowerment are a few of the other elements that seem to make this plan work for Lincoln.[7]

Similarly, the Scanlon Plan—devised in 1937 by Joseph Scanlon, a United States Steelworkers Union official—has reportedly also been successful.[8] Practitioners, though, credit more than the plan's financial bonus.[9] They also emphasize: the philosophy of worker-management cooperation on which the plan is based; the involvement system consisting of worker suggestion committees; "identity," which means focusing employee involvement by clearly communicating to all employees the company's mission and financial data; and competent, highly skilled employees.[10]

Employee Compensation in High-Commitment Firms

You can't buy commitment, but high-commitment firms know they can't get commitment without healthy hard-side rewards. Soft-side rewards like worker involvement, a sense of achievement, and the feelings of oneness that communion bring are not enough, in other words. To paraphrase psychologist Abraham Maslow, you can't appeal to someone's need to achieve until you've filled his belly and made him secure.[11] That's why all these firms offer packages of above-average pay combined with incentives and extensive benefits.

J. C. Penney's Policy and Programs

When it comes to pay, the venerable J. C. Penney Company may be one of the best-kept secrets in retailing, a situation that goes back to 1902. On April 14 of that year, James Cash Penney, age 26, opened The Golden Rule, a dry goods and clothing store in Kemmerer, Wyoming, in partnership with merchants Thomas Callahan and William Johnson. In 1903 Penney's partners offered him a one-third partnership in their new Rock Springs, Wyoming, Golden Rule store and asked him to supervise it. At the same time, Penney recommended a new Golden Rule store in nearby Cumberland and also became a one-third partner in that store. By 1907 Johnson and Callahan had sold Penney their interests in the Kemmerer, Cumberland, and Rock Springs stores, and Penney and his new partners (all former salesclerks) started building their own chain of Golden Rule stores. As the chain spread to Utah and Idaho, Penney followed the same practice of giving hardworking clerks the opportunity to manage the stores, also with a one-third partnership—the same opportunity Johnson and Callahan had given him back in 1902. When the J. C. Penney Company was incorporated in 1913, the partnership incentive was retained.[12]

Although the structure of the plan has changed, the heavy incentive value of the partnership concept remains intact today at J. C. Penney. As one manager explained,

> You start off fairly low as an entry-level merchandising-manager trainee, at perhaps $20,000 to $25,000 per year. But all of a sudden after three years or so you're making much more money than other middle managers in the industry and the gap continues to widen as you move up the chain of command.[13]

As Don Finn, the firm's compensation officer told me, "In this industry, we're unique: We pay modest salaries and high incentive payments."[14] The proportion of salary that comes from bonus payments depends on the person's job and the size of the store. For store managers in the smallest J. C. Penney's stores, for instance, 90 percent of their annual pay would typically derive from salary, and only 10 percent from bonus, with a total annual pay of perhaps $110,000. For some of the biggest stores, however, only about $80,000 of the manager's pay would come from an annual salary, and about $110,000 would come from an at-risk incentive bonus, one tied to the store's sales and gross profits.

The big bonus component reflects several differences between J. C. Penney and other major retailers. One, of course, is the partnership concept itself: Penney's wants its people to think of themselves as truly owners of the business. Responsibilities of the store manager are therefore different. At J. C. Penney, the store managers are "king" when it comes to running what amounts to their own self-contained businesses; for example, they have full responsibility for choosing and pricing the goods to be sold. That is very different from the situation in most large department store chains where central-buying offices make the decisions and store managers have relatively little discretion regarding the goods to be sold.

At J. C. Penney, central-buying officers only identify merchandise for possible sale by the firm. They then must sell their recommendations to the store managers and merchandising managers, a process that is accomplished via Penney's in-house TV network. Orders aren't placed until store management decides what they want to buy. The heavy bonus component therefore is based on the fact that the store's sales and profits still reflect the decisions of the store's managing "partners."

Bonuses are paid to store managers (first-level personnel) annually, usually in February or March. Second- and third-level management personnel are paid a monthly bonus tied to sales and gross profits. For example, senior merchandising managers who might earn $35,000 to $40,000 a year receive about 70 percent of that from salary and about 30 percent in monthly bonuses. Third-level merchandising managers get about 80 percent of their $30,000 pay in the form of salary and about 20 percent as bonus. (As we'll see in Chapter 10, by the way, these managers' job responsibilities also reflect the heavy bonus component. For example, merchandising managers have a big say in the goods bought by a store for their departments and they are expected to run those departments as if they are actually theirs to run.)

The heavy bonus component of managerial pay has two main consequences. First, of course, it provides a substantial incentive to improve performance, reflecting as it does the manager's and the store's performance. Second, by putting much of Penney's wage expense "at risk," it allows the firm to shrink its costs in difficult times without laying off employees.

In terms of each manager's salary (the fixed portion of their pay), each position (such as merchandising manager, store manager, and so on) has an associated pay range. For example, pay for a senior merchandising manager may range from $30,400 to a maximum of $45,600, with a midpoint of $38,000. However, salary increases are not automatic from year to year. Every manager is told, "You should recognize that your earnings will reflect your performance. Earnings increases are not entitlements but rather a recognition of your accomplishments."[15]

In order to facilitate such a "recognition of accomplishments," Penney's appraisal process is comprehensive and well documented. Manuals explain how to set performance goals for each supervisory position and how to complete the performance-appraisal forms. All supervisory appraisals are then based on the results achieved by the manager in relation to goals set at the start of the planning period. In addition, the manager is also rated on several generic supervisory skills, such as leadership, sense of urgency, and judgment.

Federal Express's Policy and Programs

At Federal Express, quarterly pay reviews and periodic national and local salary surveys are used to maintain salary ranges and pay schedules that are competitive. Internal equity is maintained through the use of the Hay system of job evaluation. (Under the Hay system, all salaried Federal Express positions are evaluated on three factors: know-how, problem solving, and accountability. For each job, points are assigned for the three factors; the total number of points establishes the grade-level rating for that job. That is, each grade level is given a range of job evaluation points.)

The result of this system of job evaluation is a set of salary ranges such that salaries for each Federal Express position tend to be equitable relative to other Fed Ex jobs. At the same time (thanks to the salary surveys), the base salaries are highly competitive as compared with similar jobs in the market.

While base salary alone would make the pay competitive with market rates for virtually all Federal Express positions, there is also a heavy emphasis on pay-for-performance. As one manager put it, "We are convinced people want to see a relationship between performance and reward....I think people want to know that when they knock themselves out to reach their part of our 100% customer satisfaction goal, their efforts will not go unnoticed."[16]

Federal Express has several pay-for-performance programs:[17]

Merit Program.   All salaried employees receive merit salary increases based on their individual performance. Many hourly employees also receive merit increases rather than automatic step increases. As at J. C. Penney, a careful performance-appraisal process at Federal Express provides the means for rating employees' performance and for "making pay increase recommendations based on sustained performance."

Pro Pay.   Many hourly Fed Ex employees can receive lump-sum merit bonuses once they reach the top of their pay range. Pro Pay is paid only if the employee has been at the top of his or her pay range for a specified period of time (normally six months), and it's paid only if he or she has had an above-average performance review.

Star/Superstar Program.   Salaried employees with a specified performance rating may be nominated for a Star or Superstar bonus. Employees who are designated a Star or Superstar receive a lump-sum bonus. Stars represent the top 10 percent of performers in each division, while Superstars represent the top 1 percent of performers in each division.

Profit Sharing.   Federal Express's profit-sharing plan distributes profits on the basis of the overall profit levels of the corporation. The board of directors annually sets the amount paid, based on pretax profits. Payments can be in the form of stock or cash, or both, and are usually made semiannually in June and December. The plan is designed to integrate with the firm's pension and savings plans to provide a comprehensive retirement program.

MBO/MIC and PBO/PIC Programs. These are individual incentive plans for managers and professionals. They were developed to provide management and many exempt (supervisory or professional) employees the opportunity to receive financial rewards for helping attain corporate, departmental, and divisional objectives. The MIC (management incentive compensation) and PIC (professional incentive compensation) components generally reward achievement of divisional and corporate profit goals. The MBO (or PBO) bonuses are tied to individual attainment of people-, service-, or profit-related goals. Thus for a regional sales manager, a people-related goal could be an improvement in the manager's leadership index score on the firm's annual SFA survey.[18] (Fed Ex's SFA survey is discussed in Chapter 4.)

Bravo Zulu Voucher Program. The Bravo Zulu Voucher Program gives managers the ability to provide immediate rewards to employees for outstanding performance above and beyond the normal requirements of the job. ("Bravo Zulu" is borrowed from the U.S. Navy's semaphore signal for "well done.") Bravo Zulu vouchers may be in the form of a check or in some other form of reward (such as restaurant vouchers or theater tickets). It's estimated that more than 24,000 times a year a Fed Ex manager presents an employee with one of these Bravo Zulu awards. The typical award is about $50.[19]

Golden Falcon Award. The Golden Falcon Award goes to permanent employees who demonstrate service to customers that is above and beyond the call of duty. Candidates are usually nominated on the basis of unsolicited internal company or external customer letters citing the candidate's outstanding performance. Nominated candidates are reviewed by the Golden Falcon committee, and the final selection is made by the chief operating officer. Winners are announced monthly through company publications and/or video programs. They receive a Golden Falcon lapel pin and shares of Federal Express common stock.

With the exception of the merit program, all of these pay-for-performance programs are forms of variable compensation. In other words, Pro Pay, Star/Superstar, Profit Sharing, MBO/MIC, PBO/PIC, Bravo Zulu, and Golden Falcon awards are paid as one-time lump-sum awards, separate from base pay. They thus let the firm reward outstanding performance without permanently increasing its fixed payroll costs. The variability can also reflect changes in business conditions and allow Fed Ex to react to adverse economic conditions while maintaining its full-employment policy.

Like other high-commitment firms, Federal Express also offers a feast of worker benefits. Their health plan provides medical, dental, and vision benefits to all permanent employees at company expense. (There's a $100 deductible.) Medical and dental coverage is also generally available for eligible dependents at an additional cost to the employee. The firm offers short-term disability benefits if a permanent full-time employee becomes disabled for any period longer than 40 consecutive scheduled working hours; long-term disability benefits kick in after 26 weeks. Permanent employees have life insurance provided at no cost. The firm provides accidental death and dismembership insurance, as well as business travel accident insurance.

The firm's retirement benefits are exceptional. Retirement benefits at Federal Express actually consist of several plans: The pension plan, profit-sharing plan, and employee stock-ownership plan (as well as company-sponsored savings plans) combine to provide employees with a good income at retirement. The firm's pension plan alone provides employees with a fixed percentage of their salary. The normal retirement benefit payable at age 60 is 2 percent of the employee's final average pay times the employee's years of credited service (up to 25 years). That means that the pension benefit of a 60-year-old employee with 25 years of service with the company will be 50 percent of that employee's final average pay. "Final average pay" is the average of the total compensation received during the highest-paid five consecutive years of the employee's last 15 years before retirement or disability. And that means highest-average *total* pay, including overtime and incentives.

All full-time permanent or part-time employees who have completed at least three consecutive months of employment with Federal Express can also participate in the firm's employee stock-purchase plan. This lets them purchase Federal Express stock without commission through payroll deductions in an amount varying from 1 percent to a maximum of 10 percent of the person's total salary. These deductions accumulate for a designated period, at the end of which time Federal Express purchases the shares of stock for all participants.

There's more. The firm's tuition-refund program lets any permanent employee with one year of continuous service receive financial reimbursement up to a maximum annual amount for his or her continuing education. Employees earn two weeks of vacation after one year with the firm, three weeks after five years, four weeks after ten years, and five weeks of vacation after twenty years with Federal Express.

But for some employees the best bonus is Fed Ex's discount travel program. Federal Express participates with other airlines to offer interline flight benefits. Employees who have completed a minimum of six months of continuous service in a permanent status are eligible to participate. And—in a benefit that J. C. Penney, Saturn, and even Goldman, Sachs would find hard to match—permanent employees are eligible to use Federal Express aircraft jump seats for travel. Whether they're planning to travel for personal or business purposes, they make their arrangements through the jump-seat reservations office in Memphis, which takes and confirms the request by phone. There is also a computerized system called "Free Bird," which lets employees make the reservations themselves. Having made the reservation, you need only be at the airport two hours prior to the flight time, and away you go.

Ben & Jerry's Policy and Programs

There are several unique aspects to Ben & Jerry's compensation plan. Entry-level employees and those in the lower managerial ranks have salaries pegged at about 120 percent of comparable jobs in the community. This helps to ensure a constant flow of applicants in what is generally a low-employment geographic area. Top managers, however, have salaries pegged at about 65 percent of comparable jobs, which ensures that Ben & Jerry's attracts applicants who buy into the firm's social values. The net effect is to help lock in employees at the lower levels with a healthy pay scale and to lock in top managers with the value system.

In addition, regular full-time and regular part-time employees who have at least six months' continuous service can purchase Ben & Jerry's stock through a payroll deduction, at 15 percent below the stock's current market price. Ben & Jerry's also has a healthy annual profit-sharing plan. Under current board of directors policy, 5 percent of the company's annual pretax profits are placed in the plan, and each full-time regular employee receives a share of that money, based on his or her time with Ben & Jerry's, *not* on his or her salary.

Toyota's Policy and Programs

As befitting an automobile plant with Japanese roots, Toyota's pay plan has three unique features. First, everyone at Toyota is salaried.

Theoretically therefore all employees receive a biweekly fixed salary. However, nonexempt (generally nonsupervisory or nonprofessional) plant and office employees receive "salary reductions" for absences and tardiness. In other words, if the nonexempt Toyota employee misses time from work, his or her biweekly salary is reduced by the appropriate hourly rate. (The only exception to this practice is in the case of paid time away from work such as vacations, holidays, jury duty service, and funeral leave.) Nonexempt employees also earn overtime pay calculated on the basis of time-and-a-half (the person's regular rate) for all hours worked in excess of eight hours a day.

There are no time clocks, though. Each week all nonexempt team members are given a time report, which is to be completed daily by recording the straight-time hours worked, the overtime hours worked, and the hours lost (time off, etc.), along with the appropriate code for the lost time. At the end of the week, employees summarize the information, sign the report, and submit it to their group leader or supervisor for review and approval.

Second, there are only a handful of job titles at Toyota. Consistent with this, they don't use job evaluation systems, like the Hay system at Fed Ex, to compute point values for jobs or to classify jobs by pay grade. As Sam Heltman, Toyota's personnel officer told me, this is because "with a point system, you can't move people as easily from job to job."[20] (With the sort of carefully calibrated point system and multiple job titles found, say, in the typical GM plant, workers' jobs are clearly delineated and assigned a number of points—in which case, moving employees from job to job becomes problematic, a situation Toyota studiously avoids.)

Only three plant job classifications are utilized at TMM. Division I includes all production team members. Division II includes all general maintenance team members. Division III includes all tool-and-die team members. Various team members elect their own team leaders. The team leaders are not supervisory personnel in the traditional sense, but do receive a premium of 5 percent of their base rate for being a sort of "first among equals" on their team. Several team leaders report to the first real supervisory level in the plant, a cadre of workers TMM calls "group leaders." Group leaders then report to assistant managers, who report to managers, who in turn report to assistant general managers. A general manager has charge of the overall plant operation.

There are four job grades in the office compensation system at Toyota, with each job grade based on the person's individual experience, knowledge, and related factors. There are two job grades for nonexempt personnel and two grades for exempt supervisory and professional employees.

The third feature of Toyota's pay plan is its pay-for-performance component. This is aimed at bringing team members up to and then beyond market wage rates. For example, plant employees earn base salaries that usually amount to about 88 percent of market rates for similar jobs. On top of this, they can earn a performance award equal to just over 15 percent of their base pay. This is awarded on the basis of the person's attendance, productivity, safety, and quality consciousness as well as on the company's overall performance. Specifically, "performance areas that will be evaluated include the quality of work produced, the quantity of work produced, safety, attendance, and the contribution made by each team member to the success of his/her team."[21] Base pay plus the performance award would normally bring team members a little above comparable market rates for similar positions. In addition, however, all team members are eligible for discretionary bonuses based on individual and company performance.

The pay plan is similar for nonexempt office workers. Here, however, the performance award needed to bring the person up to or just beyond market rates is smaller—about 8 percent—although nonexempt office employees can still earn discretionary bonuses. Exempt employees don't earn performance awards, but they can earn merit bonuses that may amount to about 15 percent of their total compensation.

Toyota's emphasis on pay-for-performance translates into at least two benefits for the firm and its employees. First, while the bonus doesn't approach the gargantuan 40 to 60 percent paid by some firms in Japan, it still provides the flexibility to reduce labor costs in bad times without layoffs. Second, the performance awards and bonuses, of course, provide an incentive and a sense of ownership and commitment to the work and the firm.

Toyota supplements the bonus plans with a comprehensive list of benefits. As regular full-time team members, employees and their dependents are eligible to participate in TMM's company-paid group comprehensive health and medical plans. The firm also provides each full-time member with a basic life insurance benefit in addition to an accidental death and dismemberment policy. Team members are eligible to enroll for short-term disability benefits on their first day of active employment; after six months of continuous employment, regular full-time team members become eligible to participate in the firm's long-term disability insurance program. The firm pays all premiums for the company's dental care plan and has a defined contribution pension plan as well as an available 401K savings plan. Team members presently are eligible for up to 10 consecutive days of vacation and receive 12 paid holidays each calendar year. They are also issued Toyota uniforms (the wearing of which is voluntary).

Last, but not least, full-time team members who have completed six months of service may purchase vehicles for themselves or their dependents at dealer cost. They can buy up to two vehicles per year but title of the vehicle must be retained by the purchaser for at least nine months before the car can be sold.

Saturn's Policy and Programs

Saturn's pay is also built on the three principles of salary, few classifications, and pay-for-performance. All employees are salaried, and there are no time clocks at the firm. To report your time, you go to a keyboard and type in the number of hours worked. While there are some checks and balances, the process is basically an honor system. "What it comes down to," says Joe Caldwell, an operating technician, "is a matter of trust."[22]

There are also relatively few job classifications at Saturn. Virtually all the assembly employees are in the classification of "operating technician," the same classification to which all non-skilled-trades members such as machinists are assigned. In addition, there are four additional classifications for skilled-trades members.

Under the reward system originally envisioned in the memorandum of agreement between Saturn and the UAW, about 20 percent of each employee's pay was to be "at risk." Specifically, each employee's base compensation was to equal 80 percent of straight-time wages of the average competitive rates in the U.S. auto industry. Over and above that, a reward system was to be developed that would be based on factors such as achievement of specific objective productivity targets; performance in terms of individual and work-unit performance; quality bonuses; and, eventually, a "Saturn sharing formula" through which profits were to be shared above a specified level of return to Saturn. At a minimum, therefore, 20 percent of each person's pay was to be at risk and to be earned only if the individual and the firm met productivity goals. On top of that, a profit-sharing formula was to kick in.

At the present time, a slower than expected start-up at Saturn has forced the firm to reduce the at-risk component and thus boost the "guaranteed" component of the pay. When I was at the plant, only 5 percent of an employee's wages was at risk, and workers could earn that 5 percent by meeting specified training goals—attending training sessions, improving their skills, and so on. Everyone I spoke to, however—

from executives to operating technicians—expected to phase the at-risk factor back up to 20 percent in the near future. As one operating technician put it, "That's what we want. The thought process is that if the economy turned way down, all would work, but at 80 percent of pay, that's the main thing."

As with most high-commitment firms, Saturn also provides a long list of benefits. There are eight paid holidays; up to four weeks' vacation after 20 or more years; company-paid HMOs; a retirement plan; and an individual savings plan under which any Saturn employee can contribute up to 15 percent of base compensation (Saturn will match up to 6 percent of the base at a rate of $1 for every $2 contributed by the employee). The firm also offers life insurance benefits and extended disability benefits.

Mary Kay's Policy and Programs

For its full-time employees Mary Kay Cosmetics begins with above-average salaries. Beyond that, one compensation manager says that in 1990 and 1991 a "very generous 15 percent of payroll" went into the firm's profit-sharing plan for each employee, to be obtained at retirement. There are also Christmas bonuses of around 5 percent of an employee's salary each year and gifts of company stock on each fifth-year anniversary. The bonuses themselves are based on the firm's "EBD+T"—earnings before depreciation and taxes. Employees make no contribution for the firm's medical and dental insurance, and the firm provides various other benefits, including life insurance, short-term and long-term disability, and tuition reimbursements.

But it's the army of Mary Kay "beauty consultants"—200,000 strong—that most people think of when they think of Mary Kay. In fact, it was supposedly the idea of giving career-minded women a chance to achieve their ambitions that inspired Mary Kay Ash to found her firm. For a relatively small investment they can have their own business and be their own boss, with all the products, training manuals, and sales support they would normally expect to spend a lot for if they were buying, say, a franchise.

Throughout the direct-sales industry—including Mary Kay itself—turnover of sales consultants is huge. But for those who stick with it at Mary Kay, the hard-side rewards can be substantial. For example, the firm estimates that by providing three hostess shows per week, giving one facial a week, and calling on a given number of new customers, a beauty consultant's yearly profit will be approximately $30,000 for a 20-

hour week. As the beauty consultant recruits new consultants and moves up the hierarchy—to team manager, director, senior director, executive senior director, and finally national sales director—income grows dramatically. Many of these people reportedly earn well in excess of $50,000 a year.

There is also, as most everyone knows, a mind-boggling array of special awards, recognitions, pink Cadillacs, diamond rings, trips, and all manner of hard-side rewards aimed at keeping the sales staff happy. In one recent year, for instance, directors in Mary Kay's Circle of Excellence—those reaching or exceeding the $600,000 level of unit retail production—were awarded vacations in Rome (spouses included). These superstars also receive their choice of various prizes, including diamond bar pins. National sales directors who attained career-high sales levels in 1990 were presented with 14-carat gold and pavé diamond necklaces. And there is, of course, the famous "car program." A pink Grand Prix or Cadillac is available to the sales consultant who has climbed the career ladder from beauty consultant to star recruiter, to team leader, to team manager, to director-in-qualification, and finally to director—to qualify, on the basis of sales, for the firm's signature prize.

Common Themes

High-commitment firms' compensation plans have several features in common. Most are characterized by very competitive compensation, a significant portion of which is "at risk." It may be the 15 percent profit-sharing plan at Mary Kay, the 20 percent performance pay at Toyota, or the performance-based pay at Federal Express; in one way or another most of these firms require that to reach parity with comparable firms and then exceed such pay, the employee and the firm will both have to *perform*. Some more examples: At Publix, stock clerks earn wages comparable to entry-level college grads, while cashiers earn about $11.45 per hour; managers, as we've seen, average $60,000 to $65,000 per year (and perhaps much more), about half of which is based on store performance. Stephen Friedman, Goldman, Sachs chairman, had a base salary of $210,000 in 1991, but earned about $15 million more as his share of partnership profits—and many of Goldman, Sachs' 142 partners apparently earned over $5 million in partnership profits.[23]

While it's not a universal practice, there is a tendency among these firms to keep the number of pay grades to a minimum, and to pay everyone a salary rather than an hourly wage. There is also a corresponding emphasis on self-reporting hours worked, rather than on using devices like time clocks. Finally, in keeping with the view that their employees are their most important assets, these firms all provide a broad list of benefits aimed at keeping their human resources healthy, secure, and relatively worry-free well into retirement.

A Summary: Hard-Side Rewards as a Key to Commitment

1. Offer packages of above-average pay combined with incentives and extensive benefits.

2. Build a compensation package that puts a significant portion of pay at risk. High-commitment firms put about 15 to 20 percent of annual pay at risk.

3. Emphasize self-reporting of hours worked, rather than devices like time clocks.

4. Build a pay plan that encourages employees to think of themselves as partners. This means that they should have a healthy share of the profits in good years and share in the downturn in bad years.

5. Provide a package of benefits that makes it clear that you view your employees as long-term investments and that you are concerned with their welfare. Stock-ownership plans, pensions, above-average health plans, and similar benefits contribute to this sense that the firm views its employees as part of "the family" and wants them around for the long haul.

6. Institute stock-ownership plans that encourage your employees to make a significant personal investment in your firm.

References

1. Frederick W. Taylor, "What Is Scientific Management?" reprinted in Michael Matteson and John Ivancevich, *Management Classics*, Goodyear, Santa Monica, Calif., 1977, p. 5–8.

2. Frederick Herzberg, "One More Time: How Do You Motivate Employees?" *Harvard Business Review*, vol. 46, no. 1, 1968, pp. 53–62.

3. Based on Arthur D. Sharplin, "Lincoln Electric Company, 1989" in Arthur A. Thompson, Jr., and A. J. Strickland III, *Strategic Management: Concepts and Cases*, Richard D. Irwin, Homewood, Ill., 1990, pp. 839–861.

4. Sharplin, p. 846.

5. Ibid., p. 839.

6. Ibid., p. 842.

7. Ibid., p. 850.

8. Brian Moore and Timothy Ross, *The Scanlon Way to Improved Productivity: A Practical Guide*, Wiley, New York, 1978, p. 2.

9. J. Kenneth White, "The Scanlon Plan: Causes and Correlates of Success," *Academy of Management Journal*, vol. 22 (June 1979), pp. 292–312.

10. Moore and Ross, pp. 1–2; see also Steven Markham, K. Don Scott, and Walter Cox, Jr., "The Evolutionary Development of a Scanlon Plan," *Compensation and Benefits Review*, March–April 1992, pp. 50–56.

11. Abraham Maslow, "A Theory of Human Motivation," *Psychological Review*, vol. 50, 1943, pp. 370–396.

12. *The Tradition Continues*, Publications Division, J. C. Penney Company, Inc., pp. 1–2.

13. Personal interview with Mike Lynch, October 1991.

14. Personal interview with Don Finn, October 1991.

15. *J. C. Penney Management Compensation*, company document, p. 6.

16. *Blueprints for Service Quality: The Federal Express Approach*, AMA Membership Publication, New York, 1991, pp. 31–32.

17. "Compensation at Federal Express," company document, pp. 8–9. Unless otherwise indicated, this section on pay-for-performance is based on this document.

18. *Blueprints for Service Quality*, p. 32.

19. Ibid., pp. 34–35.

20. Personal interview with Sam Heltman, March 1992.

21. *Team Member Handbook*, Toyota Motor Manufacturing, U.S.A., February 1988, p. 35.

22. Personal interview with Joe Caldwell, March 1992.

23. William Power and Michael Siconolfi, "Goldman Chiefs Made Over $15 Million Each," *The Wall Street Journal*, July 22, 1992, p. C1.

10
Actualizing

Actualizing in Theory and in Practice

You will come to a point when you will ask if you've achieved all you could have achieved, given your skills and your gifts and your dreams, for yourself, and woe to the firm that prevented you from doing so. Few needs are as strong as the need to fulfill our dreams, to become all we are capable of becoming. Firms that don't cater to this need lose their best employees and drift along with increasingly bitter, unhappy ones. It was the psychologist Abraham Maslow who said that the ultimate need is "the desire to become more and more what one is, to become everything that one is capable of becoming." Self-actualization, to Maslow, meant that "what man *can* be, he *must* be....It refers to the desire for self-fulfillment, namely to the tendency for him to become actualized in what he is potentially."[1] The ultimate key to gaining commitment is thus to help your employees to actualize—to become all they can be. Saul Gellerman put it this way:

> The ultimate motivation is to make the self concept real: to live in a manner that is appropriate to one's preferred role, to be treated in a manner that corresponds to one's preferred rank, and to be rewarded in a manner that reflects one's estimate of his own abilities. Thus we are in perpetual pursuit of whatever we regard as our deserved role, trying to make our subjective ideas about ourself into objective truths.[2]

Ironically, many companies not only don't commit to fulfilling this need, they actively thwart it. As a healthy person matures and approaches adulthood, said Chris Argyris, he or she moves to a state of increased activity, independence, and stronger interests. The person also becomes capable of behaving in a greater variety of ways and tends to have a much longer time perspective. And as he or she matures from the subordinate role of a child to an equal or superordinate role as an adult, the person also develops more awareness of and control over his or her actions. Often, according to Argyris, the typical company with its short-cycle jobs, autocratic supervision, and relative dearth of growth opportunities thwarts these normal maturation changes by forcing employees into dependent, passive, and subordinate roles.[3] "Let us take an example," said Toyota's Fujio Cho, "of a job where a worker takes parts off an automated machine and places them on a conveyor belt all day long. Would you be proud of your work? Would you want your family members to see you working?...Too often [firms] make people do as they are told without letting them think. People are often treated as unthinking robots."[4]

Not surprisingly, high-commitment firms don't organize their jobs this way. They all engage in actualizing practices, practices that aim to ensure that all employees have every opportunity to actualize all their skills and gifts at work, to become all they can be. These practices include, first, *committing themselves* to the goal of actualizing their employees; then *front-loading* first-job challenges; *enriching and empowering employees*; and *aggressively promoting employees from within*. "Actualizing" thus doesn't mean just promotions or even career success. Certainly, these are very important. But the crucial question is whether your people have the opportunity to develop and use all their skills and become—as Maslow would say—all they can be. Training employees to expand their skills and to solve problems at work, enriching their jobs and empowering them to plan and inspect their own work, helping them continue their educations and grow—these are some other ways to achieve this.

A Commitment to Actualizing

It's what companies believe that drives what they do. To actualize your employees you first must commit your firm to doing so. Every high-commitment firm is fully and explicitly committed to helping their workers to actualize. This commitment generally stems from a firm's people-first values and can usually be found referenced repeatedly in the firm's documents and by its management. At J. C. Penney, for instance, Vice Chairman Bob Gill put it this way:

> We have an obligation to develop our people to the fullest. You never know how high is high....One of the best measures of a manager's effectiveness is the length of the list of names of those he helped to develop careerwise. For me, one of the truest measures of a Penney manager's effectiveness is how many people would put you on the list of those who helped their careers here.[5]

The emphasis on actualizing at other high-commitment firms is much the same. At IBM it's the idea that "your objectives and long-term career interests are recognized."[6] At Ben & Jerry's it's the fact that the firm "is committed to offering regular full-time employees a variety of chances to develop their skills, knowledge and professional capacities, both for advancement within the company and to achieve overall career goals."[7] These activities include career planning programs, tuition aid, company internships, special classes, seminars, and related activities, and financial planning. At Saturn, it's their commitment to training and to using their employees' skills to the fullest. Assembler Dan Dise told me as we talked on the plant floor,

> I'm committed to Saturn in part for what they did for me; for the 300-plus hours of training in problem solving and leadership that helped me expand my personal horizons; for the firm's "Excel" program that helps me push myself to the limit; and because I know that at Saturn I can go as far as I can go. This company wants its people to be all that they can be. But I'm also committed to Saturn for what I saw where I came from: the burned-out workers, the people who were so pressed down by the system that even if they saw their machines were about to break from poor maintenance, they'd say, "Leave it alone, let management handle it." This is like a different world.[8]

But it was a Federal Express manager who perhaps best described the commitment these firms have to actualizing employees. He told me that

> At Federal Express, the best I can be is what I can be here. I have been allowed to grow [at Federal Express]. People here are not turned on by money. The biggest benefit is that Federal Express made me a man. It gave me the confidence and self-esteem to become the person I had the potential to become.

The net effect is that employees become committed to their firms because they know their firms are committed to them—to their development, to their well-being, and most of all to their desire to become the people they've always hoped they could be. It's little wonder that firms committed to actualizing earn, in turn, their employees' commitment.

Front-Loading Entry-Level Positions

Employees all bring certain needs, aspirations, and hopes to their jobs, and they become committed to those employers who take concrete steps to help them develop their abilities and achieve their potential. At no time are such development efforts more important than in a person's first assignment. Young graduates or new recruits often start their jobs expecting challenging assignments to help them test and prove their abilities. In most firms they are instead shunted to low-risk jobs where they "can't cause any trouble while we're trying them out."

High-commitment firms are generally different; they front-load the job challenge. At Saturn and Toyota even assembly workers are assigned at once to self-managing teams of highly skilled and motivated colleagues where they must quickly learn to be productive team members. At Goldman, Sachs young professionals are expected to contribute at once; they immediately find themselves on teams involved in challenging projects. As one manager stated,

> Even our young people often start out handling millions of dollars of responsibility. And at a meeting with a client, the partner in charge will often not talk first at the meeting but the youngest will. At Goldman, Sachs, you take the responsibility and you're supported by the team. That's what attracts people to Goldman, Sachs, the ability to make decisions early.

The merchandising-manager trainee position at J. C. Penney's (their entry-level management position) is another good example of a job designed to engage the worker right away. A trainee almost straight out of college might be assigned the job of supervising the jeans section in the menswear department. Fresh from college, in other words, he or she would be responsible (under the guidance of his or her manager) for jeans display, inventory management, customer service, and staffing. As one Penney's manager told me, "From day one [as a merchandising-manager trainee straight out of college] I was running the 'store within a store.' The philosophy is: We'll give you some guidance but won't hold your hand—you've got brackets to work within only. You're made to feel part of a team right away, you know: 'I can buy the material and my decisions are important.'"

At Penney's new merchandise managers remain as trainees for about 12 months. During this time they are responsible for training themselves. To facilitate this they receive various training manuals, including "The Role of a First-Level Supervisor," which describes the trainee's responsibilities for activities such as customer service; sales; merchandising; visual merchandising; and sales promotion, staffing, and time management. Each new trainee is also assigned a mentor, usually a merchandising manager or senior merchandising manager. The mentor provides guidance and weekly appraisals. The training program, however, is self-administered: The trainee is responsible for teaching himself or herself the job's details.

As mentioned, trainees are appraised weekly by their mentors according to a schedule. At the end of week 2, for instance, their personal selling skills are appraised. In week 3 their visual merchandising skills are appraised; in week 4, their sales leadership; and so on.

At the end of eight weeks, the trainee gets an extensive appraisal. At this point he or she meets with three people—the store manager, the merchandising manager, and the senior merchandising manager—and has what one manager referred to as a "very frank discussion." A typical comment might be, for example, "You're going to have to be much more outgoing if you want a successful career here." They "lay it on the table," as one executive said, telling the trainee where he or she stands, what sort of progress is being made, and what further development is required.

From their first day trainees participate in departmental meetings and attend all Penney's broadcasting system meetings. (Here Penney's buyers "sell" their recommendations to the store's merchandising managers; trainees can thus help decide on purchase decisions even at this early stage of their development.)

After six months, trainees usually move into new assignments, where they assume more responsibility, generally running larger departments. At the end of a year then they're ready for promotion to merchandising manager.

Not all firms believe in such front-loading of job challenge and responsibility. Delta is a case in point. Because it subscribes to a promotion-from-within policy, Delta hires virtually all future managers at entry-level positions. Most of Delta's more than 3000 managers have thus started in positions such as aircraft cleaning or flight attendant. For example, Delta's operational people normally enter as aircraft cleaners, 40 percent of them having college degrees and 5 percent having master's. Within two to three years they move into ticket agent positions, then into supervisory positions, and hence into other positions of increasing responsibility. Though certain highly specialized graduates—in accounting, for instance—might start with entry-level positions in functional departments, the vast majority start at ground level, with brooms in their hands, convinced that promotions will come and that their careers are in good hands.

Enriching and Empowering

> You don't have anyone here [on the line] who is a supervisor. You don't experience supervision. We are supervised by ourselves. We become responsible to people we work with everyday. What I do affects my people. In other firms you're treated like children and here we are treated like adults. We make up our own work schedule. We do our own budgeting and buying of tools. We decide and improve on the work process by consensus.—a Saturn assembler

Ideally, job enrichment and worker empowerment should always go hand in hand. "Enrichment" means building challenge and achievement into workers' jobs by changing job content, letting them order and inspect their own goods, schedule their own day, and so forth. "Empowerment," as the term is increasingly used, means authorizing *and enabling* workers to do their jobs. Enriching jobs should thus give employees more challenging jobs to do, while empowering employees should give them the skills, authority, and discretion they need to actually do the enriched jobs. "Enriching and empowering" thus means doing three things:

1. Changing the content of jobs—letting employees plan the work, control the scrap, and obtain the supplies, for instance

2. Giving employees the training, tools, and support they need to enable them to do their new jobs

3. Insisting that all managers follow through by actually letting the workers use their new, broader authority to do their jobs.

The total effect, as we'll see, can be exhilarating for all concerned.

Saturn provides a good example of the three "enrich and empower" components in action. At Saturn, all production work is accomplished by work teams, and the work assignments of all work teams are highly enriched. This is evident from the 30 "work unit functions" for which all team members are responsible.

A sample of the 30 functions is presented in Figure 10-1. As you can see, all teams are responsible for a broad range of functions, including planning their own work; making their own job assignments; selecting new

Each Saturn team will:

1. Use consensus decision-making: No formal leader [will be] apparent in the process....All members of the work unit who reach consensus must be at least 70% comfortable with the decision, and 100% committed to its implementation.

3. Make their own job assignments: A work unit...ensures safe, effective, efficient, and equal distribution of the work unit tasks to all its members.

5. Plan their own work: The work unit assigns timely resources for the accomplishment of its purpose to its customers while meeting the needs of the people within the work unit.

6. Design their own jobs: This should provide the optimum balance between people and technology and include the effective use of manpower, ergonomics, machine utilization, quality, cost, job task analysis, and continuous improvement.

8. Control their own material and inventory: Work directly in a coordinated manner with suppliers, partners, customers, and indirect/product material resource team members to develop and maintain necessary work unit inventory.

9. Perform their own equipment maintenance: Perform those tasks that can be defined as safe, and those they have the expertise, ability, and knowledge to perform effectively.

13. Make selection decisions of new members into the work unit: A work unit operating in a steady state has responsibility for determining total manpower requirements, and selection and movement of qualified new members from a candidate pool will be in accordance with the established Saturn selection process.

14. Constantly seek improvement in quality, cost, and the work environment: The work unit is responsible for involving all work unit members in improving quality, cost, and the work environment in concert with Saturn's quality system.

18. Determine their own methods: The work unit is responsible for designing the jobs of its team members consistent with the requirements of the Saturn production system and comprehending the necessary resources and work breakdown required.

21. Provide their own absentee replacements: The work unit is responsible for the attendance of its members....The work unit will be required to plan for and provide its own absentee coverage.

22. Perform their own repairs: The work unit will have the ultimate responsibility for producing a world-class product that meets the needs and requirements of the customer. In the event a job leaves the work unit with a known or unknown non-conformance to specification, the originating work unit will be accountable for corrective action and repair.

Figure 10-1. Sampling of the 30 Saturn work-team functions. (*Reprinted with permission from* Saturn Work-Team Functions, *a company training document.*)

team members; and determining their own methods. By documenting the 30 functions, Saturn has clarified the responsibilities of each team and helped legitimate the broad-based authority the teams exercise.

Second, the teams and their members get the skills and tools to do their jobs, since "empowerment" without "ability" is just a sham. For example, workers can't use consensus decision making and make their own job assignments without the training and decision-making tools that will help them do so. Saturn thus provides both the tools and the training. The RASI card is one example of such a tool. As shown in Figure 10-2, RASI stands for Responsibility, Approval, Support, and Inform. Teams are trained to use the RASI process to assign the level of each person's involvement as they use consensus decision making to solve team problems. For example, suppose a door-installation team decides to look for new suppliers for some item. Individual roles and responsibilities are assigned according to the RASI process: Mike and Tina might be responsible for initiating the action and ensuring it is carried out; Lynn and Karl must approve or veto the recommended action; and so on.

RASI – Clarifies level of involvement; agree who owns the task, assign that person the "R". All other group members would assume A, S, or I positions depending on their role in relation to the task. Only one "R" can be assigned per task.

	Individual Roles and Responsibilities
R Responsibility	• Owns task (accountable and responsible) • Initiates action • Ensures the action is carried out • Performs tasks or delegates to appropriate others • Involves other team members appropriately
A Approval	• Approves or vetos the recommended action • Assures members are properly involved • Ensures resources are available for implementation • Sets parameters
S Support	• Provides support and resources • Shares knowledge and expertise • Questions and challenges • Offers options and input
I Inform	• Listens to assure understanding • Uses information • Keeps feedback loops open • Questions and expresses opinions

Figure 10-2. Saturn's RASI card. (*Reprinted with permission from Saturn Corporation.*)

Training in RASI is but a fraction of the empowerment-producing training these people receive. Joy Rodes, a Saturn personnel specialist, points out, for instance, that new Saturn team members get at least 320 hours of training in their first year and receive at least 92 hours per year thereafter.[9]

> We have an immense amount of training here. New people get 320 hours, plus current employees get at least 92 hours per year, and we've tied their salaries to the amount of training they get. If they don't take at least 5% of their hours as training, their salaries will be lower than they would with the training. To earn that 5% you must get your training.

And remember that at Saturn "training" doesn't only mean how to screw in bolts or position doors. Instead, it means broadening the employee and developing new skills, with the aim of making each person "all he or she can be." The emphasis is on learning new things—for instance, with problem-solving training or with teaching the use of Pareto diagrams and basic accounting.

Third, high-commitment firms like Saturn follow through with supervisory action—they make sure their managers actually let their people do their jobs. The team members I spoke with made it clear that Saturn teams really were empowered:

> "You don't have anyone here who is a supervisor. You don't experience supervision. We are supervised by ourselves. We became responsible to people [the team members] we work with everyday. What I do affects my people. In other firms you're treated like children and here we are treated like adults."

> "If an issue comes up, the work team handles it; all on our team must be agreed or we don't leave the room until we're 100 percent committed, 70 percent comfortable."

> "When you're on a team like this, you get to know others in your group and feel responsible to them. You are responsible and thus committed to your fellow team members."

> "Here you know there's no one else to do it; if something is wrong, you must fix it yourself. We bring in suppliers if there is a problem and work with them to rectify it."

> "The old world treats you like a kid. Here, for example, we're trusted with a lot of confidential information, like the financials of the company."

"They tell you, Here is the problem; what would you do about it?"

"If a defect goes to the next business team, they'll either stop the line or call one of us over to look at it and help them fix it. We watch out for each other and for the other business team."

"There is some traditional industrial engineering here, but part of the "30 functions" is having the team do it. Even if they need a traditional IE, the team has a big input and works with the IE to make the improvement."

"It's like you draw off each other. Here our industrial engineers are the workers right on the line. In a traditional setting it would be 'let the IE do it.' Here it's the team's responsibility."

Promoting from Within

For many employees "becoming all you can be" boils down to career progress. In that sense, promotional opportunities are the ultimate manifestation of a firm's people-first values. Two-way communication, guaranteed fair treatment, a sense of sharing and commonality, job security, and hard-side rewards satisfy many needs and foster employee commitment. Similarly, front-loaded job challenges and worker empowerment help ensure that all employees' capacities are fully utilized. But in the final analysis many employees will ultimately measure their firm's commitment to them by the degree to which they had the opportunity to achieve careerwise all they were capable of achieving. All our high-commitment firms thus have comprehensive promotion-from-within programs, and most adhere to these programs tenaciously.

The distinction between promotion-from-within *programs* and *policies* is important. Like many companies, our high-commitment firms have strong promotion-from-within policies. At J. C. Penney, they state, "We believe in promotion from within whenever a unit's requirements and an associate's qualifications provide a suitable match. Promotions are based primarily on such factors as performance (including productivity), dependability, initiative, and availability."[10] At Federal Express "open positions are filled, whenever possible, by qualified candidates from within the existing workforce."[11] At IBM, "promotion is from within—and also based on merit."[12] Delta Air Lines "hires at entry-level, then trains and develops personnel to promote them to higher levels of responsibility."[13] At Toyota, where the team leader and group leader positions are stepping-stones to all management positions in the plant, "it is TMM's philosophy to consider its current workforce when attempting to fill team leader and group leader job openings. [Furthermore] TMM is committed to filling open positions in the office classifications by promotions from within whenever possible. New hires are considered only after efforts to promote from within have been exhausted."[14]

But there's much more to a successful promotion-from-within program than a strong statement of policy. At high-commitment firms "promotion from within" generally means a five-part program consisting of a promotion-from-within policy, value-based hiring, developmental activities, career-oriented appraisals, and a coordinated system of career records and job postings.

Value-Based Hiring

Promotion from within is aided first by value-based hiring. As one Delta manager explained,

> First of all, we hire for the future....The employment process favors applicants who have the potential for promotion for a good reason. Delta subscribes almost entirely to a promotion-from-within policy. Except for a handful of people with specialized skills, everyone is hired in at entry-level.[15]

The story is similar at other high-commitment firms. You can't really commit to promotion from within when you hire people who haven't the potential to eventually be promotable. Hiring people with promotion potential and values that are in synch with the firm is a requisite step in any promotion-from-within program.

Developmental Activities

Next, these firms provide the assessment and development resources needed to help employees identify and develop their promotion potential. At Ben & Jerry's, promotional development is encouraged through programs of career planning, company internships, and tuition assistance. Ben & Jerry's employees are encouraged to attend a sequence of eight 4-hour career-planning seminars, the aim of which is to help employees think about and plan their careers. Employees who have completed the seminars and want to learn about other jobs within the firm can then spend two or three days interning at another company job, on paid time. The firm offers as much as 90 percent funding in tuition reimbursement for up to three courses per year. And it provides classes, seminars, counseling and tutoring, both on company premises and off, including community and college courses; a business writing class (taught by the community college of Vermont, which includes one-on-one tutoring); computer classes, in which employees can earn certificates from Ben & Jerry's information services group; basic adult education tutoring and a high school diploma program; management development counseling, one-on-one, by invitation and by request; professional development classes and seminars; and financial planning seminars and individual financial counseling.

Our other high-commitment firms also spend lavishly on developing employees' potential. For example, IBM has one of the most extensive training and education programs in industry. In its advanced education program, IBM sponsors part-time or full-time coursework at outside colleges and universities. "Consistent with IBM's goal to encourage individual career development," employees may also receive educational leaves of absence without pay after two years of satisfactory full-time employment.[16]

IBM emphasizes that it is the employees' responsibility to make the decisions regarding their development that are appropriate, given their interests and goals. Managers are charged with determining their employees' interest in participating in these programs and with understanding their employees' development needs.[17] The company's tuition-refund plan also fully reimburses employees for tuition costs and other educational fees for approved courses and programs at any accredited college, university, or school.

At Saturn, a career-growth workshop uses vocational guidance tools (including a skills-assessment disk) to help employees identify career-related skills they need to develop. This career-growth workshop, according to one employee, "helps you assess yourself and takes four to six hours. You use it for developing your own career potential. The career disk identifies your weaknesses and strengths. You assess yourself, and then your team assesses you." Tuition reimbursement and other aids are available to help employees develop the skills they need to get ahead.

At Publix, says Jim Rhodes, the process is more informal, but the firm's commitment to it makes it work.

> When I started work here at age 17 I was told that the company was like a smorgasbord, that it would change and that more and more jobs would become available. They told me to watch and look and pick out what's best for me. At 17 that didn't have much relevance but it stayed in my data bank. And over the last 30 years this company has let me move into new positions and grow.[18]

No assessment, training, or education programs can guarantee that someone will be promoted, of course. Many employees will plateau, rising no higher at their firms. However, assessment and development programs do help guarantee that all employees can formulate realistic career goals and occupational options, and have an equal opportunity to make themselves promotable at their firms. They also make it easier for employees to make lateral moves and thus grow, by learning new subjects and meeting new challenges. That's why assembler Dan Dise said as we talked on the plant floor at Saturn:

> I'm an assembler now; I was a team leader for two-and-a-half years. My goal is to move into our people-systems [personnel] unit. I know things are tight now, but I know that the philosophy here is that the firm will look out for me. They want people to be all they can be. I know here I'll go as far as I can go; that's one reason I'm so committed to Saturn.[19]

Career-Oriented Appraisals

Next, most of these firms offer career-oriented appraisals. They don't just assess past performance. Instead, the supervisor and the appraisee are charged with linking the latter's past performance, career preferences, and developmental needs in a formal career plan. As I was told at Delta:

> Our annual evaluations are formal and include an interview. We touch on whether the employee is making progress or not, review his or her past performance, and discuss where that person is going with his or her career. The formal evaluation forces the supervisor and employee to communicate and talk about the person's career path.

J. C. Penney has the most comprehensive program in this area. As you can see in Figure 10-3, their Management Appraisal form requires both a "promotability recommendation" and "projections for associate development."

Here's how the Penney's system works. Prior to the annual appraisal, the associate and his or her manager review Penney's Management Career Grid (see Figure 10-4). The grid itemizes all supervisory positions at J. C. Penney (grouped by operations jobs, merchandise jobs, personnel jobs, and general management jobs) and includes specific job titles such as "regional catalog sales manager," "cosmetic market coordinator," "regional training coordinator," and "project manager, public affairs." The firm also provides a "work activities scan sheet." This basically contains thumbnail job descriptions for all the jobs listed on the grid.

Date & Initials Midyear Follow Up: 9/10/90 GPT / [illegible]

Management Characteristics and Strategic Directions: Fill in letter for each using ratings below. See reverse for definitions.
Ratings: O = Outstanding G = Good S = Satisfactory ND = Needs Development TN = Too New to Rate or Not Applicable

I. **Leadership** G II. **Awareness** ND III. **Sense of Urgency** ND IV. **Judgement** G V. **Planning & Organizing** G VI. **Team Process Participation** G VII. **Fashion Credibility** G VIII. **EEO Management** G

Additional Comments, Strengths and Opportunities Lee achieved very solid results in Men's -- nice sales, good team development and depth of lines. Shoes is a real opportunity for Lee. Many decisions must be made more quickly by Lee, using merchandise systems better.

OVERALL PERFORMANCE RATING 3
(See reverse for instructions)

Manager Signature	Date of Appraisal	Reviewer Signature	Date of Review	Associate Signature	Date of Appraisal	Is this associate willing to move residence? (Check One)
Garry D. Turner	4-15-9[illegible]	Phil Adams	4-1-91	Lee Smith	4/15/91	[X] Yes [ ] Not Now

See Associate Career Grid for Instructions

Promotability Recommendation: Enter letter here → B

A This Year
B Second or third year
C Fourth or fifth year
D Can grow with job
E Recommend lateral transfer
F Is at responsibility level
G Recommend less responsibility
H Promotable this store
I Too New To Rate

High Potential: Check if this associate has exceptional growth potential, top 5% in drive and ability. [ ]

Projections for Associate Development	Year 19 92		Year 19 ___	
	Position Title	Position Code/Volume	Position Title	Position Code/Volume
First Choice Projection	Sr.Merch.Mgr.	4300		
Alternate Projection				

DP. 2036 (Rev. 2/90) T.O.C. # 008-7427-1000

Figure 10-3. Portion of J. C. Penney's Management Appraisal form. (*Reprinted with permission from J. C. Penney.*)

Instructions and Use of Grid for Making Associate Projections of Development

1) Promotability - Enter the appropriate Promotability letter in the box provided. If the answer to Promotability is D, F, or I, leave the "High Potential" and "Projections for Associate Development" sections blank.

2) High Potential - The High Potential box should be checked if this associate has exceptional growth potential — is within the top 5% in drive and ability. Please keep in mind that appraisal ratings and high potential ratings while related reflect two distinct judgments — performance in current assignment versus exceptional potential for growth. A "1" rated associate, is not necessarily high potential or vice versa.

FIELD MANAGEMENT					
OPERATIONS		**MERCHANDISE**			**PE**
Position Title/Volume	Code	Position Title/Volume	Code		Po
Regional Operations Manager	1002	Manager of Geographic Markets Manager of Business Planning District Manager Store Manager 30+ D.S. Entity Store Manager Store Manager 22 - 30 D.S. Store Manager 15 - 22 D.S. Regional Business Planning Manager Store Manager 10 - 15 D.S. Store Manager Under 10 D.S.	1017 1025 1121 0109 0110 0108 0107 1026 0106 0105		Re
Regional Catalog Sales Center Manager Regional Programs Manager Regional Systems Manager	1150 1100 1027	Regional Merchandiser/Geographic Markets Store Manager 5 - 10 S.L.	1146 0104		
Regional Catalog Sales Manager District Operations Manager District Operations/Personnel Manager Regional Loss Prevention Manager Operations Manager 30+ D.S. District Merchandise Systems Coordinator	1139 2290 2310 4804 1329 2330	Business Planning Manager District Special Events & Publicity Manager Store Merchandise & Marketing Manager Store Manager 3 - 5 S.L. General Merchandising Manager 30+ D.S.	**40( )0 2800 4260 0103 4299		Re Re Re Dis Pe
D.L.D.C. Manager Operations Manager 25 - 30 D.S. Regional Loss Prevention Representative Regional Styling Salon Sales Manager Regional Maintenance Manager Regional Telecommunications Manager	3750 1328 4805 1109 1165 1028	General Merchandising Manager 22 - 30 D.S. Store Manager 1 - 3 S.L. Regional Visual Merchandising Mgr - Geo. Mkts. Regional Visual Merchandising Mgr - Metro Mkts. General Merchandising Manager 15 - 22 D.S. General Merchandising Manager 10 - 15 D.S. General Merchandising Manager under 10 D.S.	4298 0102 1085 1092 4297 4296 4295		Pe
District Loss Prevention Manager Operations/Personnel Manager 10 - 25 D.S. D.L.D.C. Operations Manager Systems Implementation & Training Manager Catalog Sales Center Manager	5620 5356 4930 1130 1010	Store Manager under 1 S.L. Multiple Unit D.L.D.C. Merchandiser D.L.D.C. Merchandiser District Merchandise Publicity Coordinator Special Lines Market Coordinator District Visual Merchandising Manager	0101 4450 3760 5580 2340 5630		
Sales Support Manager	3210	Cosmetic Market Coordinator Visual Merchandising Manager Senior Merchandising Manager Department Sales Manager Shoe Department Manager Cosmetic Manager	0700 4650 4300 3460 5590 0710		
(Functional Title) Manager	4980	Merchandising Manager Fine Jewelry Manager Multi Store Fine Jewelry Manager Fine Jewelry Merchandiser Shoe Department Merchandiser Cosmetic Merchandiser	4310 3360 4470 3370 5600 0720		
		Merchandising Manager Trainee	4330		

Figure 10-4. Portion of J. C. Penney's Management Career Grid. The Grid also lists personnel and general management positions. (*Reprinted with permission from J. C. Penney.*)

The Management Career Grid also shows typical promotional routes. As the instructions indicate, "When projecting the next assignment for a management associate, you should consider not only merchandise positions but also operations and personnel positions as well as general management positions."

Promotional plans can cross the four groups as well as up one or two job levels. Thus a senior merchandising manager might be projected for promotion to either assistant buyer or general merchandise manager. ("Assistant buyer" is classified as a general management job at Penney's, since buying is done centrally. The general merchandise manager job is a merchandise group job, two levels above the person's current senior merchandising manager position).

Career Records and Job Posting

Finally, most high-commitment firms have a career records/job posting system. Its basic purpose is to ensure that an inside candidate's career goals and skills are matched openly, and fairly with promotional opportunities.

Goldman, Sachs' Internal Placement Center (IPC) is an example of a career records/job posting system. The center's aim is to offer

> employees interested in pursuing career opportunities in different areas of the firm the resources to locate and apply for job openings. The IPC also makes it simpler for managers to consider qualified internal candidates when filling open positions, and furnishes managers with information about openings that could provide career development opportunities for their employees.[20]

There are five steps in the IPC process.[21]

Step 1. For each open position, the hiring manager can first choose to conduct an internal, external, or combined (internal and external) search; "an internal or combined search is strongly encouraged."

Step 2. The manager and recruiter fill out a job description form for the open position. The form includes job title, department and manager, a description of the position's responsibilities and duties, and a summary of qualifications required for the position.

Step 3. Listings of current job opportunities are then posted in the Internal Placement Center and in the reception area on each floor.

Step 4. Any employee interested in applying for an open position submits an IPC application and current resume to the Internal Placement Center.

Step 5. The process of reviewing an employee's application begins with the IPC coordinator and the recruiter assessing each applicant's qualifications. Within two weeks after submitting an application, the employee is informed by the IPC coordinator at his or her home address about the status of the application. (This is the case whether the employee is selected to be interviewed for a position or not.) Those chosen as candidates then start their interviews.

Federal Express has its own career records/job posting system called JCATS—Job Change Applicant Tracking System. Announcements of new job openings via this electronic system usually take place every Friday. All employees posting for the position are given numerical scores based on job performance and length of service and are advised as to whether they have been chosen as candidates.

J. C. Penney has its own career records/job posting system. First, regional managers and regional personnel managers review lists of promotable people from their store managers. The regions and districts also keep their own career-related files on supervisory personnel, and there are another 4000 files or so at the J. C. Penney corporate office. The four functional divisions (merchandising, operations, personnel, and general management) have their own files.

Who gets what files depends on an associate's chosen career path (as determined by the yearly appraisal). Thus someone who wants to move from merchandising manager to assistant buyer would have a file established in the general management offices.

J. C. Penney also has an employee database on over 18,000 managers—where they're located, their appraisal codes, their chosen career routes, and so on. A senior executive reviews all recommendations for interregional or interdepartmental transfers. The chief operating officer evaluates all the appraisals and career plans for all employees down through the director level.

The result, says Jay Hundley, one of the firm's top personnel officers, is

> An on-going dialogue between managers and associates regarding their careers. They are always discussing—at least annually, usually a lot more—what will this person be doing in the next 12 months, and what are his or her career options? And in turn, the store managers are discussing the same thing regarding their careers with their own district managers. The emphasis is always on how to help this associate grow.[22]

As Vice Chairman Bob Gill told me, this doesn't guarantee that every person will be promoted to the position that he or she wants. But it does help to guarantee that everyone is at least *considered* for the position and that if someone else gets it, the process is perceived as fair.

A Summary: Actualizing as a Key to Commitment

1. Engage is actualizing practices that aim to ensure that all employees have an opportunity to use all their skills and gifts at work, to become all they can be.

2. Commit to actualizing your employees. Make it clear to everyone in the company that you expect the company and all its people to act in such a way that each employee can say, "I can be the best I can be here."

3. Front-load the job challenge for your employees. After training and orientation, assign them at once to teams or mentors with whom they can quickly become productive, where they will be expected to contribute at once to challenging projects.

4. If front-loading isn't appropriate, make it clear that the assigned job is part of a well-considered development program.

5. Design the work so that your employees can use all their skills and gifts on their jobs. To do this, "enrich and empower":

   - Enrich employees' jobs by changing the content of their jobs; let them plan their own work, control their own scrap, and obtain their own supplies.
   - Give them the training and tools and support they need to do their new jobs.
   - Insist that all managers follow through by actually letting the employees use their new, broader authority to do their jobs.

6. Establish a comprehensive promotion-from-within program and adhere to your program tenaciously. A comprehensive program would include a strong promotion-from-within policy; value-based hiring; career-assessment and developmental activities and continuous learning; career-oriented appraisals; and a coordinated system of career records and job postings.

References

1. Abraham Maslow, "A Theory of Human Motivation," *Psychological Review*, vol. 50 (1943), pp. 370–396; reprinted in Michael Matteson and John Ivancevich, *Management Classics*, Goodyear, Santa Monica, Calif., 1977, p. 336.

2. Saul W. Gellerman, *Motivation and Productivity*, American Management Association, New York, 1963, p. 290.

3. Chris Argyris, *Integrating the Individual and the Organization*, Wiley, New York, 1964.

4. Fujio Cho, speech to the Asian Business Club of Harvard Business School, Cambridge, Mass., March 4, 1991.

5. Personal interview with Bob Gill, October 1991.

6. IBM, *The People and the Company*, p. 11.

7. *Ben & Jerry's Homemade, Inc., Employee Handbook*, p. 11.

8. Personal interview with Dan Dise, March 1992.

9. Personal interview with Joy Rodes, March 1992.

10. *J. C. Penney Associate Handbook*, p. 3.

11. *The Federal Express Employee Handbook*, August 7, 1989, p. 28.

12. *About Your Company*, IBM Handbook, p. 17.

13. *Policies and Procedures Manual*, Delta Air Lines.

14. *Team Member Handbook*, Toyota Motor Manufacturing, U.S.A., February 1988, p. 82.

15. Paulette O'Donnell, speech to Southeast Region All Hands Conference, August 1990, pp. 4–5.

16. *About Your Company*, p. 188.

17. Ibid.

18. Personal interview with Jim Rhodes, April 1992.

19. Personal interview with Dan Dise, March 1992.

20. *Internal Placement Center: Guidelines for Managers*, Goldman, Sachs and Company.

21. Ibid., p. 1.

22. Personal interview with Jay Hundley, October 1991.

11

In Summary: Using the Keys to Commitment

We've seen that creating commitment requires a comprehensive, multipractice management program, one consisting of a package of concrete actions and policies. In the absence of such a program, results from relatively one-dimensional efforts like quality-improvement programs or incentive plans are bound to disappoint.

In this chapter we summarize the eight commitment practices discussed in this book.

People-First Values

Actions are the products of values. Therefore, start your commitment program by deciding how you and your team really feel about people. Then put your people-first values in writing.

Know What You Want

Commitment-creating practices such as guaranteed fair treatment and actualizing all flow from people-first values. As one Fed Ex executive says, "You start the process of boosting employee commitment by making sure you know how you and your top managers really feel about people." You have got to be willing to commit to the idea that your employees are your most important assets and that they can be trusted, treated with respect, involved in making on-the-job decisions, and encouraged to reach their full potential. To paraphrase Fed Ex's Fred Smith, you have to be willing to put your people first in every action, every planning process, every business decision that you make. You must commit to the idea that in every decision you make and in every business (and especially personnel) practice you establish you are going to ask first, "How will this impact my people?" Your employees will begin to commit to you when they see that in every decision you make you are committed to them.

Put It in Writing

Publish your people-first values in company literature. For example, devise an employee handbook that sets forth your policies. Emphasize that:

- This firm cares about its people being "all that they can be."
- This firm values trust and respect for the individual.
- This firm believes that people want to be involved in decisions that affect them, that people care about their job, and that people take pride in themselves and in their contribution.
- This firm recognizes that every person has an inherent right to be treated with respect and dignity and that that right should never be violated.
- This firm recognizes that its people are its most important resource.

Hire and Indoctrinate

Hire, and promote into management, people who have people-first values from the start. Establish rigorous interviewing and testing procedures to screen out applicants who lack people skills and values; continually retrain managers in the use of manuals and management guides that emphasize the people-first theme.

"Walk the Talk"

Translate your people-first values into everyday actions. For example,

- Continually remind your supervisors that employees come first and that every action they take must be based on that standard.

- Eliminate symbols like time clocks that say "I don't trust you."
- Monitor each group's reactions to its supervisors' actions.
- Maintain open communications and be candid with your people.
- Invest in your people through training and education.
- Provide your people with job security.
- Promote from within.
- Work hard to make sure each employee is able to use all his or her skills to the fullest and enjoys the most successful career he or she can.

Double-Talk

Managers of high-commitment firms know that commitment is built on trust and that trust requires a flood of two-way communication. You should therefore set up programs that guarantee this kind of exchange.

Guaranteed Fair Treatment Programs

Establish a "super" grievance procedure that guarantees fair treatment of all employees in all grievance and all disciplinary matters. Encourage employees to use the procedure and make sure the procedure is easy to use and is continually supported by top management. Insist on documentation and include an executive appeals review board to facilitate the process.

Speak Up! Programs

Institute multiple, formal, easy-to-use channels which employees can use to express concerns and gripes and to get answers to matters that bother them. The Speak Up!, Open-Door, and Hotline programs discussed in Chapter 4 are three examples. With IBM's Speak Up! employees may ask questions or make comments and receive a reply without revealing their identity to anyone except the Speak Up! administrator. The form itself is a combination letter-envelope, and it is easily available to all employees. Fed Ex's Open-Door is a one-page multipart form used to express any concern regarding matters such as seniority, vacation schedules, company benefits, or area maintenance. At Fed Ex, the process is not anonymous, and senders must sign their names; the forms are then directed to the appropriate department heads. With Toyota's Hotline, employees are told, "Don't spend time worrying about something...speak up!" All inquiries received on the telephone hotline are guaranteed to be reviewed by the general manager of human resources, and all questions and answers are posted on plant bulletin boards.

Periodic Survey Programs

Use opinion polls such as Fed Ex's Survey Feedback Action to aid management at all levels in identifying and solving problems.

Top-Down Programs

Use every opportunity to tell employees what's going on in your organization. High-commitment firms provide their people with extensive data on the performance of and prospects for their operation. Use opportunities such as daily and other periodic meetings, in-house TV networks, monthly "town halls," frequent round-table question-and-answer periods, and written material to keep employees posted.

Communion

Strive to create a strong "we-feeling" among your company's employees. In other words, to create commitment you must foster a sense of communion—a sense of connectedness, belonging, and participation in a whole.

Homogeneity: We've Got So Much in Common

Foster the sense of community in part through "selective homogeneity": Use value-based hiring to select people who fit your firm's value system; also hire team players and use or encourage dress codes that reinforce a sense of commonality and homogeneity.

Communal Sharing: I Own a Piece of the Rock

Foster a sense of sharing by eliminating unnecessary status differences. Examples of practices that have proved effective here include eliminating offices or minimizing status differences between offices; banning executive parking spots, company cars, executive lunchrooms and bathrooms; capping executives' salaries; encouraging dress codes or informal dress. "We do as much as we can to minimize difference between nonexecutive and executive levels" is how one top Fed Ex manager put it.

Use profit- and risk-sharing plans to put some portion of each employee's annual pay at risk to further evoke the sense of sharing by making all employees financial "partners" in the profits of the firm. Reward acts of sharing by employees to underscore your commitment to building a sense of community. At Mary Kay, for instance, sales directors who excel at sharing their time and effort with another director's recruits are singled out and awarded the firm's Miss Go-Give Award. Keep hammering on the need for and value of sharing and collegiality.

Communal Work: Get On the Team

Encourage joint effort: Organize around small work teams; utilize job rotation; encourage everyone, top managers included, to share in even the most mundane tasks when the going gets tough.

Employees tend to develop their strongest ties to the colleagues on their teams, so stress team building. Formulate a "teamwork principle" such as Toyota's, which sets the goal for employees "to work as a team with mutual respect and equal opportunities for all."[1] Work itself can be organized around work teams, and various practices can be used to assure smoothly functioning work teams. These practices include value-based hiring to select prospective team members (where team members also assist in the selection); steeping employees—through team-member handbooks—in the terminology and techniques of teamwork; and training aimed at facilitating work-group communications and problem solving. Continually publicize the accomplishment of teamwork heroes.

Encourage job rotation, both on a companywide basis and within work groups. This encourages a better understanding of each other's work and makes for a real sharing of all the work.

Regular Group Contact: Let's Get Together

Schedule activities that bring individual employees into regular contact with the group as a whole. These can include daily, weekly, or monthly meetings, daily teleconference meetings, annual affairs, and so on.

Ritual: It's a Tradition

Encourage collective participation in recurring events of symbolic importance—in other words, rituals. Establish traditions such as new-manager inaugurations that include a solemn pledge of loyalty. New-employee end-of-orientation banquets and periodic award ceremonies to recognize employees who have symbolized important company values (such as teamwork) are some other examples of ritual and ceremony.

Transcendental Mediation

If employees are to be committed, they need missions and values to be committed to. That's why high-commitment firms excel at formulating shared transcendental ideologies, missions, and values and mechanisms for communicating these to their employees.

Create the Ideology

Create a written ideology that lays out your organization's basic way of thinking and doing things, an ideology that all employees are expected to share. Components may include:

- *A statement of mission or vision.* This generally succinctly clarifies the "business" your company is in and the way in which you plan to distinguish your firm from its competitors. At Mary Kay, for instance, the vision is "to be preeminent in the manufacturing, distribution, and marketing of personal care products through our independent sales force. To provide our sales force an unparalleled opportunity for financial independence, career achievement, and personal fulfillment. To achieve total customer satisfaction worldwide by focusing on quality, value, convenience, innovation, and personal service."[2]

- *A statement of basic values or philosophy.* At Fed Ex, for instance, the basic values are people, service, profits. At Mary Kay, the company philosophy says, in part, that "every person associated with the company, from the Chairman Emeritus to the newest recruit, lives by the golden rule, do unto others as you would have them do unto you, and the priorities of God first, family second, and career third."[3]

- *A code of ethics.* At Mary Kay, the code of ethics includes the fact that "the Mary Kay skin care program, other Mary Kay products, and all facts concerning a Mary Kay career will be presented to customers and the prospective consultants in a truthful, sincere, and honest manner."[4]

Create Charisma

Try to make your firm and its ideology charismatic. Establish a mission statement that becomes a source of pride for your employees; have it evoke "higher callings," moral values like "help your fellow humans." Ben & Jerry's relates its ideology to social and political aims, while Saturn Corporation keeps hitting on the idea of becoming an example of how American workers and manufacturing can build a world-class quality car.

Achieve Ideological Conversion

You can convert your employees to your ideology through three basic practices:

- Use value-based hiring. Clarify what your basic values are and then enforce procedures for screening new employees in the light of these values. In other words, select employees whose values and skills match the firm's ideology.

- Use value-based orientation. Institute an extensive new-hire orientation program that continually emphasizes examples of your firm's basic values.

- Use value-based training. Your training programs should not just emphasize technical skills, but should also hammer home the basic values and missions of the firm, such as quality, service, putting employees first.

Use Symbols and Stories, Rites and Ceremonials

Remember that actions speak more loudly than words. High-commitment firms continuously engage in deeds that exemplify the values and ethics they want their employees to espouse. Use symbols like Ben & Jerry's Joy Gang does. Promulgate stories like those in Toyota's newsletter about examples of teamwork heroes. Schedule rites and ceremonials at which you can symbolize your firm's values and link your employees to them perhaps by having them take vows to the firm's ideals.

Value-Based Hiring

The time to start building commitment is before, not after, employees are hired. High-commitment firms are very careful about who they hire. They use value-based hiring practices: They don't just look at applicants' job-related skills; they try to get a sense of the person and his or her personal qualities and values; they identify common experiences and values that may flag the applicant's future fit with the firm.

Start by clarifying your firm's own values and ideology so that they can be made a part of your firm's screening process. If you want to emphasize teamwork and quality, start by formalizing your commitment to these values and then create screening procedures (interview questions and practical tests, for instance) to help you identify such values in the workplace.

Make your screening process exhaustive. Even with entry-level employees get some middle- and higher-level managers involved in the interviewing; design tools such as structured interviews to help ensure that applicants are thoroughly screened. Recruit actively so that those who are hired see that many were rejected and that they are therefore part of an "elite."

Always provide candid, realistic previews of what working at your firm will be like and what the entry job entails. Remember that self-selection is important. This can involve long probationary periods in entry-level jobs; low salary ceilings (as at Ben & Jerry's); or "sacrifice" on the part of employees, such as that demanded by a long and exhaustive screening process.

Securitizing

Institute a "lifetime employment without guarantees" policy. While specifying that all employment relationships will be "employment-at-will" arrangements, emphasize your commitment to lifetime employment with statements such as "Stable employment and the continual well-being of our team members are essential and can be obtained through the smooth, steady growth of our company."

Company practices that facilitate employee security include compensation plans that place a substantial portion of each employee's salary "at risk," with yearly bonuses that shrink in harsh economic times; use of large numbers of temporary or part-time employees; and cross-training to permit and/or require employees to wear "several hats."

Hard-Side Rewards

Though attractive compensation packages are not enough in themselves to do the trick, providing hard-side rewards for your employees is one of the keys to winning and keeping commitment.

- Offer packages of above-average pay combined with incentives and extensive benefits.
- Put a significant portion of pay at risk. High-commitment firms generally put about 15 to 20 percent of an employee's annual pay at risk.
- Emphasize self-reporting of hours worked, rather than devices like time clocks.
- Build a pay plan that encourages employees to think of themselves as partners. This means employees should have a healthy share of the profits in good years but should share as well in the downturn during bad times.
- Provide benefits that make it clear that you view your employees as long-term investments and that you are concerned with their welfare. Pensions, above-average health plans, and similar benefits contribute to this sense that the firm views its employees as part of its "family" and wants them around for the long haul.
- Institute stock-ownership plans that encourage employees to see that they have a significant investment in your firm.

Actualizing

Few needs are as strong as the need to fulfill our dreams, to become all we are capable of becoming. High-commitment firms therefore engage in actualizing practices. These practices aim to ensure that all employees have every opportunity to actualize themselves—to use all their skills and gifts at work and become all they can be.

Commit to Actualizing

Make it clear to your managers that the company should be run in such a way that every employee can say, "The best I can be is what I can be here."

Front-Load

Front-load the job challenge for your employees. After training and orientation, assign new employees at once to teams or mentors where they can feel productive, where they are expected to contribute at once to accomplishing challenging projects. If front-loading isn't appropriate, make it clear that the new employee's job is part of a well-thought-out development program.

Enrich and Empower

Design the work so that your employees can use all their skills and gifts on their jobs. To "enrich and empower," you should, for example:

- Let employees plan their own work, control their own scrap, and obtain their own supplies in order to enrich their jobs.
- Provide the training, tools, and support they need to enable the employees to do their new jobs.
- Insist all managers follow through by actually letting the employees use their authority to do their jobs.
- Give substance to enrichment by documenting the enriched responsibilities given to the employees.

Promote from Within

Establish a formal and comprehensive promotion-from-within program and adhere to your program tenaciously:

- Use value-based hiring to make sure new employees are compatible in a long-term sense with your firm, in terms of both skills and values.
- Flood your employees with opportunities for developmental activities and continuous learning.
- Require career-oriented appraisals that not only review past performance but put it in a context of what the employee's future aspirations are.

- Provide a coordinated system of career records and job postings so that all employees have immediate knowledge of job openings as well as an opportunity to be evaluated for the jobs fairly and equitably.

References

1. *Team Member Handbook,* Toyota Motor Manufacturing, U.S.A., February 1988, p. 10.
2. *Cosmetics Consultant's Guide,* Mary Kay Cosmetics, p. 1.
3. Ibid., p. 2.
4. Ibid., p. 3.

The Workers Speak: Selected Comments by Employees of High-Commitment Companies

How do the employees themselves feel about the firms that use the keys to commitment? The following comments illustrate how some people feel about their work and, just as important, how each firm uses the keys to commitment. We'll listen to the employees of each of our high-commitment firms in turn.

Ben & Jerry's

On Employee Commitment

"Frankly, I think the outside world views us as having better commitment than we have. We have a lot of great stuff but it's not perfect. Why are our people committed? We're big fish in a small pond and, frankly, it's probably the best place to work in the area. We pay good salary and benefits. There's a real pride or 'wow' factor in working for Ben & Jerry's. We have good opportunity for advancement. Our communication is top-notch; you always have the opportunity to go to the department you're interested in transferring to and talk to the department head about letting you in, for instance. We have a liberal tuition-reimbursement policy. And we give people the impression that we respect and value what they say because we actually do. A lot of people who have left here have...come back [to] tell their coworkers, 'You won't find much out there.' Others compare the work they're doing here and how we treat them [with the work experience of] their spouses or other family members....One of our employees told me how his previous employer had frequently made ethnic slurs at his expense. Here there's none of that, you can be gay or ethnic or anything you want; you'll be treated with respect. People feel they can be themselves."

On People-First Values

"When push comes to shove, this company really comes through for people. You can see it in how terminations are handled, for instance, and you can see it in the policy we had toward an employee who was dying of cancer, the way the company scheduled the work and met the person's emotional needs and how the whole company and all employees worked to help her. You can also see it in our policy toward unmarried couples and how everyone in the company is treated equally. That's how I would want any company to be, so it's not hard being loyal to a company like this."

"What would I tell a manager about winning commitment? That the company must take full responsibility for all it does and always study the impact it has both on its own employees and on the people outside the company as well."

"Trust is implicit in our mission statement; we're generally fair and have very caring treatment of employees."

"Show people you treat them like human beings and that you trust them; that's what we do here."

"Here I know if I don't make it careerwise, it's because of something I did or didn't do, not because of gender or something like that. There's little or none of the usual politics. You're valued for yourself."

"We are teaching our people to say, 'What you did to me was not fair,' to speak up for [themselves] and deal with the issue on a person-to-person basis. The only way that works is to empower people to speak back. You must get your people to appreciate that it doesn't matter if you have a college degree or an executive job: 'You are a human being of power.' And it's getting better here all the time."

On Communion

"There's a very egalitarian feeling on the part of employees regarding management. [Bosses] are not isolated in a glass tower. We also do a lot of work based on cross-departmental teams, having them work together, for instance, to put together orientation and training programs, and to devise answers to out-of-stock problems."

"We started the Joy Gang a few years ago. Jerry had left the company for one-and-a-half years and when he came back he felt the company had become too much of a factory. It had changed from a small fun place in which all shared in the experience to a factory. He felt we needed something to ensure that we all could share in the joy of work, and that's how the Joy Gang got started."

"I am impressed most around here by the commitment from the top, the commitment to be involved in all phases of the operation. Last week we didn't have enough people for a shift. We all volunteered and at 2 a.m. Jerry, me, and others, we were all down in the plant. `I never would have believed that,' said one employee. This company is not hung up on titles and everyone from Ben and Jerry down will do whatever it takes to make the company successful."

"There's a very egalitarian attitude in the company."

"All employees are on a first-name basis with Ben, Jerry, and Chuck, our president."

"This is not just a business. There's a feeling of family here, a feeling that you're part of a community. Employees help each other out; they help with gas money and so forth when someone is sick and can't come to work, for instance."

On Transcendental Mediation

"We always want to be sure that...our mission is important to our employees. For example, we had some pressure a while ago from outside environmental groups. They wanted us to object to a Quebec hydroelectric plant, and there was also some pressure to do so from within our firm. We sent about eight employees up to James Bay to...get a feel for what the situation was. They came back and we made the decision that it did not make sense to support the objectors. Our rank and file wrote ads talking about how the final effect of the plant was going to be beautiful. The point is that how we create a business environment [in relation to] a long-term social cause...is very important here."

"What this company feels like is more important than what the firm does; what I personally value here is the definite culture, one I'm comfortable with. It's politically and socially progressive. We avoid some actions that are endemic to the business world; we're not just making money here. We are staffed by people who wouldn't survive [in] many business cultures."

"The only way you can get people to take responsibility for their own actions is for them to see that the institution takes responsibility too. For example, when we saw milk prices falling in 1991, we went to our suppliers and told them they were not charging enough. We felt that the effect on farmers and on the whole social fabric...would be devastating if prices were allowed to fall. We paid a premium based on the average price we'd paid for the previous few years. The point is we do the right thing. We took about $500,000 right off the bottom line but we put our money where are mouths are."

"It's tough to be committed when you don't understand the mission of the company. So our mission statement really works to make our mission clear."

"Every day I come to work I feel I make a difference....That's what people believe in here. For me this has been the greatest time of my life."

"Quality is important here. Ben is never happy with the final products and always pushes for perfection. Similarly, they're never happy with survey results....Ben always says if you don't continue to improve—continuous improvement—someone else will move to the top. You have to give your people such a philosophy....That's what we do here."

"People work here because they think they can make a difference—in the environment, etc.—and because they're proud of how we treat people. It's also fun to work here."

On Value-Based Hiring

"For me one of the most interesting things here is the concept of expanding the role of business beyond just supplying jobs and making money. We're open to things we haven't figured out. The typical business is very smug, very economic, and has a very unimaginative view of what business can accomplish. So anyone interested in what the business world can do to solve problems won't find answers in the traditional business. Here, I frequently have to speak for the company and feel comfortable talking of our shortcomings too. I know if an article quotes me as having some doubts, I won't be locked out of my office when I get back."

"I grew up in Vermont. I went to college for a few years and then got into the dairy industry working for a farmers' co-op....I came here four years ago because I felt like it was a place where politically and culturally I felt at home.

"At the office and at the plant levels we pay very competitively. But at [the] managerial levels and up is where we could run into a problem. Most middle managers come from Vermont locally. We're paid well by Vermont standards but could make two times more in most other firms. It's therefore most important that we find someone who can live with that salary limitation. We offer a comfortable wage and an opportunity for growth. But if you're looking to get rich, this isn't the place for you. As a result, we get competent people who fit in."

"This is a very prestigious job, working for this company, and that's one of the reasons we get unbelievable quantities of applicants. There were 600 to 700 applicants just for my job, for instance. That's why selection decisions here are very careful, and everyone, including the people you'll be working with, gets involved in making the decision."

"If you're motivated by money, this is not the place for you. You come here for the social side and for the values of the organization."

On Securitizing

"At Springfield we had to make a decision when demand didn't match supply for a while. We let the third shift paint fire hydrants in town....This company's impulse is to hire as carefully as possible and then to maintain employee security as best we can."

On Hard-Side Rewards

"We shower our people with recognition. We pay good salaries and benefits and then recognize them at every opportunity. We have barbecues for all three shifts, the Joy Gang gives out trinkets like small flashlights and pocketknives. We even have a 'graft box.' Whenever someone does something special, an employee can come in to the graft box and dig out something he or she likes. The box is filled up by the 'graft' we get from suppliers who give items to managers."

"The pay policy here is to pay above market for entry-level employees, about 120 percent over what they'd expect in the surrounding community. But we pay below market for top-level employees, only about 65 percent of market. Yet we have an extremely low turnover at the upper echelons of management. I came here to build and run the plant. I saw this as an opportunity to grow and to enjoy myself while working, and it's worked out that way. I feel the company respects me for what I do. Why would I go anywhere else?"

On Actualizing

"I started working here after I answered an ad for someone who liked to play with his food and keep good records. I'd been a teacher-chef at a culinary institute in Montpelier. I started out just helping Ben and the others come up with new yogurt recipes like Fire and Ice and Wavy Gravy. But the thing is, this company lets you grow, and so people here find a niche and go with it. I'd like to be able to do it more, perhaps, but I've found an outlet in working with the Ben & Jerry's Joy Gang. I get to sing every day and can try out alter egos at work. How many companies let you perform [like that]?"

"We have nine teams in the plant and we train the people in statistics and...then let them analyze the problems and make their presentations."

"We've lost eight people this year in my department alone due to promotions to other [Ben & Jerry's] facilities. We sent six off to St. Albans to set up the new plant, for instance."

"We believe in promotion from within. Some people assume that as they gain knowledge they'll...move on, but it turns out that as [they] gain knowledge our people stay—because of promotion from within and because of the firm's social values and mission."

"Chocolate Chip Cookie Dough was one of our biggest flavor successes and it was created by a team of workers. We tried it for five years and finally [it worked]! They solved all the problems. Now we're using teams to create the new distribution center."

"I love it here; I come in...at 6 a.m. seven days a week...because being here just makes me feel good. I come in and sort of get my fix, and then go back home."

"Our people really get involved. For example, we have festivals around the country, day-long celebrations for customers—in Chicago, at Golden Gate Park, and so on. We often send 20 people to these Ben & Jerry's festivals, and most of them are production people. They're good employees who say they want to go to the events. So we send them off; just giving them the opportunity is great for them. They go out and represent the company, give out free ice cream, and represent us."

"For many employees I really believe that Ben & Jerry's is the best thing in their lives. Up here in Vermont there are long, cold winters and lots of isolation. This is the place they can come for respect, and where they can make a mistake and still continue. I guess employees also get a safety net, one that they wouldn't have otherwise, in terms of our benefits and our employee-assistance plans, for instance. Some employees test us: Are you really going to do it? they ask. And they find the company usually comes through. Managers will take in the children of a single mother who's an employee here who's had a short-term problem....It can be a delicate balance, though, encouraging responsibility while helping people out."

"We train production workers to do the screening and selection for our new plant. One said to me, 'My wife said to me how lucky I am.' 'Why?' I asked. 'Because I'm making twice as much money as I would be otherwise and because Ben & Jerry's turned me into a new person and let me be who I had the potential to be.' You people want my opinion; it isn't just 'do what they tell me.' I have so much more control over my life."

Delta Air Lines

On People-First Values

"Our employees have a sense that the company is committed to them. I was speaking to one employee recently who was in here from a task force studying our flexible benefits. He said to me, 'I always know Delta will do the best thing for me, so I don't have to worry about my own career decisions.' I recently spoke to a class of new flight attendants who had come over from Pan Am when we absorbed them. I noticed that several people in the back were crying as I spoke and I asked them why. They said, 'You don't know how good it feels; we've never had a company officer talk with us before.' They sent their class instructor flowers because, they said, it feels so good to know you really care. At Delta, employees know that the company will always do the best for their employees."

On Double-Talk

"We schedule a lot of meetings. We have general personnel meetings a minimum of once every 12 to 18 months in which the top personnel officers meet in groups with all the departments. In addition to that, we have local meetings—formal meetings—in which operating managers and personnel department officers meet with all employees in groups of 20 to 40."

"We have what we call networking, which comes down in large part to a very open open-door policy. Everyone in top management is always available and welcomes comments and calls from all employees."

"I'll always reserve enough time to be visible and speak with employees when I travel. And I get eight to ten calls per week with suggestions...and [I] see about three people per week who [ask] to meet with me. We also have an effective grievance process. It's not really formalized, but everyone understands that you can go up the chain of command to your regional manager, our EEO office, etc."

"People have limited authority when it comes to disciplinary action. For example, no one can be dismissed unless that's reviewed by the division head and by the head of personnel for Delta. Supervisors can give warnings and things such as days off without pay. But to demote, reclassify, and certainly dismiss (and there are very few actions like any of these), the action must be appropriate and must be approved at the top levels."

On Communion

"The family spirit begins from the first day. At the orientation meetings, top management comes to talk to all the new classes; for instance, the head of personnel speaks to all the new employees [800 to 900] each month. We speak of our open-door policy, and what we're all about."

"There are always subtle reminders that we're all in this together. For example, the programs for free flights that employees get are based on length of service; there's no special privileges for any of our people. There are also common break areas for all our employees,...including pilots, mechanics, [and] cleaners.

"We award service...pins for the first year and then every five years of service but at twenty years we have a big banquet for all 20-year people and their spouses. The last one [was attended by] 7200 people, for instance. Our chairman speaks, most of our top management get up and speak, and we bring in the people from all over the world. We also have many other occasions to get together. We have luncheons by...department every one to three months during the year...and frequently show a short video describing the history of the department, old films showing the company's evolution, and so forth. At the 20-year banquet our top seniority people are always introduced individually. We ask them to stand and be recognized and to tell us a little bit about the history of Delta."

On Transcendental Mediation

"Our philosophy is passed on verbally, starting with the orientation meetings. We always talk about our commitment to our people."

On Value-Based Hiring

"We don't have to recruit; we get about 4000 applications per day. We do go to colleges and do have open houses for flight attendants. We have no management training program per se. Some college specialties go directly into functional areas like finance. But our operational people normally come in as aircraft cleaners. Forty percent have college degrees and 5 percent have master's degrees. Within two to three years they move into ticket agent positions....We also have some summer college internships and find many good folks through that."

"Who are we looking for? We're looking for people who can work in our team environment, who have a strong work ethic, who have the basic education required, and who are well rounded and who...can deal well with the customers. Some of our applicants say, 'We won't start at the bottom' (for instance, cleaning aircraft), and we generally end up not hiring these....What we get therefore are employees who are willing to go along with and work in our team environment."

"Personnel people are looking for team players when they interview."

On Securitizing

"We have a no-layoff policy that has been in force for 35 years."

"To help protect our no-layoff policy, we keep a small temporary workforce of about 5900 people in airport operations and regional offices. Our business has many seasonal changes,...for example, being heavy in summer. We also keep a lot of part-time people who are trained and in a 'ready-reserve' program who can work for a daily rate and are ready to step in if demand warrants."

On Hard-Side Rewards

"We pay at or above industry standards because we get more productivity, and [we] cross-utilize our people. We probably have the best pay rates and benefits program in the industry. For example, a lot of the employees from Western Airlines got as much as $800 raises when we took over that airline, and Pan Am employees got $400 to $500 per month raises. In general, and amongst specialties like flight attendants,...there's very little turnover because they get great pay relative to the industry. We feel if we take care of their financial needs, they can concentrate on our customers."

On Actualizing

"We have a bid system for new jobs. Any nonmanagement, supervisory position is posted and you can bid for the job. For management and supervisory positions, the...employees here are generally chosen by the managers in charge. Especially for department head and other key jobs, there is a list of key people maintained in personnel, and we make this information available internally, sharing the names of potential candidates."

"We're careful about selection, in part because promotion from within drives our whole company."

"Our annual evaluations are formal and include an interview. We touch on whether the employee is making progress or not, review his or her past performance, and discuss where that person is going with his or her career. The formal evaluation forces the supervisor and employee to communicate and talk about the person's career path."

"We use a lot of task forces and similar types of groups. They make presentations to senior management on how we can solve problems."

Federal Express

On Employee Commitment

"I don't just work for Federal Express; I *live* [for] Federal Express because of what the company does for me."

"How do we keep our top commitment? That's the biggest question I get, and when I thought about it I came up with an answer that surprised me. We make our employees our business partners. Most employees want to do a good job and will if they're properly motivated. We hire good people, tell them how our rules work, and try to give them what they want—a good working environment, an opportunity to get ahead, job security, and we keep our people informed. Our people feel it's their company."

"Our people are very committed. For example, one of our trucks broke down. Two employees jumped into two smaller vehicles, went out to the truck, put [the packages] in their smaller trucks and took off and delivered them. As another example, 75 employees in one of our stations had to operate for a while with only one manager. The station basically continued to operate as it always did; they took care of all customers, and everything went smoothly although several managers were gone."

"I was with several other airlines but I've only seen one, Federal Express, that works at treating people as fairly as we do here. Others talk about treating people fairly, but we really do it. There are a lot of specific examples of this: our Open-Door policy; the guaranteed fair treatment policy; a very careful selection process; the promotion-from-within policy; our training, in particular the leadership institute; the fact that all managers are required to take 40 hours of training per year; encouraging all our hourly people to take periodic technical training; the fact that all our officers and managers must take a test every six months on our products and also make sales calls; extensive communication, including Fed Ex TV, publications, what the company is up to, and so on. We have an open, informal culture. Anyone can walk into Fred Smith's office without an appointment—no appointment is required. And this is true up and down the line. Employees are encouraged to interact with managers, and managers are encouraged to go to the stations and chat with people. We care about them and are accessible. You also can't discount people's success here as a big motivator: We've grown fast and people have had lots of promotional opportunities. We also try to maintain above-average wages and benefits, as good or better than our competitors. Last but not least, most of our people here—our officers and managers—are good people. Office politics is minimized. Federal Express also expects you to take your vacations and so people here are pretty well rounded, nice people."

"What would I tell owners of another firm that wants to win their employees' commitment? First, that you must start at the top. It costs a lot of money to institute a program like this, but it's worth it. It also takes a lot of time, and I can't really say you're going to save X number of dollars. Here at Federal Express we're getting better at putting costs on human resource management, but it's still hard to put a dollar value on the results."

"It's important to have commitment in this business because the unexpected at Federal Express happens all the time."

On People-First Values

"Our basic values here are people, service, profit. We know we can't have great profitability if we neglect our people because one services the other. If you take care of your people, they will take care of your customers, and that's the philosophy that drives this firm."

"What would I tell owners about winning employees' commitment? You have to begin by asking yourself, How do you really feel about people?"

"What would I say is the key to commitment? Make sure to have your employees involved in the decision-making process, and make sure you work for your employees, not that they work for you."

"Our basic value here is in the *Managers' Guide*. It says, 'I have an inherent right to be treated with respect and dignity, and that right should not be violated.'"

"Everything else the company does is a spin-off from the basic idea that I have an inherent right to be treated with respect and dignity and that that right should not be violated. The question for companies is, 'How can you make sure all else comes from that?' We do it here with things like our leadership institute, our TV network, our annual surveys, and with our guaranteed fair treatment process. But everything stems from our people-first values."

"Much of what we do here is to make sure our realities and our ideals are as much in synch as possible. For example, people see they can seek redress if there's a problem."

"At Federal Express the biggest problem a manager can have is not taking care of his or her people. That's one of the things the leadership training and [the] survey-feedback-action process are for. We'll help them get their house in order and develop an action plan."

On Double-Talk

"Our guaranteed fair treatment program is based on the idea that you have to foster feelings of individual significance and importance amongst your employees. And that all stems from our core people-first values. There's no way to generate this from the bottom; you must espouse it from the top down. And so it's Fred Smith's values, his people-first values; he fosters it and we've institutionalized it."

"The heart of the system is respect for the individual, our justice system, and our survey process. We put our people first. We have the guaranteed fair treatment process that helps guarantee all grievances are dealt with. And we use the survey-feedback-action survey process to continuously monitor our employees as a sort of manager's report card. With SFA, when people are fair they come out OK. The trick is to treat your people right."

"It's important that we get information about the company to the employees before the information gets public. That's one reason we have the daily Federal Express TV. Seventy percent of our employees see it daily, and we replay it every day."

"We have a very open-door philosophy. People do not hesitate to come to the manager. We rarely have to use the guaranteed fair treatment process because of this open-door philosophy."

"We have a lot more people in personnel than most firms—700 to 800 in personnel out of about 100,000 employees total. And remember, we also have another 100 to 200 people separately, just in our communications area. People can therefore call in and ask questions at least once per month in a process that Fred Smith calls 'one on one.' If there's a reorganization or something, the 'one on ones' might [come] more often."

"We encourage people to learn the process, to write to the chairman and take advantage of our open-door process whenever they need to. And our supervisors and managers soon learn that you have to keep that open-door process open and follow our values or you don't get into or stay in management."

"Our guaranteed fair treatment process is a grievance procedure that allows and encourages grievances to go up the management hierarchy to an appeals board at the top. The team will review all complaints based on unfairness issues. Employees know that the worst that can happen to them is that the top people will review their complaints. The process ensures fairness. We also have an annual survey—SFA—each year that monitors employees' views of the company, compensation, leadership, recognition programs, and generally how the company is doing. It's like a report card for bosses."

"There is a lot of communication around here. People therefore see they have a great stake in the firm. [We have] at least one meeting per week in which people can call in with opinions. Some questions that managers get at these meetings are really tough. But they're handled right on the TV broadcast. For example, someone might call in and say, 'I'm John Doe on-line from Tallahassee. Why are we putting money on new planes when we're cutting back on our compensation?' Questions are handled immediately, on-line."

On Communion

"One of the things our front-line employees look for is whether their manager is willing to help them. We've got to be willing to help them, and we need to get back to them if they have a question or comment. Most important, though, we'll get right out there and chip in with them, loading the trucks, etc. We'll work right along with them if need be."

"We are not your typical hierarchical company here. We are loose and open, and while there are some perks for officers there's nothing blatant, even for Fred Smith. For example, Fred Smith has no parking spot; there are no company cars and certainly no image of a privileged few. There's no executive lunchroom. Our officers have modest offices; they're nice, but not spectacular. We do as much as we can to minimize the differences between the nonexecutive levels and the rest of the employees."

On Transcendental Mediation

"Our LEAP process is used to prepare people for management. Do you take into consideration the employees' feelings? That's important here. To be eligible for management you have to get through LEAP, and only about 50 percent get through [that] program."

"Fred Smith has laid out what we expect managers to do in our *Managers' Guide,* and we're tested on it periodically. We keep testing on the management principles and our different processes to make sure all our managers stay in touch with our policies. And for every policy, the *Guide* says, Here is the policy and here is why we have it."

"Most firms have their values posted, but these are real values here that govern our business. I suppose that no company can ever have their real values completely congruent with their ideal ones. But at Federal Express there's less of a gap—and more of an ability to reduce the gap—than anywhere else that I'm familiar with. In most other companies you see managers doing one thing and saying another. Here gaps like that are very, very small."

"How do you change people's values? Most of our people grew up here and learned our values that way. When the Flying Tiger people came in, some of the older guys didn't believe a thing that we said. I've seen a remarkable change in the Flying Tiger people: They're starting to say,...'This does work.' We did this by making sure they all had the *Manager's Guide,* by giving them our leadership classes. We built in our norms."

"One of the key roles of our leadership institute is to translate our culture and values into meat-and-potato terms, to try to get it down to 'What does it mean?'"

"All our managers go through the leadership institute. The management guide is the 'bible' of the company. In the leadership institute we'll emphasize what the company stands for—its values, what it expects of you, the obligations of management, management integrity, ethics, quality, and dealing with diversity."

On Value-Based Hiring

"Supervisory selection is very careful here. I just hired two new managers and they have to go through 11 weeks of training. They get leadership courses that all managers are required to take periodically."

"Leadership selection is very careful. We look for validated leadership dimensions. We start with a one-day 'Is management for me?' program. This helps people determine 'if they can do it' by, for example, presenting situations such as 'What would you do if...?' About 20 percent of our people fall out after this day. We then emphasize self-appraisal of their skills by management candidates, we send out peer-assessment questionnaires (we pick out three to ten of the person's peers and let them assess him or her), and set up a panel interview of senior managers and directors to interview the person."

On Securitizing

"We have a no-layoff policy; they'll do their best not to lay off employees. Layoffs are something that Mr. Smith and Mr. Perkins are committed to avoiding."

"We have a no-layoff *commitment*, not a no-layoff *policy*. If we get in times that are so bad, we might have to downsize, but we've never done that and probably never will. Our people therefore get a sense that the company cares for them and protects their interests."

On Hard-Side Rewards

"We give a lot of recognition awards. There's Bravo Zulu awards, pins, stickers, Golden Falcon awards for those who go above and beyond the call of duty to keep the customer happy, Gold Star awards for the five top employees in the company each year (who get from $3000 to $25,000 for doing a great job), and a suggestion award program, among others."

On Actualizing

"Our employees participate to unprecedented levels. We have quality-action teams, which we pull together, and [we] use the process to find the root causes of problems. For example, in one location we had a problem in that we couldn't get the packages off the planes fast enough; they were often 15 minutes late. It turned out the people solving the problem were the workers; they all had an opportunity to participate, and they improved the process."

"Career opportunities are posted each week. They list the specifications, and you apply, sending the job-change application to the hiring manager, who may get as many as 300 [applications]. Managers weed through these and decide who they want to interview. You really only use the personnel department as a resource in assisting us."

"One of the things the couriers like here is the employee involvement. They have the freedom to do their jobs—to decide how to run their route. It's their business to run. It's great; you have 'your customers.' We also have quality-action teams to analyze problems and make suggestions. The result is high commitment. You'll get an employee coming in and saying, 'I'm going to midtown; I'll take that package for you and drop it off when I get there.'"

"We have a strong promotion-from-within policy. Internal candidates always have an opportunity for promotion. All our managers have grown up in the company. Everyone knows that if you work hard and learn, you can succeed here."

"The best I can be is what I can be here."

"We have a problem in America; we put employees on a job, then don't let them use their minds. You have to empower employees. You have to empower them and get them to the point where they are willing to fail, if need be."

"I have been allowed to grow. People here are not turned on by money. The biggest benefit is that Federal Express made me a man. It gave me the confidence and self-esteem to become the person I had the potential to become."

"That's what Federal Express does for its people. It gives you the confidence, the self-esteem."

"One question is how do you keep people from getting burned out in their jobs—how can you take their work and change it and keep them satisfied? People, like some in our call center, have expanded their jobs while others have gotten involved in team-based quality efforts. The idea is to keep giving them the opportunity to broaden themselves and their jobs."

Goldman, Sachs

On People-First Values

"One of our most important principles is 'Our people are our greatest asset.' And we follow through with this in our actions."

"Top management has done a lot to show that employees really are our greatest asset. For example, people here don't get threatened by other people at work. There's no mental intimidation here; you can't tell someone, 'I'm firing you,' without going through a careful approval process first."

"It's the personal interest we show to all people that underscores this."

"How you treat people is very important here."

On Double-Talk

"It's a meritocracy here and not a pyramid, really very horizontal. You're on a team and most importantly you must 'post' each person on what's happening all the time. You must call anyone below, at, or above your level to make sure everyone is posted on what's happening on your project. This ease of communication is essential, and everyone here therefore knows what's happening. This stress on 'posting' is impressed on everyone from the top."

"You can call any of the top 10 people in the firm, and they'll call you right back."

"Employees get a list of all employees' home addresses and phone numbers and that includes all the top partners."

On Communion

"People are made to feel part of something here; you're part of a team."

"We have a very flat organization here, so that everyone gets exposed to all areas and all decision makers very quickly."

"Orientation begins almost at once with the Goldman, Sachs in Perspective program, which takes one week. Everyone begins working together and meeting together at lunch, breakfast, cocktail parties, etc. From the start, everyone learns to share information. Everyone learns that this is a relationship business and a relationship organization and that everyone needs to be involved."

"At the end of the day everyone shares in the process. Everyone here is working long hours; no one hands you work and walks out the door."

On Transcendental Mediation

"We're very careful here that all is done right; we never get sloppy."

"It's clear to everyone that we have a commitment to excellence."

"You won't find any memos saying things like 'You said this or you said that.'...At Goldman, Sachs, your word is what counts."

On Value-Based Hiring

"As with all of our human resource activities, we take our responsibility for selecting new hires very seriously. Every year, the firm nominates team captains, an appointment which is considered an honor, to help us build a positive relationship with each school at which we recruit. Each campus visit includes time set aside for getting to know the professors, having dinner with students and faculty members, in addition to extensive interviewing both on and off campus. After passing an initial interview, a candidate typically goes on to meet with 10 to 15 other people before he or she is hired. Although this requires a great deal of time and energy, we believe it is well worth the extra effort. And everyone is more than happy to get involved in the process, including our most senior-level personnel. Ask 10 partners to attend a meeting to discuss recruiting, and all 10 will do whatever they have to do to be there. Why? Because they really do believe that Goldman, Sachs can only be as good as its people."

"We're looking for candidates who are intelligent, team players, flexible, self-confident, and who have a sustained pattern of success, be it in athletics, music, civic commitments, or some other. We also want people who are creative and who have good interpersonal skills. We hired from over 50 undergraduate schools last year."

"One common experience many of our candidates have is some solid prior work experience."

"We don't do any formal testing but do very careful background checks. After an offer is made, our investigating agency checks for possible criminal background, actual school experience, etc. The person's boss does not review this background information, however. The investigations are in part due to the very responsible nature of our business, and in part due to the governmental regulations governing those hired in the securities and banking industries."

"You must want to be challenged and must thrive on wanting to be successful to work here."

On Hard-Side Rewards

"The firm bonus is equal to 20 to 25 percent per year of your base salary, but as you become more senior you also get a merit bonus and then, for some, the bonus soon begins to exceed the salary. There's also profit-sharing contributions to our retirement plan for everyone."

"Goldman, Sachs compensates everyone very generously. No one talks first about money here, however. They come here for the culture and because they want to be on the best team."

On Actualizing

"People really understand that Goldman, Sachs as a whole is willing to take a chance with people from the inside. It's not formal, but we all understand that we bring in people and then promote from within."

"We have developmental reviews that get at the question 'Where would I like to be?'"

"New employees are assigned to a 'deal team' almost at once."

"At a relatively young age our new employees get enormous responsibility very quickly."

"Autonomy and independence to do one's job comes almost at once; no one is looking over your shoulder here."

"Even our young people often start out handling millions of dollars of responsibility. And at a meeting with a client, the partner in charge will often not talk first at the meeting, but the youngest one will. At Goldman, Sachs, you take the responsibility and you're supported by the team. That's what attracts people to Goldman, Sachs, the ability to make the decisions early."

"Every day you must be willing to get up early and play, and you must be 'on' every day. I think it's unique; expectations are high and things are different every day. Everyone here is really sharp; they're bright, team players, and enthusiastic."

"The work here is interesting, challenging, and we think we hire the brightest and best people and then encourage them to work with their teams."

IBM

On People-First Values

"Respect for the individual has always been used as a criterion in everything we do here."

"Creating commitment is not just programmatic, just your recruiting practices, and so on. It has more to do with the environment you create, and that depends on communications and the competence of management. That's one of the reasons we stress communications skills, even of first-level supervisors, because the supervisor-employee link is essential. Obtaining commitment also depends on a strong network of values and beliefs...that give the process integrity. It's not just our system of full employment."

On Double-Talk

"We think our employees are much more empowered and autonomous today. We use our survey to find out how empowered they think they are. We've created an index (Latin America is highest in participation and empowerment, for instance) and also monitor how committed are our people to the company."

"I don't think you can ever listen enough, and you must have a formal way to do that. That's partly what empowerment is all about."

On Transcendental Mediation

"Our officers host the top patent people, for instance. It's very symbolic."

"All we do flows from our basic values; you must have the basic values and beliefs."

"When a unit's morale goes down, the only reason can be management neglect. That's why we spend so much on training in values and beliefs."

On Value-Based Hiring

"We tell recruiters, 'Think of how much you're encumbering this company for: If you were buying real estate, you'd have to go to the board of directors of IBM to get approval for the kind of investment you're making in the person you are hiring.' Our people thus have tremendous pride in working for IBM."

"In hiring, all our people are very intelligent. We also sort out the colleges that lead the parade for electrical engineers, mechanical engineers, etc., and then urge our units to get a high percentage of recruits from these schools. We look for achievement-oriented people, so grades are very important. We're looking for high GPAs from the right schools and the right disciplines. Our new people also have to buy into IBM's values, or you quickly self-select out."

"We believe that the destiny of our company is the quality of people who come to work for us. That's part of our creed. That's why we put so much stress on being the employer of choice in the areas in which we recruit. We...want everyone to take great pride in our company."

On Securitizing

"We are still deeply committed to job security and full employment, and I believe our employees will still rank 'full employment' as one of the top manifestations of our respect for the individual."

"With today's downsizing, we've had to do many unusual things. We've retrained over 70,000 people, for instance."

On Hard-Side Rewards

"We are a meritocracy and I think we run the closest thing to that in the world. We're striving more for pay-for-performance today so that pay here is a function of the employee's own performance and that of his or her unit as well as the company as a whole."

"All our employees have been on salary since 1958."

"IBM has always been heavy on rewards and recognition, in other words, heavy on monetary awards, sales recognition, and special events to recognize performers."

Mary Kay

On People-First Values

"Why are we committed here? I think it's the deep culture and philosophy of the company. You identify with a company and a person who 'walks their talk' and here we know we all follow the Golden Rule for our sales force and our management team. As a supervisor, you know you must not take unfair advantage and must see that you act judiciously. Do the right thing is everything here."

"We work hard to make sure the Golden Rule is followed here. We try and attract the right people. Technical aspects are secondary. The main thing is what kind of a person is this. We're not big on staff meetings, and we're not at all bureaucratic. We have lots of good role models. We're big on supervisory training. We conduct attitude-feedback surveys. And management works hard to stay in touch by walking around and speaking to employees."

"The Golden Rule flows to all we do and is the basis for everything we do. We try to instill it in all our employees, the fact that this is the core value."

"What would I tell a president" To go back and see how you treat your employees. Are you fair? Go back to your basic people values and policies. All our people are committed to doing that and in human resources part of our job is communicating that culture."

On Double-Talk

"We have a very explicit open-door policy here. Employees know they can always go to Mary Kay and to the other top executives; they can go right to them."

"In disciplinary matters, the last recourse is a committee of executive vice presidents. In some dismissal cases, for instance, we've reinstated the people because we felt they hadn't been treated right."

"We have open-door appeals for disciplinary matters but they generally don't go beyond the person's own head of his or her department. I'd go to the supervisor's boss, or to an officer, but beyond that it would go to a committee of executives and that generally does not happen."

On Communion

"It's a nice company. People are nice to each other and, really, my best friends are at Mary Kay."

"There is a feeling of shared ownership here. We have a common mission—serving the beauty consultants, being nice..., profit sharing, and taking care of all of our employees (all our plants are air conditioned, for instance)."

"We have lots of group meetings. There's an annual luncheon for recognition of perfect attendance. There's a luncheon once per year for those with 10 or more years with the firm, which Mary Kay and Richard Rogers attend. There are annual employee meetings; the president speaks of year-end results, goals, and our profit-sharing plan and the whole financials of the company."

"Our highest award is the Miss Go-Give Award. It's for the individual who has shared the most with the most people. She's nominated by her peers in a giving and loving spirit. Sales directors are eligible. Miss Go-Give is a person who has supported her own consultants and other consultants too. Remember, we use the adoption system. A sales director does not get any remuneration for another's consultants. It's the Golden Rule in action."

"We don't talk about selling cosmetics. It's more a sharing and caring approach."

On Transcendental Mediation

"If my phone rings and it's a sales rep with a first order who needs a product delivery fast, I'll get it for her because we all know we're part of something that's bigger than we are, and that's serving the customer."

"We work hard at telling stories and showing videotapes and talking up how the company was when Mary Kay started it. The whole firm is rich with stories of how she succeeded."

"In addition to the Golden Rule, we never forget who our customers are; they're our independent beauty consultants-contractors. And we remember that we have to support them because that's our mission. Supporting these people drives this entire company. How you answer the phone, returning calls quickly, taking care of that customer, that's everything here. That beauty consultant needs to feel that she has a touchstone here and that if she has a problem we'll fix it. That is drilled into our people, as is the fact that they can each make a difference."

"We emphasize the Golden Rule. We give Mary Kay's book to all our employees and her autobiography as well. So from the first minute with the company you're involved with her philosophy."

"There is much communication of our values. For example, the president meets with the sales force and continually identifies and emphasizes our core values. And we have Mary Kay always talking of the Golden Rule in person or on video."

"Orientation is important here. We have a one-day introduction and overview to the company, and Mary Kay personally speaks to them. She always talks values and Dick Bartlett talks about the need for communication. We have some discussion of company rules, but the big weight is on what this company is all about. On the first day you also learn something about our benefits."

"The essence of what we keep talking about in our orientation sessions is how dependent we are on a highly motivated sales force. We won't have our jobs without quality products and customer service, and we need to focus on delivering those products. 'No matter who you are you somehow touch those people' is what we emphasize. We also talk about ethics and the importance of people's values and in particular fair treatment to everyone. We emphasize that this is a good place to work and that our jobs all touch people's lives and make their lives better. Something in this company attracts people; it's a very positive company."

"What accounts for our commitment? Talking about our values and the essence of our company over and over again. Even if Mary Kay may be telling the same story, even if you've heard it for 10 years, it all emphasizes the tradition, and our beliefs and values are handed down from generation to generation. That's what we want here, and that's what we want to emphasize, so we're constantly communicating that, and our values and beliefs will live on."

"The first thing I would tell a CEO who wants to get commitment is to ask, 'What's important to you? What do you want? What is the most important thing to you?' I'd tell them they have to have a mission, something that [their] people can identify with and effect. And I'd tell them to live it, to communicate it in ways they understand and then train their people in how to do it. Keep reinforcing it, keep associating what you want with good stuff, not with negatives. Remember that people do want to work hard for you and do the right thing. Be honest about the values you communicate and how you do it. Remember, you can't do it with smoke and mirrors."

On Value-Based Hiring

"Selection differs from job to job. With assemblers, our biggest problem is to sort through the applicants; it's sometimes hard to cope with the numbers. We look here for employment stability and maturity, not job experience. We do little testing, just test for drugs and use Equifax. Our personnel group does the initial interview, then there's a second interview with the supervisor. In hiring phone people, we do some initial screening in which we're looking for a positive attitude for our phone service people. For professionals we do no testing. The candidates talk to several people, and we don't have any structured interview formats. It's about 30 minutes for the first interview; then the second interview might take two hours. Higher-level professionals might be interviewed for a full day and possibly a second day."

On Securitizing

"We had to lay off 50 to 60 people in 1985 but that was the only time we had done so in 30 years. Since then we've emphasized using part-time and temporary employees to avoid layoffs."

"We tried when we had to lay off our people in 1985 to lease them to another company. It was a very unpleasant experience. We have since then tried to stay lean and to depend on temps and only hire when it's absolutely needed. We're also much smarter about hiring part-time people now."

"It's really hard to be terminated here, because there's always ample opportunity to bring performance up to standard."

On Hard-Side Rewards

"We did an attitude-feedback survey and our profit-sharing plan came out number 1. It's very generous and in 1990 and 1991 we put in about 15 percent of the employees' pay. After about 10 years, even assembly workers could leave with $60,000 to $70,000 in their fund."

On Actualizing

"Our promotion-from-within system is very effective. We use job posting and there are may success stories in here—for instance, secretaries [who] moved up to management."

"We use what we call CAT teams—creative-action teams—which involve exempt and nonexempt employees in specific projects to improve the company. We started these in R&D and now use them all over—in human resources, in manufacturing, and so on."

"We have always empowered people because we trust them to do the right thing. 'I can make a difference' is what we believe here, and I feel that way here."

"People here can achieve their career potential. Look at me. I started in a branch and moved up to vice president."

"We have a job opportunity program. All our open jobs are posted three times a week. In our appraisals, which are once a year, we ask how can our managers help the employee with his or her career, but in truth we encourage employees to manage their own careers."

"Our creative-action teams are groups that we put together to look at the issues. There are always about 200 teams working, especially in distribution. People are chosen by self-selection and by assignment. One team is now working on our entry into Japan, plant workers are working on plant problems, and so on. In fact our CAT teams do almost all our outside activities such as market planning now."

"We're working on empowerment. We have two pilot groups who still have a supervisor but are basically self-directed. The supervisors are becoming coaches."

"The thing is, for our independent beauty consultants, they all run their business as they choose."

"For our independent beauty consultants, anyone can advance at her own pace, based on her own goals and abilities. It's unlike other firms. In other firms the boss might not like how you part your hair. Here you set and meet your own requirements. And we emphasize for these people that we know they're great."

J. C. Penney

On Employee Commitment

"Even today, you come here and you'll find people shut off the lights when they leave and reuse partly used pages by erasing them. There's a feeling that 'The company is mine.'"

On People-First Values

"There's a high commitment to people, to treat them fairly."

"The commitment comes from the respect for the individual, a commitment on the part of the company to its associates. That produces commitment. It goes back to the Penney idea: Test every action in this wise, Is it fair? That question is brought into our management process on a regular basis, in every decision we make."

"We always try to be honest with our people, and fair in our appraisal of how they're doing."

"The key human resource value here is Mr. Penney's Golden Rule: Do right by your people. We are trying hard to maintain that philosophy. All Penney's people are nice people—they have a heart, and you would relate to them. If they're not nice, they'll be filtered out in the evaluation process. One was alienating people she had to work with; she was pushing them too hard and was too demanding. I told her, 'You must work with people,' because she did not, I guess, perceive herself as unfriendly. She did change her attitude and her relationships."

On Double-Talk

"We try to continuously get employee feedback—about how fair our pay is, benefits, etc. There's a real effort to bring people into the process."

"We have a survey and the chairman does get information and suggestions from the survey and that information is used."

"We have no written appeals process. Before someone is dismissed the dismissal must go through personnel where we review appraisals, time in service, and so on."

On Communion

"Our pay system stresses team playing. Early on we pay in part based on how the unit does—about 15 percent of the person's pay at first-level merchandise manager, 30 percent at senior merchandise manager level, and 30 to 50 percent at the store manager level."

"The team process is important. You're a member of the team, and your vote is as important as anyone's else's. It's the J. C. Penney partnership concept. It's not just one individual but a team that is important."

"A camaraderie is built up here—people liking people and treating people as human beings. They all know they're treated well, and we hear that even more from people who have left us to go elsewhere. Nothing's ever hidden here; any question you ask is always answered."

On Transcendental Mediation

"Penney's is built on tradition and loyalty. We use orientation programs. There's a little museum with Mr. Penney's desk, but the main thing is we're run by managers who have been around for years and the legend gets passed on."

"Communicating our traditions is important. We use orientations, the HCSC meetings, departmental meetings, reading material, our associates' handbook, and keep emphasizing the traditions of management. We especially communicate our traditions by our statement of business ethics, a list of do's and don'ts for our company."

"Mr. Penney used to say, 'You've demonstrated your honesty and value system; now we think you're ready to manage your own store.'"

On Value-Based Hiring

"We use certified interviewing, and our main entrance for our employees is usually through the stores. We tend to look for generalists. We don't usually hire MBAs. Our feeling is we can mold people who are good citizens, who have decent grades, who have high energy levels, and who want jobs at entry-level that are exciting even though initially they don't pay much—about $20,000 to $25,000."

"We are looking for a Penney-type person. You have to like people, be willing to learn, have good interpersonal skills, be outgoing, and be willing to take direction. We are not looking for mavericks."

"We do spend a lot of time asking, 'Does this person fit?' And then we spend a lot of time appraising and training this person to make sure they do fit."

"We're looking for Penney-type persons. They're hard-working, self-motivated, loyal, committed, honest, fair, company-oriented, competitive, and team players."

"We're not looking that much for 'fast-trackers.' We want family-type people, people who may have to move around a lot, people who are good solid people and a lot like our customers."

"The merchandise manager's job is highly time-consuming. If they survive that, they stay and go on to run departments and buy and sell for other departments. Once they go through that initial stage, they usually stay."

On Securitizing

"There's no guaranteed job security but layoffs are very, very infrequent. Perhaps 25 percent of our new trainees leave after a year or so, but after that the turnover is very low and after 10 years with us it's very, very low."

On Hard-Side Rewards

"In the 1960s, store managers may have been paid 90 percent of their pay in incentives. 'It's your business,' they were told."

"Part of the reason we're highly committed is that we get very good pay. All of a sudden, after three years or so, you're making much more than other mid-managers in industry. There's also a lot of recognition via opportunities to move ahead."

"In this industry, we're unique: We pay modest salaries and high incentive payments."

"For senior people, about 30 percent of their pay is based on bonus and about 70 percent on salary. For merchandise managers, about 80 percent of their pay is salary, and 10 to 20 percent is bonus. First-level senior merchandising managers and merchandising managers are paid for their departmental responsibilities, and on a shorter time frame—about 12 times per year. District managers are paid based on the aggregate sales and profits for their districts. They in turn report to regional managers, who are paid based on the sales and profits of all in their region— usually about 70 percent salary and 30 percent bonus. In the corporate offices here we were all paid based on total corporate results up until 1990. Now our pay is based on the performance of our divisions, and there's more discretion built into our pay."

"Lots of things account for our commitment. There's promotion from within, the ability to grow, and the fact that your personal income is very good and tied to performance. We pay better than anyone else in our business, and our store managers make more than anyone else. Similarly, our people in a shipping center will be the highest paid. There may be lean years in the beginning when you're first starting out, but once you move up, your pay is much higher than it would be."

"The pension plan here is such that you have a long-term opportunity to build yourself a meaningful career and also build assets through our profit-sharing plan of a million dollars or more and then retire at age 56 or so."

"The profit-sharing plan is very reassuring. Sometimes when store managers retire from smaller stores they actually retire with more pay or as much as 85 percent of their pay compared to when they were working. They keep working for the love of it."

"For our retirement plan, the last four years are very heavily weighted. You might get 55 percent of your last four years average pay, for instance."

On Actualizing

"We stress promotion from within. It's very, very unusual to hire any management person above senior merchandising manager from outside the company, and we never hire store managers or second-level store managers from outside."

"We are a meritocracy and we're judged on our numbers, much more so than most."

"We do a good job of sitting down with a manager and saying, 'Where do you want to head with your career?' Then after about three years the district manager and store manager sit down with a third-year person and discuss his or her options. At the trainee level, the store manager sits down with the trainee every week to clarify the prior week's training and to provide feedback. At weeks 10 and 21, the store manager must fill out a formal evaluation on the trainee. After that, it's once per year. All this opens up a two-way communication: Here's what I think I'm good at, and the manager of the store says yes or no, here's how you're doing. The process lends itself to career goal discussions. The manager might say, for instance, 'Here's what you've got to do to get to that level job.'"

"From day 1, I was running the store within a store. The philosophy is, We'll give you some guidance but won't hold your hand. You've got brackets to work within....You're made to feel part of a team right away. You know, 'I can buy the material and my decisions are important.'"

"We give people the opportunity to make decisions."

"Regional managers or personnel managers give lists of people who are promotable into corporate positions to the people doing the hiring. The associate will often go to the store manager (or his or her own boss) and say, 'I really have an interest in moving into such and such.' Personnel will then get a minifile on the person, including his or her appraisals,...and review it."

"The Management Resource Inventory is part of every appraisal. It covers where you see yourself going in the company and makes projections into particular jobs. They use the Work Activity Scan Sheet to help fill out the MRI."

"We have an obligation to develop our people to the fullest. You never know how high is high. It's our job to unlock that potential....If you ask them, 85 to 90 percent of our associates would say the company has always been fair to me, given me an opportunity."

"We try to find out what people want to do. I used to ask each of my people, 'What do you want to do 10 years from now?'"

"There's no formal recognition of managers for helping a subordinate's career. We do state that our best managers are those that perpetuate the company, though. On the wall is a Hall of Fame showing our graduates, and there's a tremendous pride in the fact that an officer of the company trained under one of our store managers."

"I tell young people, 'A point of time will come when you cross a bridge, and at that point you will have committed yourself to the Penney company: This is where I want to stake my career.'"

"I gave a talk a few years ago on 'How do you rate a manager?' One of the best measures of a manager's effectiveness is the length of the list of names of those he or she helped to develop careerwise. For me, one of the truest measures of a Penney manager is how many people would put you on the list of those who helped their careers here."

"There's an ongoing dialogue between the managers and associates.... They are always discussing, 'What will this person be doing in the next 12 months, and what are his or her career options?'"

"We promote from within. Ninety-five percent of profit-sharing level jobs are filled by in-company people."

"When I graduated college, my dean told me that he understood I had accepted a job with Penney's. 'What are you going to do?' he said. 'It's a five-and-ten operation. You're starting at $60 a week,' he said, 'but you had offers from Procter and Gamble and GM and IBM that would have started you at twice that amount or more. You'll be at the bottom of the salary ranks forever,' the dean told me. I told him I asked for a description of what the job opportunities would be at Ford and the other companies, and they always said I'd have to wait. As it turned out here I was able to be as good as I could be. Not everyone can be number 1 or 2 in their company, but the important thing is that here you can be as good as you can be or want to be, and you know you'll end up where you should be."

"The promotion process here is fair. If three apply for a job, one will get it, but persons 2 and 3 won't leave the organization [because they didn't get it]. They see that there's a high respect for individuals, and they will have a high respect for the person who got the job because they know he or she earned it."

"I'm a second-generation Penney's person. My father went to New York City in 1915 as an Irish immigrant. He had to drop out of high school and go to work and stumbled into J. C. Penney. He went upstairs and they hired him as a messenger. Then someone gave him invoices to add up, and he did it and became a bookkeeper. They encouraged him to get his high school certificate and then promoted him again and moved him to merchandising. He sold patterns and notions. Then they promoted him to assistant buyer and to buyer and to merchandising manager and all the while he was putting two kids through college. I never realized he had no high school degree or started as a messenger until years later. And when I graduated college I thought that if he could do it and the company could recognize him, how much easier it would be for me with education and hard work to get ahead here, and it was. And many people can tell you stories like that here."

"As a company our people in the stores always had individual store responsibility. They were always in charge of selecting and selling the merchandise and choosing from what was offered."

"There are always opportunities—to become district manager, regional manager, or move into corporate. There's a great deal of opportunity for personal growth, and with our profit-sharing plan you can go into a great retirement, all funded."

"Our initial assignments were always challenging at the merchandise-manager position, even 35 years ago. Back then you had to add up all the stock by hand and had to do that over the weekend while you were running the department during the week. It's a very, very busy job, but with a good merchandise manager you get great experience."

"It's really exciting, to be able to manage your own department right from the beginning. You might, for instance, manage the order for luggage in the Tacoma store. You order it, lay it out, and then watch the customers buy it."

"The new trainee is assigned to a merchandising manager or senior merchandising manager who mentors him and provides guidance. It's a self-administered training program, though. Week by week it's self-administered and you are responsible for your development. After eight weeks the trainee is evaluated. He sits with the store manager, merchandise manager, senior merchandising manager and discusses what needs improvement. They all lay it on the table and tell the trainees where they're weak. If it's in leadership, for instance, the suggestion might be 'Have you thought of a Dale Carnegie course?' or 'You must be more outgoing.'...If the person is already outgoing, the problem might be that he's got to develop his analytical skills. The point is, it's a very frank, outgoing discussion."

"In week 12 the trainees go to Dallas for a training session. They put it all together there and see what their job is all about. After six months we try to change their assignments, to put them in an area where they can assume more responsibility, perhaps running a whole department. At the end of 52 weeks they should move in as merchandise manager. During the first six weeks they're already attending all Penney's Broadcast System [PBS] broadcasts and may help decide on assortment buying. They'll remain as merchandise manager for two or three years and then move on to senior merchandise manager. Meanwhile they're evaluated annually: We set goals at the start of the year—individuals participate in setting them—then midyear we sit down to say, 'Is this where we are?' At the end of the year our comments and results are put down in writing. The process is not time-consuming and works quickly."

"At Burdines or Saks,...the merchandise manager and sales manager jobs are split, one does the buying and the other develops the promotions. Here at J. C. Penney our merchandise manager does it all. He has total responsibility for an area. He buys via the PBS. The merchandise manager knows his projections, his sales estimates, etc. He watches the PBS, knows his history, and might see 300 dress shirts he likes. 'That's what I'll buy for my assortment plan for my store,' he says. He enters all his data into a computer and in come the purchases a while later. He then must work with his people to lay it out and to train his people and keep track of what's selling and what isn't."

"The Penney's management position is the best-kept secret in the world. You don't just operate the store, in a sense you 'own' it. You must have the mentality though; you can't just do jobs in sequence. You're always juggling six balls in the air at once."

"Our people may move around. They may be promoted to general merchandise manager after three to five years as merchandise manager, and then switch to personnel manager. Then they might move to operations manager for a few years."

"We believe here that if you don't make it, it's no one's fault but the person in charge. It means the merchandise manager or senior merchandise manager didn't have the heart to tell the truth earlier in the process."

Publix

On People-First Values

"It's like dealing with your family. My respect is unconditional, even if there still has to be discipline at times."

"You have to put your customers second, after your employees."

"Our real job is to not lose sight of who's really doing the work—the employees. We don't just get them for 40 hours per week. We must deal with the full person. We try to be there if they do have a problem. We have a basic understanding here: If you can't get it across that the employees are respected and worthwhile, and that you want to give them an opportunity to grow and find out what they want in life and help them get it, then you're not doing your job."

On Double-Talk

"Communications are very important here. Management always tells us the truth; there's no deception even when the news is unpleasant. There's always a line of communication because we feel everyone must always know what's going on, why we're doing what we're doing. We send videotapes out all the time, have meetings, and just talk with all the employees. We always want to know what we can do better, or more."

"When I talk with people, it's amazing what they tell me. The important thing is you have to create an environment where people trust you to tell you what they think. The company understands from the bottom of its heart that only by being honest and open will it grow."

"With discipline, it's 'you and me against the problem.'"

"We continually seek inputs—from meetings, from climate surveys, by meeting with hourly workers and supervisors, and so on. These meetings are sometimes like confessions and they tell us everything. Then we'll get back to the managers and tell them what they are doing wrong and they'll usually change."

"All employees know they can call anyone at any time, and they often do."

On Securitizing

"In 62 years we've never laid off a full-time associate. In our company about 60 percent of the employees are part-time, and 40 percent are full-time. In most of our competitors, it's 80 percent part-time and 20 percent full-time."

On Hard-Side Rewards

"We pay more in salaries than our competitors, but we're more efficient. We pay competitive or above-competitors' wages."

On Actualizing

"When I started work here at age 17 I was told that the company was like a smorgasbord, that it would change and that more and more jobs would become available. They told me to watch and look and pick out what's best for me. At 17 that didn't have much relevance but it stayed in my data bank. And over the last 30 years this company has let me move into new positions and grow."

"We don't have budgets here, but you're still accountable. And our store managers do a lot more decision making than they do in most competitors' stores."

Saturn Corporation

On Employee Commitment

"The assumption here is that you're part of the business. Everything you do makes a difference. For example, if you drop a nut you must pick it up because it costs money. Everything you do must be cost-effective."

"I would tell union leaders that if you aren't willing to work twice as hard now, don't do it; this is the toughest job we've ever had. You need total dedication to the plan. But it doesn't mean a loss of power, it's a reaffirmation to really represent people. The union is not giving up all their power. Unions used to watch out for behavior but not be involved in running the business. Here we understand the business and do help run it. Here we represent the majority of people, not just a minority. We have 100 percent union member participation."

"What if there weren't any more promotions and Saturn didn't continue to grow? I never did what I did for career growth. I did it for Saturn. If I was told I couldn't go anywhere, it wouldn't matter. It's not the career or the advancement. I'm doing it because I believe in Saturn and what they're doing here. It makes me mad to hear that Japanese are superior at building cars. We've led the world and will do it again."

"The keys to commitment here are worker involvement, opportunities for career growth, opportunities for training, developing team norms— their own rules to live by on things like attendance—and the chance to always change things by talking about it."

"What would I say to a business owner? Don't fear the voice of the worker. You must be willing to give up some traditional power. Also be sure you're ready to stay with it; it's better to stay with what you have than to start this and go back. We could not get our people to start producing bad cars now."

"You get out on the floor and if you didn't know it was a represented team member, you'd never know it; he's working like an owner."

On People-First Values

"In the late 1970s and early 1980s Japan was eroding the U.S. GM market. The challenge for us was, Could GM build a small car? We put together a team of '99' to look into the fact that there must be a better way than we were doing it then. We went out to find benchmarks and to look at the best practices; we went to Harley Davidson, the Nummi plant, and so forth. What we found was that people seemed to be the key. They wrote a 'Phase 2 Report,' which was the foundation of what we should be. It also described what the UAW-management partnership should be in terms of hiring practices, the risk and reward balance, benefits and well-being, and so on. But the main thing was teamwork. They found that people want to be involved in decisions that affect them, and so we work hard at having a flat organization, consensus management, and trying to get input. That's one of our basic guideposts: Do we get our people's input?"

"Even our ads stress Saturn people-first values. They're ads that project the heart and soul of Saturn—people, quality, commitment."

"I would tell another top manager trying to put in a program like this that you must have the commitment of top management to the people that the program impacts."

"The top management philosophy here is 'The people are an integral part of the business.' That's why they give you continuous training, and you get the feeling that they're really investing in you."

"You go into the keyboard and punch in the numbers of hours you worked. It comes down to trust."

"The company is committed to its people, so its people are committed to it. People had to quit GM to come here; that's commitment."

"Managers are different here. The question is 'Do you really believe in people? Do you really believe their input is important?'"

"One of the main factors leading to high commitment is what you feel about people. From that, you build your job design, your layout, and what you need to support that—what training, what structure, what personnel guidelines, the way people are paid and their attire, whether you need time clocks, where they park, where they eat, their working conditions, the outside environment, everything."

On Double-Talk

"Power is spread throughout the organization. They don't have a long hierarchy here. The point people on each team find the resources they need."

"We have town hall meetings once per month, which are broadcast. We have 500 to 700 people. We try to bring everyone's knowledge base up and you had better know the facts."

On Communion

"In staffing our new company we had a few guiding principles. We were trying to create an equal society—no special parking spots in the parking lot, a cafeteria for everyone, the same clothes for everyone. Most importantly, you can't see who's a manager and who's not."

"We hire all on our own team. Applicants get screening with simulations, and so forth, and then the team makes its decisions on who to hire onto the team."

"On the fourth day of orientation there is a dinner for the new employees and their families."

"The team hires its own members, so once a person is hired in there's great ownership created about who's there and about sharing of work."

"If an issue comes up, the team handles it; all on the team must be agreeable or we don't leave the room until we're 100 percent committed, or [until] at least 70 percent are comfortable with the decision. We know we are responsible to make our jobs more cost-effective, more ergonomic, and so on. So we have much consensus."

"When you're on a team like this you get to know others in the group and feel responsible for them and to them. Now you know you're responsible and thus committed to your team members."

"If a defect goes to the next business team, [they'll] either stop the line or call someone over to look at it and fix it. We watch out for each other."

"All here are salaried, not hourly. There are no time clocks, no security guard. In the old world, we had barbed wire leaning in to keep people from stealing. They don't check to see if you're stealing here; they treat you like adults."

"The partnership [between Saturn and the UAW] makes a big difference. In another company [someone] might represent the union and I'd be the manager and we'd spend 50 percent of our day arguing, not on the floor improving quality and so forth. Here we work toward the same goals. Even how our performance is appraised is the same. We work shoulder to shoulder. We don't necessarily have to be at the same meeting, don't both always have to be there together. When one of us is traveling we take over for each other. We assume responsibility for each other. There's none of that 'This is my role, this is yours.'"

On Transcendental Mediation

"There's a five-day orientation program. On days 1 and 2 we discuss benefits, safety and security, and such things as overview of materials management. On days 3 and 4 we emphasize teamwork, the Saturn mission, and the Saturn philosophy. We have leaders come in to explain what these all mean. Top managers usually do this, and the president of Saturn does it if he's here. We also discuss the risk-and-reward program and the importance of quality and the fact that training is required. We spend time talking about conflict resolution."

"All employees get a copy of our mission card, and go through an exercise to discuss each point on the card. There is another exercise in which they're asked, 'If you saw a team member doing this…what would you do?' or 'If you saw a member living this value, what would you see?' We then brainstorm the answers and discuss them. All the while they're working in teams doing the exercises."

"They do take time to explain to people what they're committing to. Their philosophy is 'We care about the people, and it shows.'"

"What would I tell a business owner? You have to have a philosophy and a mission; you must have that first."

"Our mission is to be a car company but we take a different approach. Our philosophy is to give people a real stake in the business. You might not see any difference [between] our mission and philosophy and [those] at other plants. But here we're trying to give action to these words. We've tried to bring life to a different kind of value system. Your actions will be guided accordingly. You must create a value system that encourages the kind of behavior you want. You must put in an actionable value system that changes how people build cars. You must build the value system. How do we do that? Identify the big or little things that may undermine those values—executive parking spots, executive cafeterias, things like that. If you really want to trust people, you have to also eliminate all those things that say, 'I don't trust you.' If you start with the premise that you trust people and they will do a good job, it takes you in a whole new direction."

"Watch out for the spread between the existing value system and the operative value system—what the organization will actually let you do. People are guided by their values. But don't go by flowery descriptions of a company's values. You must go out to see what are actually the operative values."

"Values are tied to behavior. So you must change values, but do that through your behavior. You cannot create it just with a new philosophy or mission. You must say what is OK to do and then you must work through the actual behaviors. For example, when I started as a supervisor, the values were 'stress efficiency 100 percent' and 'quality is OK if you can get it.' So when people asked, 'What's it really OK to do?' the answer was 'Stress efficiency.' You must change values via behavior—What's OK to do? What's not OK to do? What you've got to do thus isn't so mysterious, once you know where you're going."

"The notion of values is so strong it controls you even when you're not told what to do."

"Another big source of commitment here is a big desire to reinstate our manufacturing base as a leader for the United States. We feel we in auto plants must play a part in that. We can demonstrate that we are really going to make it as a country."

"Someone said, 'It sounds like you're in a cult.' But we're really not. We do not blindly follow. We have hired in real independent thinkers who have real individuality. They are strong-willed, strong-minded. We must manage that so it's not divisive. We're strong individually and want to be good at teamwork. The Japanese are good at teamwork, but are trying to become more individualistic."

On Value-Based Hiring

"For our represented workforce, all have, and will, come from General Motors. They are people who join and who cannot go back to GM and who are physically moving, uprooting themselves and their families. They're people from 130 different plants and 30 different states. They're risk takers to begin with. The typical hourly employee just stayed in one place, in one town."

"The hiring practices here are not extremely innovative. All employees come from GM, so to that extent they're already screened. We have testing—about three-and-a-half hours' worth. There's a four-part battery of math, reading, mechanical comprehension, and spatial relationships for skilled-trades employees. There's other assessment—group exercises in problem solving and team interaction, for instance, which take several hours. There's a team interview. They really decide who gets hired onto their teams."

"It was our hope all along that we'd hire a well-qualified workforce that would fit our environment. Our ownership-commitment philosophy was what we wanted, and taking risks was important too."

"We do prescreening first. We research files, check references, have phone interviews between team members and candidates [using a structured form] and then put them through problem solving, team interviews, and specific skills testing and exercises. Even the nonrepresented workforce goes through careful screening. They don't get testing, but they do get assessment. The interviews are less structured and often the nonrep leader will involve his or her UAW partner in the hiring decision."

"We only want to bring in nonrepresented management type persons who will work as partners with the UAW—collaborative persons. We look for team interaction, problem solving, and therefore use different exercises. But the basic question is always can they work effectively in the partnership area?"

"You make a personal commitment to come here; you give up a lot of things and must move."

"I'm committed to the environmental aspects of what Saturn is doing, things like the bluebird houses [around the plant]. It fits my personal values, and I'm proud of it—the replanted trees, and so on. All kinds of things that show we're responsible."

On Securitizing

"We have 80 percent job security. No more than 20 percent can be laid off. Job security is within my control. If we keep productivity up and quality up, we'll stay here. So we have fewer people and run a tight ship. But quality is a main concern. Remember, we have a 30-day return policy, no questions asked."

"If you build the best car in the world, people will buy it, and you'll stay in business."

"What happens to a person made redundant by work improvements? He might work as a sort of consultant to other team workers, or go on the third shift, or move into other work. Our big concern is getting teams as competitive as possible, and no one will get laid off unless there's a disaster."

On Hard-Side Rewards

"From the beginning we wanted to put compensation at risk. We believe how we pay folks means as much as anything to create commitment. Since putting more at risk goes with more ownership in the business, we're phasing in more of our risk-and-reward system. This year employees have 5 percent at risk, and they can earn that back by meeting their training goals. But there's also a reward potential, with payment based on things like quality. We hope we can phase the risk up to 20 percent, but then employees could also earn much more."

On Actualizing

"We have an immense amount of training here. New people get 320 hours, plus current employees get at least 92 hours per year, and we've tied their salaries to the amount of training they get. If they don't take at least 5 percent of their hours as training, their salaries will be lower than they would with the training. To earn that 5 percent, you must get your training."

"All our employees say this is the toughest job they've ever had."

"Our people are really in charge. They can stop the line; the team works with the supplier to come up with better products; and our teams are responsible for doing 30 work functions. We don't have a quality department or QC program here; quality is the team's everyday task."

"We've done things to give assembly workers bigger jobs. For example, they ride along a platform with the car as it's being assembled, so they have 6-minute jobs instead of 60-second ones. And each team decides how they do their jobs."

"We have flexible manufacturing here, and also people who are flexible."

"We have a formal career-growth process here. You self-appraise yourself and your leader reviews you. You look at the position description and job specs of the position you're interested in. It's your responsibility to get a self-assessment, your team's assessment, and your team leader's assessment in determining whether to move on to a job you're interested in."

"The career-growth process consists of several things. There is a workshop [to which prospective leaders must come but others can volunteer]. Here we use tools such as the skills-assessment disk. People are assessed on 30 different criteria by themselves, and their leaders, and their team [peers]. We use gap analysis tools to compare the person against the job profile. Our employees can do 'window shopping' to consider different jobs here. There's then a coaching session with the team leader prior to and after these sessions."

"They do a lot of things to get such commitment. Part of what they do is their philosophy: We'll look out for you. There's a lot of training and we're taught problem solving, leadership, and they expand our personal horizons with the Excel program, for example. They push you to your limit here. In the plant where I came from you saw burned-out workers: 'Leave me alone' is what they all said. Here the question is 'Have I gone as far as I can go?' They want people to become all they can be."

"The work unit here is run as a business. The company is like 200 separate businesses."

"All team members are responsible."

"People are involved in decisions that affect them."

"You don't have anyone here [on the line] who is a supervisor. You don't experience supervision. We are supervised by ourselves. We become responsible to people we work with every day. What I do affects my people. In other firms you're treated like children and here we are treated like adults. We make up our own work schedule. We do our own budgeting and buying of tools. We decide and improve on the work process by consensus."

"What would I tell your readers? That they should listen; that involvement must be day in and day out. That you must make your people responsible or there's nothing to be committed to. And that they must trust you to do the job. You have to build in ownership. In other firms they talk 'ownership,' but if you needed a part you needed your supervisor's OK. Here you don't."

"Everyone here has something to contribute; the old world treats you like a kid."

"We're all trusted with a lot of confidential information such as the financials. They tell you, Here is the problem; what would you do about it?"

"The career-growth seminar workshop helps you assess yourself. It helps you develop your own career potential. There is a computer disk that helps you analyze your weaknesses and strengths; you assess yourself and your team assesses you. All jobs are posted and the best person gets the job. We also have career counselors; you can go to them as if they're 'head hunters.'"

"They are taking advantage of our skills."

"There is some traditional industrial engineering, but part of the 30 functions is having the team do it. You're really making each person an industrial engineer, and they can use [this skill] 50 hours per week. It's like you draw off each other. Here our 'industrial engineers' work right on the line. In a traditional setting, it would be 'let the IE do it.' Here it's the team's responsibility."

"We're doing all we can to grow our people and use their minds."

"I came here a couple of years ago and the opportunities were thrown at my feet. People never said, 'Do it.' I just took the ball and ran with it. The sky's the limit. It's been one exciting opportunity. I've grown as a person. They've given me training and skills that have given me new insights. I enjoy coming to work; each day it's something different."

"The number 1 thing is involving your people in decisions that affect your people."

"In the traditional organization...we kept making the same mistakes. We felt then there was a tremendous amount of experience in the hands of the people doing the job, but no one ever went back to the people. We put equipment out in front but never used the human resource. Here at Saturn it's different. Teams have overall responsibility for performing to budget, quality, team development, training, everything in the building really. What's different is how we achieve our objectives. We take what the teams suggest and we implement that. So as they work with tools, for instance, they give us feedback. We use that untapped resource, our people, by involving them. Here we get the people involved and avoid the time wasted in grievances and things like that."

"You must get people involved in decision making early on; that leads to commitment. How can you be involved in creating a system and then not be committed to its sources?"

"We build involvement in several ways. With the 30 work functions, and with letting the teams actually do those functions. With keeping the job classifications down to only four. By showing [that] our engineers won't design anything without input and involvement from the teams. With our RASI process. Involving people is essential, and RASI is used for making sure all the team members are involved and that stakes and equities of team members are projected."

"We actually have an advantage over the Japanese because our people can participate in more decisions than do the Japanese, who tend to focus just on their jobs. Here they're involved in choosing suppliers, and so on."

Toyota Motor Manufacturing, U.S.A.

On Employee Commitment

"A medical doctor in practice nearby said that ours are the most dedicated people he's ever seen. He said, 'If I'm running late they all come to my window and say I have to get to work, and they're all like that.' Mr. Cho's favorite example of commitment happened during a snowstorm. The first shift was afraid the second shift wouldn't get here on time so they volunteered to stay, but the whole second shift got here early! If you want to see other examples of commitment, watch our quality circles at work; watch the teams work."

"Toyota is different from other firms. There's great team strength and great trust. Employees feel part of everyday's activities. But the biggest difference is the use of the total person, not just manual dexterity but their minds and suggestions too. Team members have the authority to stop the line, and team members then go to address the problem. And employees see they can trust us. We're fair. There's the Hotline. We're always developing them; we have a lot of communications; there's job security."

"Here's what I would tell your readers. First invest in your people. I've worked in places where they don't give a day's training. The work here is not glamorous at all but we know they're committed to us. We know we have an input. Even if you make a mistake, they make a positive out of it; there's no pointing fingers, [so] no one is afraid to make a mistake."

"Here's what I'd tell the head of an existing plant. First, the entire philosophy must change. There has to be more emphasis on human resources, on operator empowerment, on the training programs needed, and on finding out what the employees need. Forget the high tech. Ask yourself, 'What does the employee need to do his job and what must I do to support it?' But if the budget officer says no—to training, [for instance]—then it won't work. But you have to build trust. You need the ability to have team members suggest ways to get people to cut out people without fear of firing someone. Here team members know that if they eliminate a person from a process that won't cost him a job."

"You could do it in an existing plant with existing people. But if the company is in a loss position, forget it, it's too big a hit. If you're unionized, you must make it clear you'll help them [the union] maintain their union base. You'll need a no-layoff policy. You must train your people. You must put in a new system from the top; the top manager must have a vision. I'd change the industrial engineering department into a training department; we'd have no more time studies. You should train the team members themselves to do the standard worksheets. You'd need lots of training."

"It's a system, a philosophy. You cannot attack it a piece at a time. You must develop a total system for your plant and implement it; it is not 'just in time' or 'the stop line' or 'quality control.'"

"They feel they *are* the company; they are not *working for* the company."

"One of the big differences between GM and us is that a lot of their employees don't care about the company making money, just themselves. Here the people are the company. Toyota made us part of the company. Our people look at the future, 20, 30, 40 years down."

On People-First Values

"Top management watches out for the employees. You have to develop that trust—for instance, the trust that you can work yourself out of a job and still not lose your job here. We can go to a team and say, 'We'd like to Kaizen two people out of the process,' and they'll do it."

"They always express their trust in human nature. We have traditional machinery, but we put the person first. Mr. Cho always says, 'Team members must be first,' and every other action must be adapted to that. I must manage around that."

"To me the Toyota production system is the most people-oriented and successful because of operator involvement."

"Toyota has a total commitment to its people. They live it. Trust is built in."

"The Japanese are fair and honest and they care."

On Double-Talk

"Each new person we hire gets the phone number of the head of personnel, and he does get calls. And we discuss communication—how to speak so others will listen."

"We have many communications enhancers—round-table discussions, daily meetings with supervisors, the newspaper, our in-house TV center. All are aimed at building mutual trust. Mutual trust is something you earn; you trust that others will make the right decisions, you trust management to keep our jobs, and they trust you to do your best."

"We have a TV set in each break area; it runs continuously with news. There are also monthly updates that can be broadcast by each department. And twice a day we have five-minute information meetings within each team, as well as monthly meetings."

"We have a concern resolution system. This allows for higher and higher reviews. You can go to your human resource rep who acts as a representative for the employee. The head of personnel is the final level, but we search hard for compromise."

"Discipline involves corrective-action steps. There's a formal conference in which we sit with the supervisor, employee, and HRM and a letter goes to the employee. Then there's paid leave for one day to think about it, and you should come back with a written plan on how to correct the disciplinary problem. If it persists, a termination recommendation is made with peer review [three peers and two managers]. This is a voluntary review board. They can call anyone in and document it. The panel gives human resources a recommendation which we have always followed so far. Using drugs at work, however, means you're out."

"We listen to people."

"We have lots of communications. There's the TMM video in the plant; the information board in 10 places; our newsletter; team meetings each day—two per day minimum; quality circle meetings after the shift, for which employees are paid; round-table meetings, which are quarterly meetings between selected employees and top management. You can see the vice president, president, and so on. There's a Hotline—a phone number anyone can call to mention their concerns anonymously, anything they feel is important they can report. With the Hotline, all the comments are published along with the answers, and in terms of trust, you can't beat it. We follow up on all comments, but specific names are not mentioned. There's our concern resolution process. If you went to your team leader or group leader with an idea and it didn't get done, you can take it to a vice president. We've changed policies as a result of this. Hundreds [of problems] usually are solved at the group-leader level, but we always meet with the people to talk about it."

"Our team members know they're going to be listened to. People are so accessible. Any team member will even stop Mr. Cho. Open communications and closeness is very important."

"There are lots of ways we find out what's happening: The newsletter. The departmental meetings. The round-table meetings. Mr. Cho is often in the plant. Mr. Cho is at ceremonies that we hold. Toyota news network."

"We make some mistakes, but we listen. As long as we as managers talk one on one, even if the answer is no, it will be OK. The key is being honest and sharing everything with them even if it's 'confidential.' The Japanese taught us we must talk from our heart, not just our minds."

On Communion

"We do a lot of things to promote teamwork. We have casual dress and uniforms, a navy shirt and khaki pants, and we sell about $20,000 worth of Toyota stuff per month. This helps break down barriers, not having a shirt-and-tie policy. We're all on a first-name basis, although not Mr. Cho—but he's helped out a lot, his style contributes to the friendly atmosphere. There's an open office and people can stay much more in touch. There's no executive dining room and no private parking spots; in fact, the office people, including Mr. Cho, must park far away because the first plant shift comes on at 6:30 in the morning. We stress open communications and the saying 'Knowledge is power' doesn't apply here. There's a lot more sharing of ideas."

"People here feel they're part of the team. They see the product and the customer feedback and they feel part of it. We have a commitment to a common direction."

"The teamwork here is important, each team member depends on another. What helps is we rotate on a regular basis, and this gives you more opportunity to do your job better. The most satisfying thing is that we're all working and even working overtime, so we know we must be doing something right."

"All here are on the same level. You can go to a manager, specialist, engineer, etc., and talk with them regarding a problem. So when something goes down I can go to specialists."

"There's a lot of commonality—in the parking lots, the open offices, the uniforms, the lunchrooms, the bathrooms. And everyone, including top managers, walks the line. They're always coming by and asking for input."

"When the managers became students with the team members and learned along with them, it bred trust. They worked with them on the line, and there is no pretense."

On Transcendental Mediation

"From the first day, we concentrate on quality; you have to recognize it and feel it. From the first day, everyone is told that quality is the basis of our future."

"We all have a common direction—quality, safety, productivity, teamwork. And every day Mr. Cho sets goals for the company; then we make our department goals."

"We have goals like 'the facility should be the number 1 plant in North America,' and each department then has to decide how to do it. The most important part is we have a common direction, all must work toward the same thing. The big point is all in the company are aware of our goals and where we're heading; that affects teamwork and morale."

"Remember, goals here aren't just met; it is a process of continual improvement. We raise our goals another notch and that separates Toyota from all other firms. We're always asking, How can we improve more?"

On Value-Based Hiring

"Most firms take selection too lightly. Each assembly worker here is a million-dollar decision. Ours is the most extensive [screening] system I've ever seen. Applicants also learn much about us; there's self-selection during the simulations, videos, when they see the hard work and listen to the group discussions and do the individual problem solving. That itself requires commitment: 'I'm willing to work there and am willing to put up with these tests.' But to do this you must first know what you want. We define it and profile it."

"Our profile includes several things. Interpersonal skills—there's an exercise where applicants must interact with others and we look for a willingness to communicate—others should work somewhere else. We want people who are well educated; those who had the best educations did best in our simulations. We have college degrees in the plant, including assembly workers. They know there are growth opportunities here; they can go to the team leader, group leader, etc. We look for reasoning skills, problem-solving skills. They must do work layouts, standardized worksheets, details of how jobs are done. There's a physical component; every 50 seconds we build a car and the work is highly routine, hard work. We look for a quality commitment; overall the person must be committed to quality and to how to do it better. We're looking for flexibility, people who have an eagerness to learn and a willingness to try it your way, then my way. Remember, training is a lifelong commitment we make to our people. We're not looking for job skills; someone with experience might do OK, but I doubt it. Typical manufacturers don't look for problem-solving skills. We're also looking for an eagerness to learn and to keep learning."

"Those that want to become group and team leaders must take 50 hours on their own of training, and then go through assessment—by their supervisors and by their peers. Meanwhile, everyone knows that the job-instruction training, leadership training, etc., that they take affects their possibilities for promotion."

"One of the reasons our people are so committed is the hiring process itself. We're looking for the cream of the crop, and when they finally reached the front door, it was a feeling of 'We've made it!' It was like they found the last job they'd ever have to look for, and they felt good that they'd accomplished something. We treat each employee like a million-dollar project."

"You know you weren't given this job; you earned it."

"We select a different kind of manager here. You must be a people manager. My managers spend hours in meetings with team members and group leaders. You must find people-oriented managers or you're doomed."

"The Japanese were very careful in how they selected their managers."

On Securitizing

"Other firms talk of how important employees are, but then lay them off. We work hard to keep them here. The last thing we do is let people go."

"Job security is important because no one can do their best if we have to worry about our job. We have a no-layoff policy. There's no guarantee, but we would cut management's salaries before we laid off someone."

"They always say they'd never lay someone off. We'd make money doing something else. In lean times, we'd be kept on to make the process more efficient."

"The GM system was good in its time. When I look back, if they had had a different philosophy about layoffs and encouraging employees to be successful, they would have been OK. They should have encouraged workers to improve. At GM workers wanted short-term layoffs. GM built themselves into short-term layoffs. Here all work to put the shop in shape."

On Hard-Side Rewards

"We don't use a point system like the Hay system because we found you can't move people as easily. For instance, as our 'specialist' we can move you from engineer, to personnel, etc.; that's one reason we have a very broad rate range. There are basically two ranges at the nonexempt level and one range at the exempt level. We also have very few job titles."

"With the suggestion system there's a form to fill out. You diagram the process, what you're trying to accomplish, and it goes to the training center after it goes to the team leader and group leader. If it's approved, you'll get a gift certificate, and if it's an improvement, you'll get points. You can earn over $500 in cash and get one month's savings. That's tied in with the teamwork. All team members share in the improvement, whether 2 people or 20 people are involved."

On Actualizing

"The important thing is to empower them, to expect them to do well."

"The big stress is on how we treat people."

"When you have a workforce with very bright people, you must keep them challenged. They tell us they are happy to be here, but you must always keep them challenged."

"If we don't cross-train people, we hear about it. Here the highest skill level is to train others."

"There's real pride. All employees compete for promotional opportunities. We promoted hundreds of people last year."

"Our commitment to training includes on- and off-the-job training. It's about 40 to 50 hours per year for each employee and we have 30 people working in our training facility. We concentrate a lot on teaching problem-solving...tools like Pareto and fishbone diagrams and practical problem-solving techniques. We also teach the Toyota production system course—how to do a standard job sheet, Kaizen, and how to analyze waste and develop solutions. Everyone is encouraged to learn."

"We rotate other jobs...in the office too. For example, our personnel manager was the former accounting manager. Our college recruiter will write the *Toyota Topics* newsletter."

"Rotation is important. It helps retention because people keep learning and keep growing, and in a flat organization more people need to be rotated around. People who rotate make better decisions, also. They're not just from one area but instead are encouraged to get a broad development in all areas."

"Our suggestion system is very effective. Ours works. We implemented 20,000 suggestions last year; last February alone we had 3000 suggestions. On smaller [ideas] the group leader himself can sign off. For big ones there is a big presentation; 'Go try it,' we usually tell the team. We implement 98 percent [of suggestions]. In addition to the suggestion system, we have quality circles. In other places quality circles is just a program, not a way of managing like here. Here they are trained....Circles get one hour per week but they work a lot more themselves. Two teams got together and eliminated a team leader; they knew that if they eliminated someone, that person doesn't get fired though."

"I think it's essential to find out what people want from their careers. The key is to train the group leader to elicit that information and see possibilities. We have training programs, tuition reimbursement, and so on."

"We have a lot of recognition programs. There's a promotion ceremony—two per year—for those who are promoted, and all those in higher positions attend the ceremony. The top suggestions make it to the top managers. There are periodic luncheons for our quality circles. For those with perfect attendance (which means no lateness, no absences) there's a big meeting and a drawing in which 10 Camrys go to the winners; about 2000 people were eligible this year. There's also a lot of recognition from the direct supervisor, it comes daily. It's a skill good leaders must have and it's part of their training."

"There are a lot of promotions. In 1991 we promoted about 200 production workers to the office or to team leader or group leader, out of about 3200 in the plant."

"We solicit their ideas, use their minds, ask for suggestions, and we follow it up with teamwork. To me, teamwork and trust [are] the most important dynamic there is. We've amazed Toyota Worldwide with what we've accomplished here."

"When people join TMM, they do so with the expectation that we'll develop them, even if there's a downturn. That's why we have multi-skilled team members, and the training opportunities are unlimited."

"I've never seen a manufacturing organization with this level of education. Taking a workforce like this and keeping them challenged will be a major challenge in the years to come, but we'll do it. People do feel they're an important asset, that the company has invested the time and resources and we are an asset."

"Thirteen years after I'd been working for that other company, they never looked at me as anything more than a line worker. I left where I entered. Here they look at the individual."

"My wife would tell me, 'You worked so hard at that company and you would be passed over due to politics, etc.' It's my wife who sent in my application to Toyota."

"Why do I like to work here? Each person on the line has the ability to make more decisions, and stop the line. There's teamwork. On every other job, I had people who wouldn't contribute, but it's the complete opposite here. They keep busy, there's no boredom, and they teach you much. There's a lot of communications and meetings. I've even been to Japan for training. We have teamwork, and because we have much robotics, they teach you all about robots. They teach you how paint is mixed, and if you have a question they'll answer it. We have an open management."

"They sent me to Japan to learn how to install million-dollar robots, and I make day-to-day decisions here. I program the robots and Toyota lets me make the decisions."

"We make most of the process-improvement changes right on the line. We can check out a parts problem and collect data. For example, a wire harness was too long, so we measured it and [told] the supplier to shorten it. We redo the standardized worksheets for each job."

"All our team members are high school graduates, and about 17 percent are college grads, so we have a highly educated workforce. The real concern is can we keep them challenged? There's plenty of challenge now. There's the suggestion system, line speed changes, the new plant we're building, the potential for promotion, and the excitement of our expansion."

"Operators are empowered, and you are ultimately in charge of that job. There's the Andon cord control line, and the fact that you are responsible to develop the work sequence and do the required study. You're encouraged to learn and to make other changes. Safety, quality, productivity improvement is up to you. You may also have to get others to agree on the change. In a traditional place there's an IE chart in the IE office but the workers do the job differently. Here you follow the chart at the workstation."

"We use decision making by consensus here; it's based on trust. In another facility I'd have much more power (as a supervisor) than I do here, for instance, when it comes to promotions and terminations. You could say the workers are more empowered here, the managers less."

About the Author

In addition to *Winning Commitment*, Gary Dessler is the
author of nine other books on personnel management,
human relations, and productivity improvement, including
his widely read *Personnel/Human Resource Management*. He
also wrote the popular syndicated "Job Talk" column for *The
Miami Herald* for over ten years and is a professor of business
at Florida International University in Miami. Dr. Dessler con-
sults in the areas of commitment building, personnel/human
resource management, and strategic planning, dividing his
time between Miami and New York.

Index

Actualizing, 10, 20, 133–151
  at Ben & Jerry's Homemade, Inc., 135,
    143–144, 170–171
  commitment to, 134–136, 150, 162
  at Delta Air Lines, 137–138, 142, 143,
    145, 174
  enriching and empowering, 134,
    138–142, 150, 162
  entry-level position front-loading, 134,
    136–138, 142, 150, 162
  at Federal Express, 135, 142, 148–149,
    180
  at Goldman, Sachs & Company, 136,
    148, 183–184
  hard-side rewards and, 142
  at IBM, 135, 142, 144
  at Mary Kay Cosmetics, 189–190
  at J. C. Penney, 135–137, 142, 145–149,
    194–198
  people-first values and, 134–135, 142
  promotions, 134, 142–150, 155, 162–163,
    180
  at Publix Supermarkets, 144, 199
  at Saturn Automobile Corporation, 135,
    136, 138–142, 144, 145, 205–208
  securitizing and, 142
  summary, 149–150, 161–163
  theory and practice, 133–134, 149
  at Toyota Motor Manufacturing, U.S.A.,
    Inc., 136, 142–143, 215–217
  training, 84–85, 114, 141, 150, 155, 159,
    162
  value-based hiring and, 89, 136, 143,
    150, 162
Airline industry, 3–4
  (*See also* Delta Air Lines)
Albrecht, Karl, 6
Allen, Robert, 6
Amana Society, 54

Amburgey, Tammy, 32
American Airlines, 4
American Management Association, 106
Andon cord, 31
Appraisals, 145–148, 150, 162
Argyris, Chris, 133–134
Arthur, Greg, 32, 48
Ash, Mary Kay, 65–66, 70, 129, 158,
  186–188
  (*See also* Mary Kay Cosmetics)
At-risk salary (*see* Hard-side rewards)
AT&T, 6
Automotive industry, 4
  (*See also* Saturn Automobile Corporation;
    Toyota Motor Manufacturing,
    U.S.A., Inc.)

Balance of trade, 4
Banking industry, 3, 4
Barksdale, James, 39, 40
Bartlett, Richard C., 70, 188
Beasley, Barbara, 59
Ben & Jerry's Foundation, 79
Ben & Jerry's Homemade, Inc., 9, 165–166
  actualizing, 135, 143–144, 170–171
  communion, 56–59, 63, 64, 166–167
  hard-side rewards, 125, 169–170
  people-first values, 166
  securitizing, 113, 169
  transcendental meditation, 78–81, 85–86,
    159, 167–168
  value-based hiring, 81, 101–103, 160,
    168–169
Boruff, Bob, 33, 84–85
Braniff, 3
Bravo Zulu Voucher Program, 123, 179
Brazilian rainforest, 79
Buchanan, Bruce, 17–18

Burdick, Walt, 112
Burdines, 197
Burpo, Sandy, 60

Caldwell, Joe, 33, 128
Callahan, Thomas, 58, 119, 120
Cantrell, Cliff, 33
Career records, 148–150, 163
CAT (creative-action) teams, 189, 190
Ceremonials (*see* Ritual)
Certified interview, 29, 97–99
Cho, Fujio, 27, 30–32, 49, 57, 108, 134, 208, 210–212
Chocolate Chip Cookie Dough ice cream, 170
Chocolate Fudge Brownie ice cream, 79
Chrysler, 4
Circle of Excellence, 130
Code of ethics, 158–159
Cohen, Ben, 65, 79, 167, 168, 170
Commitment theory, 8, 9, 15–21
  actualizing, 133–134
  commitment creation, 19–20
  utopian communities, 15–17
  workplace, 17–19
Commitment wheel, 10, 13
Communication (*see* Double-talk)
Communion, 9, 10, 20, 53–68
  actualizing and, 142
  at Ben & Jerry's Homemade, Inc., 56–59, 63, 64, 166–167
  communal sharing, 54, 55, 57–60, 64, 66, 142, 156–157
  communal work, 54, 55, 60–64, 66, 67, 157
  at Delta Air Lines, 56, 63, 172
  double-talk and, 57
  dress codes, 55–57, 66
  at Federal Express, 56–58, 61, 64, 157, 178
  at Goldman, Sachs & Company, 55, 56, 58, 61, 63, 181–182
  group contact, 54, 55, 64, 67, 157
  homogeneity, 54–57, 64, 66, 142, 156
  at IBM, 56
  management practices and, 53–54, 63, 66, 67
  at Mary Kay Cosmetics, 55, 56, 58–60, 64–66, 157, 186–187
  at J. C. Penney, 55–56, 58, 61–63, 65, 191

Communion (*Cont.*):
  at Publix Supermarkets, 58
  ritual, 55, 64–67, 158
  at Saturn Automobile Corporation, 57, 58, 61, 63, 201–202
  summary, 66–67, 156–158
  at Toyota Motor Manufacturing, U.S.A., Inc., 56–58, 61–64, 211–212
  in utopian communities, 16–17, 54–55
  value-based hiring and, 55–56, 66, 89, 90, 156
Compensation, 117–119, 131
  CEO, 53
  employee, 119–130
Competition, 3–14, 20
  change, 3–4
  commitment wheel, 10, 13
  downsizing, 7, 105–106
  management practices, 4–7, 9–12
Computer industry, 4, 111
  (*See also* IBM)
Concern Resolution System, 41–43
Continental Airlines, 3
Corning, 6
Corporate charisma, 70, 78–81, 87, 159
Corporate goals, 26–28, 33, 153–154
Corporate philosophy, 158
Creative-action (CAT) teams, 189, 190
Cross-training, 114
Culture building, 85
Currency prices, 4

Da Prile, Mike, 29, 30, 95
Debt, personal and public, 4
Delta Air Lines, 4, 8
  actualizing, 137–138, 142, 143, 145, 174
  communion, 56, 63, 172
  double-talk, 44–45, 171–172
  hard-side rewards, 173–174
  people-first values, 171
  securitizing, 106, 109–110, 113, 173
  transcendental meditation, 82, 173
  value-based hiring, 82, 101, 103, 173
Dise, Dan, 135, 145
Dodge, Mike, 49, 83
Double-talk, 9, 10, 20, 37–51
  actualizing and, 142
  communion and, 57
  at Delta Air Lines, 44–45, 171–172

Double-talk (*Cont.*):
  at Federal Express, 38–41, 43, 45–50,
    155–156, 176–177
  at Goldman, Sachs & Company, 181
  guaranteed fair treatment programs,
    38–43, 49, 50, 142, 155, 176–177
  at IBM, 42–46, 155, 184
  at Mary Kay Cosmetics, 45, 186
  at J. C. Penney, 49, 191
  personnel policies, 49–50
  at Publix Supermarkets, 46, 49, 198
  at Saturn Automobile Corporation, 37,
    48, 201
  speak up programs, 38, 43–46, 49,
    155–156, 177, 209, 211
  summary, 50, 155–156
  survey programs, 38, 46–50, 123, 156, 177
  top-down programs, 38, 48–49, 156
  at Toyota Motor Manufacturing, U.S.A.,
    Inc., 41–43, 46, 48–49, 210–211
Downsizing, 7, 105–106
Drake Beam Morin, 7
Dress codes, 55–57, 66
Drucker, Peter, 5
Duncan, Kenny, 27, 29, 48

Eastern Airlines, 3
Electronics industry, 3, 105
Employment:
  in Japan, 113
  in United States, 105
  (*See also* Securitizing)
Employment Solutions, 113
Empowerment, 134, 138–142, 150, 162
Entry-level positions, 134, 136–138, 142,
  150, 162
Ethics, 158–159

Federal Express, 9, 174–175
  actualizing, 135, 142, 148–149, 180
  communion, 56–58, 61, 64, 157, 178
  double-talk, 38–41, 43, 45–50, 155–156,
    176–177
  hard-side rewards, 121–126, 130, 179–180
  people-first values, 26, 28–31, 153, 176
  securitizing, 110, 113, 179
  transcendental meditation, 158, 178–179
  value-based hiring, 29, 179

Finn, Don, 58, 120
Flying Tiger, 178
Free Bird, 125
Freeland, Mariellen, 84
Fresh Georgia Peach ice cream, 79
Friedman, Stephen, 130

Gellerman, Saul, 133
General Mills, 6
General Motors (GM), 103, 204, 209, 214
  (*See also* Saturn Automobile Corporation)
GFTP (Guaranteed Fair Treatment
  Procedure), 38–41, 43, 45, 176–177
Gill, Bob, 30, 135, 149
GM (*see* General Motors)
Go-Give Award, 59–60, 65, 70–71, 157, 187
Gold Star Award, 179–180
Golden Falcon Award, 123, 179
Golden Rule, The, 26, 58, 119
Goldman, Sachs & Company, 9
  actualizing, 136, 148, 183–184
  communion, 55, 56, 58, 61, 63, 181–182
  double-talk, 181
  hard-side rewards, 130, 183
  people-first values, 181
  securitizing, 113
  transcendental meditation, 71–73, 81,
    182
  value-based hiring, 81, 100–103, 182–183
Graft box, 169
Graham, Sean, 32, 33
Graves, Kim, 32
Green teams, 79
Greenfield, Jerry, 63, 64, 79, 85, 167
Greystone Bakery, 79
Grievance procedures, 38–43, 49, 50, 142,
  155, 176–177
Grimaldi, Cindy, 60
Grove, Andrew S., 4
Guaranteed Fair Treatment Procedure
  (GFTP), 38–41, 43, 45, 176–177
Guaranteed fair treatment programs,
  38–43, 49, 50, 142, 155, 176–177

Hard-side rewards, 10, 20, 117–132
  actualizing and, 142
  at Ben & Jerry's Homemade, Inc., 125,
    169–170

Hard-side rewards (*Cont.*):
 benefits, 16, 58, 66, 122–125, 131
 compensation, 53, 117–131
 at Delta Air Lines, 173–174
 at Federal Express, 121–126, 130,
  179–180
 at Goldman, Sachs & Company, 130, 183
 at IBM, 185
 at Mary Kay Cosmetics, 129, 189
 at J. C. Penney, 119–122, 193–194
 at Publix Supermarkets, 130, 199
 at Saturn Automobile Corporation,
  128–129, 205
 summary, 131, 161
 themes, 130–131
 at Toyota Motor Manufacturing, U.S.A.,
  Inc., 125–128, 130, 214
Harley Davidson, 200
Harris, Louis & Associates, 37
Hay Research, 37
Hay system, 122, 126, 214
HCSC inauguration, 65, 86, 192
Heltman, Sam, 42, 48–49, 56, 81–83, 94, 95,
 126
Herzberg, Frederick, 118
Hiring practices (*see* Value-based hiring)
Hirsch, Paul, 7
Hoover, Robert D., 6
Hospital employee commitment, 18
Hotline, 46, 49, 50, 155, 156, 209, 211
Hundley, Jay, 149

IBM, 4, 9, 20
 actualizing, 135, 142, 144
 communion, 56
 double-talk, 42–46, 155, 184
 hard-side rewards, 185
 people-first values, 28, 184
 securitizing, 106, 111–113, 185
 transcendental meditation, 184
 value-based hiring, 184–185
Internal Placement Center (IPC), 148

J. C. Penney (*see* Penney, J. C.)
James Bay, 167
Job Change Applicant Tracking System
 (JCATS), 148–149
Job postings, 148–150, 163, 180

Job rotation, 63, 66, 67, 109, 157, 215
Job security (*see* Securitizing)
Johnson, Jeri, 32
Johnson, William Guy, 58, 119, 120
Jones, Dick, 84–85
Joy Committee, 85
Joy Gang, 64, 85–86, 159, 167, 169, 170
Joy grants, 85–86

Kahn, Robert, 82
Kaizen system, 27, 77, 83, 90–95, 102, 103,
 108, 215
Kanter, Rosabeth Moss, 5, 15–17, 54–55,
 64, 69, 71, 81
Katz, Daniel, 82
Kenan Systems Corp., 6
King, Dawn, 32
Kirkpatrick, Sue, 60

Labor force growth in United States, 4
Laura, Bob, 32
LEAP process, 178
LeFauve, Skip, 57, 84
Licon, Marlinda, 60
Lifetime employment without guarantees,
 107–112, 114, 160
Likert, Rensis, 60–61
Lincoln Electric Company, 118
Lind, Peter, 85
Lonerghan, Liz, 80

Management Career Grid, 145–148
Management incentive compensation
 (MIC) program, 123
Management practices, 4–7, 9–10
 commitment theory and, 17–19
 communion and, 53–54, 63, 66, 67
 key factors, 11–12
 securitizing and, 114
Management Resource Inventory (MRI),
 194–195
Manufacturing industry, 3, 19
Mary Kay Cosmetics, 9
 actualizing, 189–190
 communion, 55, 56, 58–60, 64–66, 157,
  186–187
 double-talk, 45, 186

Mary Kay Cosmetics (*Cont.*):
  hard-side rewards, 129, 189
  people-first values, 185–186
  securitizing, 113, 189
  transcendental meditation, 70–71, 86,
    158–159, 187–188
  value-based hiring, 101–103, 188–189
Maslow, Abraham, 119, 133, 134
MBO program, 123
MIC (management incentive compensa-
  tion) program, 123
Midvale Steel Company, 117
Miller, Jim, 56, 80
Miss Go-Give Award, 59–60, 65, 70–71,
  157, 187
Mission statement, 158
Morin, William, 7–8
Morrow, Bob, 62
MRI (Management Resource Inventory),
  194–195

Northwest Airline, 3

Ochab, Steve, 33
One Percent for Peace, 80
Oneida Community, 15, 54
Open-Door (Federal Express), 45–46, 50,
  155, 177
Open Door (IBM), 42–43
Opinion Research Corporation, 37
Opinion surveys, 38, 46–50, 123, 156, 177
Orientation, 26, 29, 34, 82–84, 87, 154, 159,
  188
Ouchi, William, 113

Pan Am, 3, 174
Parker, Alan, 80
Part-time employees, 109, 113, 114
Passamaquoddy Indians, 79
PBO program, 123
Penney, James Cash, 26, 29, 30, 58, 65,
  119–120, 191, 192
Penney, J. C., 9, 190
  actualizing, 135–137, 142, 145–149,
    194–198
  communion, 55–56, 58, 61–63, 65, 191
  double-talk, 49, 191

Penney, J. C. (*Cont.*):
  hard-side rewards, 119–122, 193–194
  people-first values, 26, 29, 30, 190–191
  securitizing, 113, 192–193
  transcendental meditation, 71, 86,
    191–192
  value-based hiring, 29, 97–99, 101, 103,
    192
Penney Idea, 86
Penney Partnership, 86
People-first values, 9, 10, 19–20, 25–35
  actualizing and, 134–135, 142
  at Ben & Jerry's Homemade, Inc., 166
  corporate goals, 26–28, 33, 153–154
  at Delta Air Lines, 171
  at Federal Express, 26, 28–31, 153, 176
  at Goldman, Sachs & Company, 181
  at IBM, 28, 184
  at Mary Kay Cosmetics, 185–186
  at J. C. Penney, 26, 29, 30, 190–191
  personnel policies, 26, 30–34, 154–155
  at Publix Supermarkets, 26–27, 198
  at Saturn Automobile Corporation,
    27–29, 32–33, 200–201
  summary, 33–34, 153–155
  at Toyota Motor Manufacturing, U.S.A.,
    Inc., 27–32, 95, 210
  value-based hiring and, 26, 29, 34, 90,
    102, 103, 154
  written documentation, 26, 28, 34, 154
People Systems, 97
People's Express, 3
Perkins, Jim, 40, 179
Personal debt, 4
Personnel policies, 26, 30–34, 49–50, 154–155
Peveler, San, 60
PIC (professional incentive compensation)
  program, 123
Plato, 15
Power, J. C., 81
Pro Pay, 122, 123
Professional incentive compensation (PIC)
  program, 123
Project 767, 110
Promotions, 134, 142–150, 155, 162–163, 180
  appraisals, 145–148, 150, 162
  career records, 148–150, 163
  developmental activities, 143–145, 150,
    162
  job posting, 148–150, 163, 180

Public debt, 4
Publix Supermarkets, 9
  actualizing, 144, 199
  communion, 58
  double-talk, 46, 49, 198
  hard-side rewards, 130, 199
  people-first values, 26–27, 198
  securitizing, 110–111, 113, 199

Quebec hydroelectric plant, 167

Rainforest Crunch ice cream, 79–80
RASI (Responsibility, Approval, Support,
  and Inform) card, 140, 208
Resource balancing, 111
Rhodes, Jim, 48, 49, 110, 144
Rites (*see* Ritual)
Ritual:
  communion, 55, 64–67, 158
  transcendental meditation, 70, 85–87,
    159–160
Rodes, Joy, 141
Rogers, Richard, 187
"Role of a First-Level Supervisor, The,"
  137

Sahin, Kenan, 6
Saks, 197
Salary at risk (*see* Hard-side rewards)
Sanderson, Jeffrey, 100–101
Saturn Automobile Corporation, 8–9,
  199–200
  actualizing, 135, 136, 138–142, 144, 145,
    205–208
  communion, 57, 58, 61, 63, 201–202
  double-talk, 37, 48, 201
  hard-side rewards, 128–129, 205
  people-first values, 27–29, 32–33, 200–201
  securitizing, 108–109, 112, 113, 205
  transcendental meditation, 69, 71, 73–75,
    80, 83–85, 159, 202–204
  value-based hiring, 29, 95–99, 102, 103,
    204–205
Scaffede, Russ, 30
Scanlon, Joseph, 119
Scanlon Plan, 119
Scientific management, 117–118

Securitizing, 10, 20, 105–115, 155
  actualizing and, 142
  at Ben & Jerry's Homemade, Inc., 113,
    169
  at Delta Air Lines, 106, 109–110, 113, 173
  at Federal Express, 110, 113, 179
  at Goldman, Sachs & Company, 113
  at IBM, 106, 111–113, 185
  lifetime employment without guaran-
    tees, 107–112, 114, 160
  management policies and, 114
  at Mary Kay Cosmetics, 113, 189
  at J. C. Penney, 113, 192–193
  at Publix Supermarkets, 110–111, 113,
    199
  at Saturn Automobile Corporation,
    108–109, 112, 113, 205
  strategies, 113–114
  summary, 114, 160–161
  at Toyota Motor Manufacturing, U.S.A.,
    Inc., 106–109, 112–114, 214
  value-based hiring and, 89–90, 106, 109,
    113, 114
Service industry, 3
SFA (Survey Feedback Action), 47–48, 50,
  123, 156, 177
Shakers, 15, 54
Sirota, David, 53
Smith, Fred, 26, 28, 39, 40, 45, 49, 57, 154,
  175–179
Speak Up!, 43–45, 50, 155
Speak up programs, 38, 43–46, 49,
  155–156, 177, 209, 211
Spotlight on Success Seminar, 65–66
Star program, 122, 123
Steelcase Office Furniture Company, 37
Steers, Richard, 18
Stemple, Rick, Jr., 32–33
Stories (*see* Ritual)
Superstar program, 122, 123
Survey Feedback Action (SFA), 47–48, 50,
  123, 156, 177
Survey programs, 38, 48–50, 123, 156, 177
Swan, Naomi Lawson, 60
Symbols (*see* Ritual)
Systematic soldiering, 117

Taylor, Frederick, 117–118
Team work, 60–62, 66, 67, 157

Telecommunications, 3
Thompson, Gary, 31
Time Warner, 53
TMM (*see* Toyota Motor Manufacturing, U.S.A., Inc.)
Top-down programs, 38, 48–49, 156
Toyota Motor Manufacturing, U.S.A., Inc. (TMM), 9, 208–209
  actualizing, 136, 142–143, 215–217
  communion, 56–58, 61–64, 211–212
  double-talk, 41–43, 46, 48–49, 155, 156, 210–211
  hard-side rewards, 125–128, 130, 214
  Kaizen system, 27, 77, 83, 90–95, 102, 103, 108, 215
  people-first values, 27–32, 95, 210
  securitizing, 106–109, 112–114, 214
  transcendental meditation, 71, 73, 76–78, 80–83, 86, 159, 212
  value-based hiring, 29, 81–82, 89–99, 101–103, 213–214
Toyota Network News, 64
Toyota Topics, 62, 80–81, 86, 215
Toyota Worldwide, 216
Trade balance, 4
Training, 84–85, 114, 141, 150, 155, 159, 162
Transcendental meditation, 9–10, 20, 69–88
  at Ben & Jerry's Homemade, Inc., 78–81, 85–86, 159, 167–168
  corporate charisma, 70, 78–81, 87, 159
  at Delta Air Lines, 82, 173
  at Federal Express, 158, 178–179
  at Goldman, Sachs & Company, 71–73, 81, 182
  at IBM, 184
  ideological conversion, 70, 81–85, 87, 159
  ideological creation, 70–78, 87, 158–159
  at Mary Kay Cosmetics, 70–71, 86, 158–159, 187–188
  at J. C. Penney, 71, 86, 191–192
  ritual, 70, 85–87, 159–160
  at Saturn Automobile Corporation, 69, 71, 73–75, 80, 83–85, 159, 202–204
  summary, 86–87, 158–160
  at Toyota Motor Manufacturing, U.S.A., Inc., 71, 73, 76–78, 80–83, 86, 159, 212
  in utopian communities, 16, 17, 69
  value-based hiring and, 81–82, 89, 159
TWA, 3

U.S. Air, 3
UAW (*see* Saturn Automobile Corporation)
Utopian communities, 15–17
  communion, 16–17, 54–55
  investment, 16
  sacrifice, 16
  transcendence, 16, 17, 69

Value-based hiring, 10, 20, 89–104
  actualizing and, 89, 136, 143, 150, 162
  at Ben & Jerry's Homemade, Inc., 81, 101–103, 160, 168–169
  communion and, 55–56, 66, 89, 90, 156
  at Delta Air Lines, 82, 101, 103, 173
  entry-level positions, 134, 136–138, 142, 150, 162
  at Federal Express, 29, 179
  at Goldman, Sachs & Company, 81, 100–103, 182–183
  at IBM, 184–185
  at Mary Kay Cosmetics, 101–103, 188–189
  part-time employees, 109, 113, 114
  at J. C. Penney, 29, 97–99, 101, 103, 192
  people-first values and, 26, 29, 34, 90, 102, 103, 154
  at Saturn Automobile Corporation, 29, 95–99, 102, 103, 204–205
  securitizing and, 89–90, 106, 109, 113, 114
  self-selection, 101–104
  summary, 103–104, 160
  testing and screening processes, 16, 93, 103–104
  themes, 102–103
  at Toyota Motor Manufacturing, U.S.A., Inc., 29, 81–82, 89–99, 101–103, 213–214
  transcendental meditation and, 81–82, 89, 159
Value-based orientation, 26, 29, 34, 82–84, 87, 154, 159, 188
Value-based training, 84–85, 114, 141, 150, 155, 159, 162
Values and Beliefs seminar, 84–85

Waltz, Dennis, 62
Warren, Alex, 89
Watson, Thomas J., Jr., 111
Western Airlines, 173–174

Wild Maine Blueberry ice cream, 79
Work Activity Scan Sheet, 195
Worker comments (*see specific corporation*)
Worth, Maurice, 44–45, 101
WOW line, 46

Young, Kelvin, 31–32, 62

ZAP mail, 110
Zimet, Michael, 43